P9-CFS-794

heart&soul

Australia's First Families *of* Wine

Graeme Lofts

WILEY

John Wiley & Sons Australia, Ltd

First published 2010 by John Wiley & Sons Australia, Ltd
42 McDougall Street, Milton Qld 4064

Office also in Melbourne

Typeset in Electra 10.5/15 pt

© Graeme Lofts 2010

The moral rights of the author have been asserted

National Library of Australia Cataloguing-in-Publication data:

Author:	Lofts, Graeme.
Title:	Heart & Soul: Australia's First Families of Wine/Graeme Lofts.
ISBN:	9781742469249 (pbk.)
Notes:	Includes index.
Subjects:	Australia's First Families of Wine. Wine and winemaking — Australia — History. Wine industry — Australia — History.
Dewey Number:	338.17480994

All rights reserved. Except as permitted under the *Australian Copyright Act 1968* (for example, a fair dealing for the purposes of study, research, criticism or review), no part of this book may be reproduced, stored in a retrieval system, communicated or transmitted in any form or by any means without prior written permission. All enquiries should be made to the publisher at the address above.

Cover design by saso content & design pty ltd

Printed in China by Printplus Limited

10 9 8 7 6 5 4 3 2 1

Limit of liability/Disclaimer of warranty: While the publisher and author have used their best efforts in preparing this book, they make no representations or warranties with respect to the accuracy or completeness of the contents of this book and specifically disclaim any implied warranties of merchantability or fitness for a particular purpose. No warranty may be created or extended by sales representatives or written sales materials. The advice and strategies contained herein may not be suitable for your situation. You should consult with a professional where appropriate. Neither the publisher nor author shall be liable for any loss of profit or any other commercial damages, including but not limited to special, incidental, consequential, or other damages.

Contents

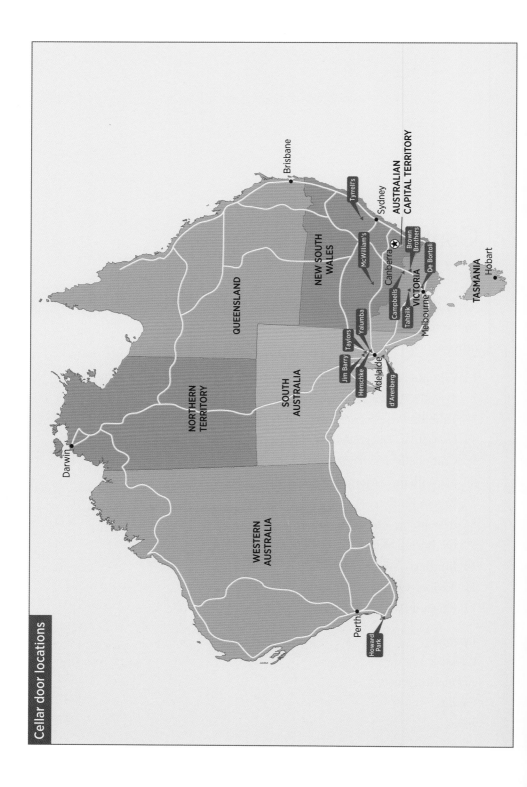

Cellar door locations

Australia's First
Families *of* Wine

About the AFFW initiative

Australia's First Families of Wine (AFFW), launched in 2009, is a collective of twelve multi-generational family-owned wine producers. Together, the families represent seventeen wine-growing regions across Australia and have more than 1200 years of experience in winemaking and forty-eight generations of winemakers.

Each family occupies a distinct niche in the Australian wine industry and its proud history, and makes a range of premium wines of character and personality — whether they be great-value varietals or single-vineyard icons. Equally, each family understands its responsibility to defend and promote Australia's pre-eminent place in the world of wine and their own custodianship of some of Australia's finest vineyards and most famous wine brands.

The aim of Australia's First Families of Wine is to showcase a representative and diverse range of the best of Australian wine with a focus on regional and iconic drops. The collective is working to engage consumers, retailers, restaurateurs and the wine industry across the globe about the real character and personality of Australian wine, and about the unique characters and personalities behind it.

The families at the AFFW launch, Sydney Opera House.

Membership of Australia's First Families of Wine is dependent on satisfying a number of criteria, which include:

✤ being family controlled as defined under the Australian Corporations Act

✤ having a history of at least two (preferably three) generations involved in the business

✤ the ability to offer a tasting of at least 20 vintages of one or more iconic brands

✤ membership of the Winemakers' Federation of Australia

✤ ownership of established vineyards more than fifty years old and/or distinguished sites that exemplify the best of terroir

✤ a commitment to environmental best practice in vineyards, wineries and packaging

✤ family-member service on wine industry bodies

✤ a long-term commitment to export markets.

Nothing but the wine.

The inaugural members of Australia's First Families of Wine are:

✤ Brown Brothers, founded in 1885, with vineyards in the King Valley, Heathcote and Swan Hill wine regions of Victoria

✤ Campbells, founded in 1870, with vineyards in the Rutherglen wine region of Victoria

✤ d'Arenberg (the Osborn family), founded in 1912, with vineyards in the McLaren Vale wine region of South Australia

✤ De Bortoli Wines, founded in 1928, with vineyards in the Riverina and Hunter Valley wine regions of New South Wales and the Yarra Valley and King Valley wine regions of Victoria

✤ Henschke, founded in 1868, with vineyards in the Eden Valley and Adelaide Hills wine regions of South Australia

✤ Howard Park Wines (the Burch family), founded in 1986, with vineyards in the Margaret River and Great Southern wine regions of Western Australia

✤ Jim Barry Wines, founded in 1959, with vineyards in the Clare Valley and Coonawarra wine regions of South Australia

✤ McWilliam's, founded in 1877, with vineyards in the Riverina, Hunter Valley and Hilltops wine regions of New South Wales, the Yarra Valley wine region of Victoria, the Coonawarra wine region of South Australia and the Margaret River wine region of Western Australia

✤ Tahbilk (the Purbrick family), founded in 1860, with vineyards in the Nagambie Lakes wine region of Victoria

✤ Taylors, founded in 1969, with vineyards in the Clare Valley wine region of South Australia

HENSCHKE

✠ Tyrrell's Wines, founded in 1858, with vineyards in the Hunter Valley wine region of New South Wales, the Heathcote wine region of Victoria and the McLaren Vale wine region and Limestone Coast wine zone of South Australia

✠ Yalumba (the Hill Smith family), founded in 1849, with vineyards in the Eden Valley and the Barossa Valley wine regions of South Australia.

Stephen Henschke, fifth-generation winemaker and Managing Director of CA Henschke & Co, observes: 'Australia's First Families of Wine is a really important part of preserving the family history of Australia — to have a commonality between a whole group of multigenerational families makes us really powerful. We have fantastic brands, great history, fascinating stories and real personalities — it's so important for the next generation and for the future'.

Foreword

For more than 185 years, Australians have been growing grapes and making wine. Over this period there have been many twists and turns as the population grew, progressively moving from subsistence agriculture to a sophisticated, affluent, multicultural society. Wine has played an important role in this transformation.

There are a number of key events that had an impact on the fledgling country and on viticulture. In the nineteenth century these included the arrival in the Barossa Valley of Silesian (German) immigrants fleeing religious persecution in the 1840s, the discovery of gold in the 1850s and the influx of thirsty miners, and the 1886 arrival of the Chaffey brothers, who planned the first irrigation systems that transformed the red desert sand along the banks of the Murray River into a verdant fruit and vegetable bowl.

The following century was just as influential. The founding of the Commonwealth in 1901 led to the abolition of protective duties imposed by each state, the aftermath of World War I saw the establishment of returned soldier settlement schemes, the growing number of immigrants included waves of Italian families moving into the Riverina and Riverland regions, World War II led to significant immigration from all parts of Europe, and the growth of migration from South-East Asia brought with it the introduction of its notably varied cuisines. All of these events have created a diverse society with an innate understanding of wine and food.

For most of the last forty years it has been commonly accepted that medium-sized, family-owned wineries will not survive. The argument is that the large companies (the top five companies crush two-thirds of total grape production) are the rock, the 2500 small wineries are the hard place and the mid-sized producers — notably the members of Australia's First Families of Wine — are wedged in the middle.

In fact, the reverse has happened, and the obvious question many are asking is why? One answer is familial pride, and the direct involvement of all the generations of each family presently alive and able to contribute. Important decisions are ultimately made by the family head, but involve all or most of the family members. Notwithstanding this consensus process, decisions can be made as quickly as needed. This is radically different from the quasi-political nature of large company decision-making, which is often cumbersome and slow, and decisions are not infrequently made for the wrong reasons.

This direct ownership has other facets and implications. Whether wine is truly made in the vineyard is a moot point, but it is certainly the starting point for great wine. Members of each of the first families will have spent time either personally working in their vineyards or talking to the chief viticulturist to decide on strategies for the future.

This link with the land is particularly strong with Australian farmers and graziers, and growing grapes is simply one form of farming. Indeed, winemaking families have a deep attachment to and understanding of the land, nurturing their precious, and often very old, vineyards. Alister Purbrick, for example, stood on Tahbilk's 1860 Shiraz vines block and inwardly wept at the destruction of many of those vines by severe frost in the spring of 2006.

There is, or there should be, a continuous link between vineyard and winery, and between winery and consumers. It is this continuity that allows the members of Australia's First Families of Wine to maximise the potential quality of the wines they produce and make informed decisions on wine style and price. The outcome is wines that routinely over-deliver on a price-to-quality ratio.

The wineries that make up Australia's First Families of Wine come from regions spread across four states. Collectively, they own more than 5500 hectares of Australia's finest vineyards and have more than 1200 years of winemaking experience. Nowhere else in the world could such a group be assembled, their history told both through the mouths of the family members and the wines they present.

The underlying rationale for the formation of Australia's First Families of Wine was the realisation that export markets had either lost sight of or had no way of knowing about Australia's rich history, its diverse regions and wine styles, and the fierce personal commitment of the best winemakers to the production of high-quality wines true to their variety and geographical origin.

As we enter the second decade of the twenty-first century, there are profound changes in the offing for the shape of Australia's export markets. These will come about partly because of adverse changes in the dynamics of the United States and United Kingdom markets, and partly because of the opportunities provided by Asia; in this context, Asia covers all the countries starting with India in the west, extending to Japan in the east, with China, the colossus, in the middle.

In June 2010, Wine Australia announced its intention to set up permanent offices in Hong Kong, Shanghai and Beijing, and suggested that by 2015 China would become our largest export market. Even if one were to substitute 'could' for 'would', this is a startling projection. China's 2010 imports are around thirty million litres; those of the United States and United Kingdom are roughly five times that.

It is far from clear whether creating the demand or finding the supply will be more challenging. Demand is surely the most important part of the equation, and here Australia's First Families of Wine is perfectly placed. The wines have none of the corporate or industrial aroma attached (no matter how unjustly) to the brands produced by the largest Australian companies.

Then there is the sheer quality of the wines made by Australia's First Families of Wine. My 2011 *Australian Wine*

Companion lists the best wineries in Australia by region, being those accorded a five-star rating. Within that rating there are three levels: five black stars, five red stars and, at the very top, those whose names are printed in red as well as their stars. There are ninety-six of the latter wineries, representing 3.6 per cent of the 2800 wineries in the companion database. Ten of the twelve members of Australia's First Families of Wine have this ultimate accolade, the other two with five red stars.

Unless my judgement is sadly astray, the future of the Australian wine industry is in the hands of the first families, and others like them. This book brings the people, their histories, their wineries and their vineyards to life. I am proud to have written this foreword.

James Halliday AM
Yarra Valley, Victoria
September 2010

Introduction

Heart & Soul: Australia's First Families of Wine tells the stories of twelve families who have put their heart and soul into their vineyards and wineries for generations. It is a book about people, their passion and the challenges they face, and their relationship with the land, their vineyards and their wines.

Family-owned wine companies have been instrumental in building the Australian wine industry into the world's fourth-largest exporter by volume, behind the much older nations of Italy, France and Spain. However, quantity is not what motivates these families. They are driven by pride in their heritage and determination to produce wine of the highest quality that rivals the best in the world.

The first commercial vineyards were planted in Australia well before 1850. Yet, until the 1960s, table wine had no significant place in the life of most Australians. Beer was the drink of choice and wine production was dominated by fortified wines (in particular, sherry and port). As James Halliday so eloquently explained in the foreword, events of the twentieth century changed that.

There is no doubt that wine is now an integral part of Australia's culture. Internationally recognised Australian wines are being carefully matched with a diverse range of food in restaurants; wine is shared at the dinner table or at a traditional Australian barbecue with family and friends, along with good food and conversation. Wine plays a role whenever there is reason to celebrate.

In Australia, wine is also an important part of the tourism industry, with cellar doors in every state and territory. Many cellar doors now offer experiences to satisfy all the senses — restaurants, art galleries, museums, live music and more. As well as providing visitors with a place to taste and purchase wine, cellar doors play a major role in educating consumers about wine and winemaking, and provide an opportunity to talk to the people who make the wine.

To become a winemaker you need an understanding of chemistry and biology; however, winemaking is also an art. The winemakers of Australia's First Families of Wine paint pictures with their wines. Every bottle of wine they create is a thing of beauty, and every bottle tells a story — and it all begins in the vineyards.

Families have been the traditional custodians of vineyards in Australia, as they have been throughout most of the world. Families nurture their vineyards, get the best out of them and overcome the challenges served up by Mother Nature, including frosts, hail, droughts, floods, destructive insects and vine disease. Many Australian winemaking families have also fought hard to survive economic depression, labour shortages, grape surpluses and personal tragedies.

When describing the history of these families, the much-overused terms 'blood, sweat and tears' and 'labour of love' really do apply. By their very nature, multi-generational winemaking families have a long-term vision and are willing to take risks and fight against adversity. Each generation adapts to changing times, adding new dimensions to their enterprise and paving the way for the next generation. Darren De Bortoli, third-generation managing director of De Bortoli Wines, puts it best: 'Family companies tend to have a mindset formed by the passage of time and family folklore. We can give a unique customer offering in that we represent core values of several generations of family stewardship giving a direct link to the past through oral and written histories'.

Alister Purbrick, inaugural chairman of Australia's First Families of Wine and fourth-generation chief winemaker and chief executive of Tahbilk, explains further. 'As family winemakers we all value our independence, but we also share the same ideals, beliefs and a passion for creating wines of character, interest and quality.'

Each of the twelve members of Australia's First Families of Wine was founded by pioneers with a passion for the land. That passion for their 'patches of dirt' — their heart and soul — is passed on from one generation to the next, and you can taste it in their magnificent wines.

Yalumba
Beating the odds

'We grow grapes and make wine with passion, and we are prepared to go to any length to deliver wines of the highest quality and personality.'

Robert Hill Smith, fifth-generation Yalumba proprietor

More than 160 years after it was founded in South Australia's beautiful Barossa Valley, Yalumba is a thriving, continually evolving, dynamic winery, led by the indomitable Robert Hill Smith. Throughout its history Yalumba has repeatedly overcome adversity with true grit and determination, ingenuity and passion.

Yalumba is the oldest family-owned winery in Australia. It is also one of the most innovative, introducing new white wine styles such as Viognier and Vermentino. Yalumba sources its fruit from its vineyards in the neighbouring Eden Valley and from external growers across the Barossa Valley, South Australia's Limestone Coast, north-eastern Victoria and Tasmania.

The story of Yalumba began when Samuel Smith, a successful brewer from Dorset, England, set sail for Australia in 1847 in search of a new life for his family. With him went his wife and four children. After several months at sea, the Smiths arrived at the remote and unfamiliar destination of South Australia. They settled briefly on the banks of the River Torrens in Adelaide, then headed north by bullock dray to the small settlement of Angaston in the Barossa Valley. There Samuel found work as a gardener for George Fife Angas, after whom Angaston was named.

By 1849 Samuel was ready to start out on his own, having saved enough money to lease a thirty-acre property on the outer edge of the settlement. He built the family home, which he named 'Osborne Cottage' after his wife, Mary Osborne, and planted a garden to grow produce for sale. He also planted some grape vines using cuttings given to him by John Howard Angas, the son of his former employer. The Angas family was instrumental in promoting horticulture in the region and considered growing grapes for the production of wine to be of primary importance.

> ❛ God gave me wonderful strength and my wife helped me in every possible way. ❜
>
> Samuel Smith

Samuel made a reasonable living selling his vegetables and dried fruits, but in 1851 his market began to dry up as people streamed out of the district to join the gold rush in Victoria and New South Wales.

His income declining, in 1852 Samuel made his way to the goldfields of Bendigo, Victoria, with his fifteen-year-old son, Sidney, intending to make enough money to buy more land. After four months of hard labour he had enough gold to purchase a further eighty acres of land and more farming equipment. He was also able to set aside a tidy sum to build a more spacious homestead for his family. He named the property 'Yalumba', an Indigenous Australian word for 'all the land around'. Together with Sidney he planted the first Yalumba vineyard, working during the day and at night by moonlight with a candle wedged in the front of a wheelbarrow. Samuel also built the new family home, which is now known as 'Percy's' after one of Sidney's children.

Samuel Smith made his first wine — primarily red wine and port — on his newly acquired property in 1853. A thatched hut served as his cellar.

Founder of Yalumba, Samuel Smith (1812–1889).

The ensuing years saw an extraordinary expansion of the vineyards at Angaston and a growing reputation for Samuel's wine. He won numerous awards throughout Australia for both fortified and table wines, and during the 1860s Yalumba wines were being exported to New Zealand and England. Samuel also won awards for his produce, including apples, dried fruits, onions and honey.

The original, modest cellar was replaced in the early 1870s by a large stone cellar, driven into the side of a hill to allow a gravity-feed system. On the upper level, wagon loads of grapes were weighed and pitch-forked into the receiving trough, and then shovelled into a crusher.

By 1875 Samuel had forty-four acres of vineyards dominated by Frontignac, Shiraz and Albilleo (sherry) fruit, and had extended the cellar. He was also purchasing grapes from fourteen other Barossa Valley growers to satisfy the demand for his wine. Only a few years later Yalumba wines were receiving accolades and winning prestigious awards for 'full-bodied wines' in London, Paris, Bordeaux and Philadelphia.

Samuel and Sidney formally sealed their 'unofficial' partnership in 1877 when the entity of S. Smith & Son was established. Six months before his death in 1889, at the age of seventy-six, Samuel relinquished control of the company to Sidney. At the time of Samuel's death, S. Smith & Son had more than 100 acres of vineyards, a winery, forty acres of orchards, a fruit-preserving factory, more than forty employees and about sixty external grape growers.

Sidney was only ten years old when the family migrated to Australia. He had seen the good times and the bad alongside his father during the early days in Adelaide, at the Victorian goldfields and then at Yalumba. Sidney derived a great deal of pleasure from working on the land — the blue skies and open spaces were in stark contrast to the cold and damp of Dorset. He had helped plant the vineyard and watched with fascination the process of transforming grape to wine. He developed the same passion for winemaking as his father and eventually became assistant winemaker. During the years before his death, Samuel had been gradually giving Sidney more and more authority.

The Smith and Hill Smith families, circa 1890. From left: Archie Smith, Mona Smith, Dr Henry Arthur Powell, Katie Powell (nee Smith), Sidney Smith (seated), unknown (behind chair), Eleanor Smith (nee Caley, Sidney's wife), Frederick Caley Smith (lying down), Ada Smith (seated), Tom Temple, Ida Smith (nee Caley, seated) holding baby Sidney Hill Smith, Walter Smith, Lizzie Smith (seated) holding baby Donald Hill Smith and Sidney (Burney) Smith.

At the age of fifty-two, with a wealth of experience and knowledge of viticulture and winemaking, Sidney was well placed to take charge of S. Smith & Son.

Sidney steered the business forward in the face of a severe depression in the early 1890s, and continued to receive accolades for Yalumba wines and fruit. In 1895 his belief in the future success of the company led him to register the Yalumba brand name. Sidney and his wife, Eleanor, had raised ten children, and it was the four eldest sons who were destined to take Yalumba into its third generation of winemaking excellence.

From the beginning of his time at the helm of the company, Sidney was remarkably adept at delegating responsibility to his sons Fred, Percival (known as Percy), Walter and Sidney (known as Burney) — all of whom had spent much of their childhood and adolescence working at Yalumba. Father and sons were constantly forging new paths within the wine industry. As the demand for their wine increased, they began to use more external growers, encouraging local farmers to plant vineyards. Their success inspired other winemakers to push the boundaries.

Working in the vineyard, circa 1890.
Walter Smith is second from the right.

In 1902, at the age of sixty-five, Sidney assigned the business, goodwill and plant to Percy and Walter due to ill health.

A new building plan was implemented under the guidance of Percy and Walter. It began in 1902 with the construction of a new corrugated-iron winery incorporating huge fermenting tanks and underground tanks used for storage before the wine was pumped into the old cellars. Icy-cold underground water was used to cool the fermenting wine. In 1908, the second phase of the new building began, including the picturesque clock-tower building that was to house the Yalumba cellars, bottling facilities and offices. The bluestone used for the walls was quarried on site and bricks for features such as corners and arches were manufactured in nearby Penrice.

The third generation of Smiths provided some high achievers and memorable characters. The eldest son, Fred, was a gifted communicator and an internationally recognised expert in vineyard and orchard management, particularly in the control of disease. He saw himself as an ambassador of Yalumba. He spent most of his adult life abroad, promoting Yalumba wines and canned fruit whenever the opportunity arose. After returning home from his travels he became restless and moved to the Adelaide Hills, where he turned to his original passion of horticulture, growing and selling flowers. He married Myra Hill in 1910 and died less than three years later at the age of forty-eight.

The clock-tower building, completed in 1908, has become a Barossa landmark.

Second son, Percy, was best known for his winemaking skills and worked tirelessly at Yalumba, gaining a reputation for the quality of his wine and the cleanliness and efficiency of the Yalumba cellars. With younger brother Walter, he supervised the construction of the clock-tower building. Unlike his brothers, Percy valued his privacy. His wedding in 1912 to Jenny Trescowthick, nineteen years his junior, went almost unnoticed, even by some relatives. A mysterious trip to Melbourne followed and it wasn't until Percy's twilight years that the family discovered the couple had a son, Lance, who had been fostered in Melbourne for his entire life.

Like his older brother Fred, Walter spent many years travelling abroad, promoting the family label. His role at the company was exporting, and he looked to the colonial markets to grow Yalumba's reputation. In between extolling the virtues of Yalumba wines, he pioneered a walking trail in New Zealand and trekked in the Himalayas, while his passion for big game hunting took him to India and earned him the nickname 'Tiger'.

Walter Smith was an adventurer throughout his life. This caricature by Adelaide cartoonist John Chinner depicts Walter in his later years.

Reprinted from The Saturday Journal, January 22, 1927.

NOTABLE CITIZENS.

Mr. Walter Smith, of wine and big game fame.
Yalumba Vineyards, South Australia.

Walter married Ida Hill, a formidable woman from a well-known Adelaide sporting family. Her brother was the famous Australian cricketer Clem Hill. (Ida was no relation to Fred's wife, Myra Hill.) Walter and Ida had four children — Sidney, Donald, Jean and Wyndham. The children eventually took the surname Hill Smith because it distinguished then from the numerous other Smiths at their school in Adelaide. Sidney and Wyndham were to later play pivotal roles in successfully steering Yalumba through the Great Depression and some family tragedies during the first half of the twentieth century.

What's in a name?

When brothers Sidney, Donald and Wyndham Smith first entered the prestigious Adelaide school Saint Peters College, their classes contained no less than twelve other Smiths. To avoid confusion all of the Smiths were asked to go home and, in consultation with their families, return to school the following morning with different surnames. For the Yalumba Smiths, it was decided that their mother's maiden name, Hill, would form part of the surname, and the new family surname Hill Smith came into being.

Sidney (known as Burney) Smith was fascinated with horticulture, and enjoyed trying out new equipment and applying new techniques to the processing and canning of fruit. While Percy and Walter managed the winery at Yalumba, Burney was firmly in control of the vineyard, orchards and fruit preservation. He was also an active member of the Angaston community, filling positions on various community organisations, as well as being a church choirmaster for many years. He married Jessie Faith Orchard, and they had three sons and a daughter.

After their father assigned the business to Percy and Walter in 1902, fruit preservation at Yalumba began being pushed aside. To make matters worse the export and, to a lesser extent, local sales of preserved fruit were hit hard by World War I. During the early years of the war Burney remained at Yalumba to help fill the gap left by the young men who had gone to serve their country, working in both fruit and wine operations. By 1916 the fruit-preserving operation had almost ceased and Burney's role at Yalumba seemed limited. Eventually he left the family business and was appointed chairman of the South Australian Apple Pool.

At the time the war broke out, south-eastern Australia was experiencing one of its worst-ever droughts. Adding to the stress of war and the absence of rain — desperately needed for the survival of the vineyards and orchards — was a severe mouse plague.

Swarms of mice invaded the preserving factory and threatened the vineyards.

The sale and export of wine and preserved fruit declined markedly in the early years of the war, which resulted in Yalumba — and many others in the wine and fruit industries — beginning to struggle financially. Yalumba's employees pulled together, working longer and harder to make up for the labour shortage. Under Walter's management, Burney and Percy took charge of the fruit and wine operations; however, the occasional absence of Walter on trips to England and India while the rest of the family fought to keep Yalumba afloat caused great strains within the Smith family.

Despite their own problems, the Smith family was unwavering in its support of the Angaston community, the wine industry in general and the war effort. Both the men and the women of the family were involved in boosting morale with meetings and parades. Burney, in particular, spent a great deal of time fundraising, making speeches and encouraging men to enlist.

The Fromm vineyard – home of Yalumba's Lyndoch Barossa Shiraz.

In early 1916, all at Yalumba were rocked by the news that J McKnight, the head of the company's distribution agency in Western Australia, had been killed in battle. This was the first

recorded casualty from among the company's people. In August that same year Sidney Hill Smith, son of Walter and Ida, was seriously wounded in the head and not expected to survive. He recovered but lived the rest of his life with a steel plate embedded in his head.

Less than one month later Burney and Faith lost their eldest son, Caley, who was killed in action while serving in France. Burney threw himself into community work and encouraged other fruit growers to work together to save the industry. Deeply affected by the death of his son, Burney launched a plan to help returned soldiers settle on the land as primary producers. Shortly afterwards, he and Faith moved away from Yalumba to assist in the establishment of vineyards on returned soldier settlements along the Murray River.

Amid the grief and heartache of the Great War, the Smith family maintained the elegance and beauty of their gardens and cellars. The gardens became a popular destination for wine-lovers and provided the perfect venue for fundraising by the Smiths. The family supported a number of charities, helping to raise much-needed funds for the war effort, repatriated soldiers and the Red Cross.

As World War I raged on, another battle was looming closer to home. In 1917 the temperance movement and the Methodist Church began lobbying the South Australian government to hold a referendum on the prohibition of alcohol. Their enthusiasm was fuelled by a state referendum held in March 1915 that agreed to the six o'clock closure of hotels. A 'yes' vote in a referendum would have been a fatal blow to the wine industry. The articulate and respected Walter Smith became an influential leader in the fight against prohibition. He helped to unify grape growers and winemakers in the struggle to save the industry from the scrapheap.

The prohibitionists responded with a campaign against the wine industry, painting it as insignificant in size and making accusations of corruption. To Walter, such accusations were like a red rag to a bull. He enlisted the support of farmers and members of any trade or profession that would be even slightly harmed by the collapse of the wine industry. These included coopers, ironworkers, bricklayers, accountants and even members of parliament. The debate raged on until 1921, when the South Australian government finally pledged to encourage and support the wine industry.

> ❛ It is the plain duty of every government, and every member of parliament in the Commonwealth, to declare itself and himself, without any equivocation, in support of the wine industry; they cannot afford to neglect their duty to Australia by half-hearted support. ❜
>
> Walter Smith

While Walter was leading the fight against prohibition in 1920, his eldest son, Sidney, married Christobel Keckwick. After his return from the war Sid, as he was known, planted new vineyards in the neighbouring Eden Valley and took on a variety of roles in the winery. He was well respected by the employees at Yalumba and the Angaston community. Following Sid's wedding, his Uncle Percy gradually withdrew from his winemaking role at Yalumba, finally retiring in 1923. The company became incorporated as S. Smith & Son Ltd with Walter Smith as chairman and Sidney Hill Smith as managing director.

Following the victory in the bitter battle against prohibition, the future of the wine industry and Yalumba began to look brighter. Yalumba continued growing and everyone at the winery continued working overtime to keep up with the demand for its fortified wine. However, by the end of 1924 the rapid expansion of vineyards and overproduction of wine was creating yet another threat to the wine industry. Growers, many of them having planted new vineyards after returning from the war, were faced with an uncertain future. Wine companies, including Yalumba, were also struggling to survive. In April 1925, the Smith family was dealt another blow when the youngest Hill Smith, Archie, died at the age of forty-four, having never married.

Thanks to the shrewd leadership of Walter and Sid, the introduction of new technology, expansion of the cellars and the loyalty of staff, production was increased and cash flow was maintained. New products were being launched and exports of fortified red wine to the United Kingdom were booming.

The Yalumba cellars in 1925, with a shipment of hogsheads awaiting transportation.

Then came the Wall Street crash of October 1929 and the Great Depression. Economies the world over went into freefall. In Australia grape growers and other primary producers were among the worst affected. Export prices plummeted and unemployment grew dramatically. At Yalumba, the bank was demanding a mortgage over all of S. Smith & Son's assets, but the company held its ground by reducing costs, employing some clever marketing and being downright stubborn. Walter and Sid talked up the wine industry, advertised heavily and supported grape growers by allowing them to process their grapes at one of its crushing facilities. The first signs of economic recovery in Australia appeared in 1933, but the effects of the Depression lingered until well into the 1940s. The long and proud heritage of Yalumba and the loyalty and determination of its people — from the chairman, to the growers, winemakers, cellar hands, gardeners, and the sales and office staff — had steered the company safely through the Great Depression.

Although Walter maintained an active involvement in the business, by 1936 his sons were in control, with Sidney at Angaston, Wyndham managing the office in Perth and Don looking after the Adelaide offices. Wyndham and Don were now directors of the company. Wyndham was particularly successful in Western Australia, demonstrating a flair for business development as well as his other passion — cricket. In fact, during the infamous 'bodyline' series between England and Australia in 1932–1933, Wyndham played in an Australian XI that included such illustrious players as Sir Donald Bradman, Jack Fingleton and Stan McCabe. He distinguished himself as a batsman and was credited with saving Australia from defeat.

When Walter Smith died in April 1938 after a long battle with cancer, Sidney Hill Smith was appointed chairman of the company. He retained his position as managing director. Tragically, less than six months later Sidney was killed in a plane crash on the outskirts of Melbourne along with other wine industry leaders Thomas Hardy and Hugo Gramp. They were part of a delegation to put a case for federal government support for the stabilisation of the wine industry. All on board the plane, including a federal government cabinet minister, perished in the crash. The people of Australia — in particular, the Barossa Valley community — were shocked by the disaster.

With the deaths of Walter and Sid it was left to the ebullient thirty-year-old Wyndham Hill Smith to lead Yalumba at what could have hardly been a worse time. The banks were once again threatening to call in the company's debts. Fortunately, Wyndham — determined to bring Yalumba back from the brink — persuaded the banks to allow him five years to turn around the company's fortunes. The outbreak of World War II in 1939 sent export sales plunging. Wyndham's response was to concentrate on the local market with a boost in advertising and a new brandy.

As it did during World War I, Yalumba made its property available as a way of raising funds for the war effort.

Yalumba advertised heavily during the 1930s, highlighting the characters working at the winery. This advertisement depicts cellarman Oliver Jenkinson.

Loading a truck with Brandivino for export to Dunedin, New Zealand, circa 1935.

Australian soldiers returning from the war for further training were housed near the winery and billeted in the homes of employees. When Japan became a direct threat to Australia, Wyndham even enlisted the help of locals to scan the skies to alert the armed forces to the presence of enemy planes.

After Japan joined the war in December 1941, there was an unexpected consequence for Yalumba. American servicemen were brought into the Asia–Pacific region through Australia, causing a sudden and huge increase in the male population. Sales of brandy and port boomed, and Yalumba took on Australian distribution of popular spirit brands well recognised by Americans, including Martini and Rossi Vermouth, Dewars Whiskey and Barcardi. By the time the war ended, Yalumba's cash flow was strong and it was looking forward to a potentially excellent vintage in 1946.

Despite the company's improving financial situation, the war was still taking its toll on the family. Jean Hill Smith's husband was captured by the Japanese and his whereabouts were unknown. The handful of employees remaining at Yalumba were working long hours to compensate for the absence of the many who had enlisted. There was also good news from the battlefront: Burney's son Doug had been mentioned in dispatches for gallantry in the Middle East and promoted to the rank of lieutenant.

Following the war Wyndham reconstructed his management and sales team. With renewed vitality and enthusiasm the company underwent a period of rapid growth. New offices, warehouses and distribution centres were established within the winery and in other states. The Yalumba Estate transformed into a hub of optimism and enterprise.

Wyndham also found time to indulge in another passion — horseracing. He put together a stable of fine racehorses and, true to his character, gave them names including Brandy Cruster, Vintage Port, Galway Pipe and Cellarman.

Wyndham married Helen Lane in 1947 and she very quickly gained the confidence of all at Yalumba. Her bubbly personality, willingness to pitch in where necessary, and support and encouragement were appreciated by all. The couple had three sons, Robert, Samuel and Patrick. Sadly Patrick died during infancy in 1960.

During the 1950s, 1960s and 1970s the wineries and equipment were progressively updated to cater for the demand for Yalumba's sherries and ports, and new products such as the spectacularly

Sidney Hill Smith, circa 1938.

successful Brandivino, a sweet white wine fortified with brandy. It was the sales of fortified wines and spirits that were funding the expansion of the winery to satisfy the rapidly increasing demand for table wines. The arrival of European migrants, with their tradition of enjoying table wine with meals, had a profound impact on the wine industry. Many of the old vineyards were pulled up to make way for popular table wine varieties such as Cabernet Sauvignon, Riesling and Semillon.

Yalumba's wine sales quad-rupled during Wyndham's term as

chairman and managing director. Almost all of the growth was in the domestic market, assisted by European immigration and a booming economy. Wyndham's respect for European wines and culture led him to predict the significant swing toward table wines. Yalumba was at the forefront of innovation in winemaking and a leader in promoting an understanding of wine in the community at large. Another factor that contributed to the company's massive growth was the close relationship Yalumba had with its grape growers. For many years the company had shared cuttings and knowledge with growers and had always paid fair prices for its grapes.

Social and community events on Yalumba's sweeping green lawns and in its immaculate gardens were an integral part of life at the winery. Guests at these events included royalty, artists, writers, sporting identities (especially from the worlds of cricket and horseracing) and entertainers, and were hosted by Wyndham and his wife, Helen, and Mark Hill Smith (son of Sidney) and his wife, Margie.

American soldiers on their way to war in the Asia–Pacific region or on leave 'fell in love' with Yalumba's Galway Port.

Wyndham retired as managing director in 1972 at the age of sixty-three. He retained the position of chairman. He was succeeded by Mark Hill Smith. Mark had started working in the family business in 1947, and was highly regarded in the wine industry and well respected at Yalumba. He encouraged experimentation and innovation, keeping the company at the forefront of the Australian wine industry. Unlike his father, Sid, and his uncle, Wyndham, Mark was inheriting the management of a debt-free company. However, for Yalumba to progress there was a desperate need for capital investment in expansion of the winery and new equipment.

Major changes were taking place in the marketplace in the mid 1970s. The movement of huge volumes of wine through a

proliferation of discount chains meant reduced profit margins for wine producers. As a consequence, many family-owned wine companies were forced to reassess their viability. Some saw no other solution than to sell out to large corporations. Yalumba, also facing declining sales in Brandivino and fortified wines, held its ground and decided to pull back from new investment. The company had no choice but to reinvent itself. During the remainder of the 1970s Yalumba moved further away from the fortified wine market, turning the focus to creating a niche for itself in quality still and sparkling table wines.

The next decade saw the emergence of youth at Yalumba. Wyndham's son Robert, representing the fifth generation of the family, and Mark's son Michael, representing the sixth generation, were appointed directors at the ages of thirty and twenty-seven, respectively. Although Mark maintained control, Robert and Michael's influence was immediate. Robert had returned to Yalumba after completing a degree in business administration, and by changing the approach to marketing quickly made a positive impact on sales in the British market.

Helen and Wyndham Hill Smith, and Wyndham's mother, Ida Smith, at the Yalumba centenary celebrations in 1949.

Guests at Yalumba during the 1960s and 1970s included (clockwise from top left) the Duke of Edinburgh, Barry Humphries (also known as Dame Edna Everage), Miss Australia 1966 Tania Verstak (with Helen and Margie Hill Smith), cricketer Sir Donald Bradman (with Wyndham Hill Smith and Alf Wark) and renowned horse trainer Colin Hayes (with Wyndham Hill Smith).

Michael's passion was winemaking. In 1984 he left Australia to pursue his master of wine studies in the UK, retaining his role as a director. Michael subsequently became Australia's first Master of Wine.

The growing demand for table wines led to another new development in the wine market — the four-litre cask. Although wine in a cask was generally regarded as inferior, the four-litre cask accounted for more than half of the wine consumed in Australia. Robert, despite vigorous opposition from other directors, convinced the board to invest in the equipment to launch premium-quality varietal wine in a two-litre cask. The result: twelve-month sales projections were met within four months. The success of two-litre casks generated much excitement at Yalumba and gave Robert the confidence to continue to challenge the status quo.

Heritage in a bottle

The 1960s saw Yalumba winning many accolades and honours. Of particular note were the inclusion of Yalumba Carte D'or Riesling on the British Wine & Food Society's list—its first Australian wine—and the announcement in 1966 at the Adelaide Stock Exchange's annual dinner (at which Yalumba wines were being served) by then prime minister Sir Robert Menzies that the 1961 Yalumba Galway Special Reserve Claret was the best red wine he had ever tasted. The status of this wine immediately soared. From the 1962 vintage this wine was labelled the Signature series.

Beginning with the 1962 vintage, the Signature wines of Yalumba have saluted the very best of the vintage. They have also acknowledged the skills and dedicated service of people who have enhanced the traditions and culture of Yalumba. A distinctively Australian blend of Cabernet Sauvignon and Shiraz, The Signature has set the benchmark for this iconic style. Deep and intense, the wine displays full palate weight with powerful fruit and soft American oak, which was hand-coopered at Yalumba. A wine made for longevity, it embodies the essence of Yalumba, its people and its heritage.

If a vintage doesn't meet the standard of excellence demanded, it is not released. Since the first Signature release in 1962 there have been six vintages that did not meet the required standard.

Fittingly, the first vintage honoured the founder of Yalumba, Samuel Smith. Others to be honoured include other family members (both male and female), vineyard managers, winemakers, cellarmen, company secretaries, accountants, state managers, sales representatives, an electrician, an artist and a racehorse trainer. The 1995 vintage, released in 1999, was dedicated to 'every man and woman, girl and boy, who has ever worked or been associated with the Yalumba Wine Company from 1849 to 1999'. The citation, written by Robert Hill Smith explains:

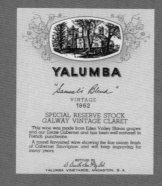

The accoutrements of the past have been shaken off, discarded or evolved but some things remain the same. Yalumba still grows grapes and makes wine for the people of Australia and the world. It also continues to employ people across a broad spectrum of race, creed, colour, skill and talent. Yalumba people stand for the history, heritage and future of this great company.

Yalumba is one of only a handful of wineries in the world with its own on-site cooperage. For more than a century, the winery's coopers have employed their ancient craft to add an extra dimension to its wines. Oak plays an important part in the winemaking process and Yalumba has full control of the quality of oak used to age its wines.

In 1985 Wyndham Hill Smith retired as chairman of Yalumba. This generated a major reshuffle of the board. Wyndham's nephew Mark retired as managing director and became the new chairman. At the age of thirty-four, Robert Hill Smith, twenty-nine years younger than his cousin Mark, was appointed managing director, the fifth generation of the family to occupy the position.

The sixth generation was also represented on the board with Michael as a director. Michael's brother Matthew also worked at Yalumba in the marketing and sales department. Robert's brother Sam had left Yalumba to manage an art gallery in Adelaide. The following year Robert married Annabel Waterman. The couple now have three daughters: Jessica, Lucy and Georgia.

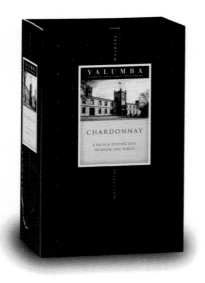

Robert Hill Smith introduced the premium two-litre wine cask to Australia in 1984.

Although sales were excellent, cash flow and profitability were down. Heavy discounting was reducing profit margins and demand for fortified wines (which were costly to produce) had fallen. Robert was forced to reduce overheads through retrenchments, cutting back capital expenditure and more efficient management. He believed that to secure the future of Yalumba executive appointments had to be made on merit, rather than on the basis of automatic accession by family members. With some strategic additions to the board, Robert set about achieving his goal of establishing Yalumba as a maker of premium wines with unique style and personality. Stretching finances to the limit, every part of the winemaking process was overhauled. Growers were paid bonuses if their grapes were of premium quality; the processes of fermentation, storage and bottling were improved; the laboratories were upgraded; outdated buildings were removed or repurposed; and the Yalumba Signature Cellar and the Family Tasting Room were constructed.

The appointment of Brian Walsh as chief winemaker in 1988 was a masterstroke. Brian revitalised the winemaking team and brought them back into contact with the grape growers and the vineyards, which he regarded as crucial to the production of quality wine. Indeed, a good relationship with growers means they are less likely to walk away to get higher prices for their grapes from rival wineries. Brian was appointed to the board of directors in 1996 and relinquished his position as chief winemaker to Louisa Rose in 2007, taking on the role of director of winemaking with responsibility for all viticultural, winemaking and production aspects of Yalumba.

During 1988 Robert became concerned that the diversity of interests and aspirations of other family members was holding the company back. He wanted to consolidate the board and management so that it shared a common passion and vision for Yalumba. Robert and Sam Hill Smith and their immediate family offered to buy out other family shareholders. To finance the buyout Robert and Sam borrowed heavily, putting everything they owned on the line, including their homes.

Not surprisingly, the initial reaction of many family members was incredulous anger and resentment. But after several months of tense and emotional discussion, on 2 June 1989 the buyout was successful.

The Hill Smith boys, 1982. Back row, from left: Sam, Robert, Mark. Front row, from left: Wyndham, Ted the dog, Matthew, Michael.

Robert and
Annabel Hill
Smith, and
daughters
Lucy, Jessica
and Georgia,
with Archie the
dog, 2008.

Mark and Michael Hill Smith later resigned from the board of directors. The staff was overwhelmingly supportive of the buyout and the new focus on the production of fine wine. The mood at Yalumba was buoyant and full of optimism. But once again, an unexpected turn of events was just around the corner.

The burden of debt and risk associated with the buyout became painfully obvious when interest rates soared to about 23 per cent, soaking up cash and obliterating profitability. Robert asked the staff, personally and by mail, to accept a twelve-month salary freeze; not a single person objected. The staff enthusiastically joined with management in meeting the challenge of reducing costs and increasing productivity. Robert and marketing manager John Auld embarked on a thirty-five week mission to increase sales, travelling on discount airfares and staying with friends to reduce costs.

When Wyndham Hill Smith passed away in 1990 at the age of eighty-one the tide was beginning to turn. Sales had improved well beyond expectations, the brand was growing and export markets were booming. It seemed that the pioneering ethos of Samuel Smith — courage in the face of adversity, innovation and determination to make the finest quality wines — was still very much alive.

In 1993 Yalumba sold its fortified wines and trademarks to Mildara Blass Limited, allowing the company to concentrate on table wines and pay off a substantial portion of its debt. During the following years there was unprecedented growth and change. The focus was on producing super premium wines, notably The Signature (a blend of Barossa Cabernet Shiraz), The Menzies (a Coonawarra Cabernet), The Octavius (a handcrafted Barossa Old Vine Shiraz) and The Virgilius Voignier. In 1999, Yalumba celebrated its 150th anniversary.

> ❛A winemaker's challenge is to add an individual element to each wine. We hope to provide enjoyable, multidimensional wines. ❜
>
> Brian Walsh, former chief winemaker

Yalumba entered the twenty-first century as an innovative maker of fine wine with a global presence. It continues to invest discriminately in cutting-edge technology and leads the way in environmental best practice, winning awards in the United States, the United Kingdom and Australia for environmental management. The Yalumba Vine Nursery, established in 1975, is Australia's largest and most reliable source of quality grafted vines.

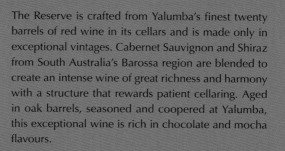

The crème de la crème

The Reserve is crafted from Yalumba's finest twenty barrels of red wine in its cellars and is made only in exceptional vintages. Cabernet Sauvignon and Shiraz from South Australia's Barossa region are blended to create an intense wine of great richness and harmony with a structure that rewards patient cellaring. Aged in oak barrels, seasoned and coopered at Yalumba, this exceptional wine is rich in chocolate and mocha flavours.

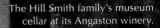
The Hill Smith family's museum cellar at its Angaston winery.

Est. VSOP 1989

Very Special Old People

This plaque honours those who have worked for Yalumba for more than twenty years.

The nursery propagates new and emerging varieties in Australia. This includes Cienna, a new hybrid variety developed in association with national science agency the CSIRO, which was working with several wineries to develop high-quality red wine grapes suited to Australian conditions.

There has been an avalanche of Australian and international awards for Yalumba since the 1989 buyout. Among the most notable are Frescobaldi Trophies won in two consecutive years for the best red wine, five vintages or older at the International Wine & Spirit Competition in London. In 2004, Louisa Rose, Yalumba's chief winemaker received the International Women in Wine Award. In 2007, at the Winestate Wine Awards, Yalumba received awards for both Winemaker of the Year (Kevin Glastonbury) and Winery of the Year. In 2010, the company was awarded the Wine Enthusiast New World Winery of the Year 'for its forward-thinking,

Poetry in a bottle

Yalumba's Voignier vines are the oldest in the Southern Hemisphere. The first commercial vines were planted in 1980, and Yalumba now makes five Viognier white wines. The benchmark is The Virgilius, named in honour of Virgilius (70–19BC), one of the greatest of the ancient Roman poets. His works often celebrated the charm of rural life, including the growing of grapevines.

The Virgilius Eden Valley Viognier, first released in 1998, is Yalumba's most distinguished white wine. The Virgilius is crafted from the best of Yalumba's Eden Valley Viognier fruit. The grapes are hand-picked and pressed directly into French oak barrels for fermenting. After fermentation the wine is aged for a further nine to eleven months. The finest barrels are then chosen for blending.

innovative leadership in the Australian wine industry and an unflagging commitment to quality and family ownership'.

Robert Hill Smith is a keen and vocal supporter of both the Australian wine industry and a number of sporting organisations. He has served on the boards of the Australian Wine and Brandy Corporation, Australian Major Events and the South Australian Thoroughbred Racing Authority, and, at the time of writing, is a member of the Market Development Advisory Committee (formerly the Australian Wine Export Council) and a board member of the South Australian Cricket Association.

Throughout six generations, and at many times against the odds, the Smith and Hill Smith families have maintained the values and heritage of previous generations, and kept the company in family hands. Yalumba has grown into one of the two equal largest family-owned wine companies in Australia (the other is De Bortoli Wines), and the family has provided ongoing support and leadership of the wine industry, the Eden and Barossa valleys, and the Angaston community.

Every generation of the family has had a strong and loyal relationship with its employees, who have shared the setbacks, sorrows, celebrations and triumphs. The Signature series, in particular the 1995 vintage — dedicated to all who had been associated with Yalumba — is testament to this, as are the two plaques inside the entrance to the magnificent clock-tower building.

When asked how Yalumba has survived for so long, Robert Hill Smith explains:

> *The Australian wine industry has been through a series of booms and busts over a period of more than 160 years. Our family has lived through all of them. You learn to 'cop it'. You can't survive without hard work and an element of luck. But it's much more than that. There must also be intelligence, risk-taking and a passion that exceeds the desire for profit. Success brings pride that must be balanced with humility — not overtaken by arrogance. Success also brings confidence that must remain under an umbrella of reality. We are cerebral, we dare to be different and we challenge the status quo.*

Running a winery is not for the faint-hearted. To survive you have to love what you do, and this is certainly evident at Yalumba. Australia's oldest winery has a proud history, and continues to go from strength to strength. The Hill Smith family's drive to produce world-class quality wine is matched by its desire to make a difference and leave a legacy. These are the attributes that will ensure it flourishes and carries on its tradition of making diverse, premium wines.

Screw caps and Yalumba

The history of Yalumba and the screw-cap closure spans more than three decades. The first screw cap used commercially was the Stelcap in 1970. Yalumba and a group of other wineries (including McWilliam's, Brown Brothers and Tahbilk) were involved in developing and improving the concept from about 1973, first using the Stelvin closure in 1976.

While the wine industry was excited about the screw cap, wine consumers were less so, seeing the metal cap as an indication of a lower quality product. As a result, in 1984 the Yalumba wines that had been sealed under screw cap reverted to cork. It wasn't until 1995 that Yalumba again began using the screw cap.

The screw cap eliminates the possibility of wine taint from cork and, as there is minimal contact between the sealing polymer and the wine, flavour absorption from the closure is not an issue. The screw cap is a wonderful seal for ensuring perfect bottle ageing of appropriate white wines; in particular, Riesling. It removes all the problems associated with using closures that are 'stuffed' into a bottle neck. As the seal doesn't allow any air into the bottle, the wine undergoes a slow but perfect ageing process. 'It offers the perfect environment, providing consistency and not allowing oxygen to influence the wine', says Louisa Rose, Yalumba's head of winemaking.

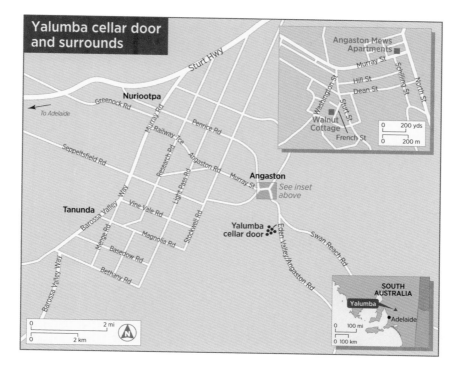

Cellar door

Eden Valley Rd
Angaston SA 5353
t: 08 8561 3200
w: www.yalumba.com
e: info@yalumba.com

Opening hours
Monday to Sunday: 10 am to 5 pm
Public holidays: 10 am to 5 pm
Closed: Good Friday, Christmas Day,
Boxing Day and New Year's Day

Accommodation options

Angaston Mews Apartments
8 Murray St
Angaston SA 5353
t: 08 8563 1000
w: www.angastonmewsapartments.
   com.au
e: getaway@grs.com.au

Walnut Cottage
8 French St
Angaston SA 5353
t: 08 8562 4556
w: www.walnut-cottage.com.au

Tyrrell's Wines

A magnificent obsession

'We have an unbroken 150-year history of winemaking. Five generations of us haven't been in this to hang our hats on homogenised, mass-produced wines.'

Bruce Tyrrell AM, managing director, Tyrrell's Wines

*T*he Tyrrell family has lived on their Ashmans vineyard in the New South Wales Hunter Valley, about two hours' drive north of Sydney, since 1858. More than 150 years later, Tyrrell's Hunter Valley winery is an amalgam of the old and the new. Rustic buildings, dirt floors and old French oak casks remain, but you'll also find shiny stainless steel vats, modern laboratory facilities and big new French oak casks used to enhance the lift and softness of its reds. Nothing at Tyrrell's winery is just for show. Everything you see, taste and smell is there to satisfy an obsession with quality that has lasted five generations.

Out of this unpretentious winery comes a collection of wines of character, flavour and integrity, including Vat 1 Semillon (the most awarded white wine of the Australian wine show circuit), Vat 47 Chardonnay (Australia's first commercial Chardonnay) and Vat 9 Shiraz (Tyrrell's flagship red wine).

Five generations of winemaking by the Tyrrell family can be traced back to 1854, when Edward Tyrrell, son of an English eye surgeon, migrated to Australia at the age of nineteen to live with his older brother Lovick.

Edward was keen to work the land and tried his hand at dairy farming before becoming fascinated with the thriving vineyards in the Hunter Valley. He subsequently purchased 320 acres of land in 1858 and began preparing the land for vineyards, clearing the native bush by hand. He planted vines from cuttings brought to Australia from the Rhone Valley in France by James Busby in 1832. Busby, a Scottish migrant, had studied viticulture and winemaking in France before making his way to New South Wales. Busby gave his cuttings to the New South Wales government for propagation at Sydney's Botanic Gardens and to distribute to grape growers.

Edward lived alone in a modest, one-room ironbark slab hut, which he built himself. The hut remains standing today. He named his property 'Ashmans' after his maternal grandmother's ancestral home in Beccles, Suffolk.

The Tyrrell's cellar door, with stainless steel vats in the background.

A lot of settlers turned to grape-growing and winemaking to make a living, no doubt influenced by the government's encouragement of the practice. Edward, like many others at the time, was a self-taught winemaker. In 1863 he built a winery from ironbark and corrugated iron in preparation for his first vintage, which was predominantly Semillon and Shiraz. Both of these varieties had already been successful in the Hunter Valley region. Later that year Edward also built an ironbark house, complete with bedrooms, a dining room and a music room.

Edward married Susan Hungerford in 1869, and in 1870 the first of their ten children, Susan (known as Molly) was born. By then some thirty acres of Semillon, Shiraz and Aucerot (regarded as the prince of white wine at the time) had been planted.

Edward Tyrrell (1835–1909).

In 1871, Edward and Susan's second child was born. Edward George Tyrrell was known as Dan from birth and later in life became affectionately known as Uncle Dan. Dan grew up in the vineyards and winery, and developed a fascination for making and blending wine. He completed his first vintage at the age of seventeen in 1889 under the guidance of his father. When his father died in 1909, Dan took over the management of the winery.

Dan adopted the same simple winemaking practices used by his father. He spurned technology, refusing to make use of refrigeration and even thermometers. While other wineries were concreting their floors, Dan insisted that hard dirt floors were an important element in wine maturation and flavour.

Keen to learn all he could about winemaking, Dan spent time with the great Hunter Valley winemakers Philobert Terrier, Maurice O'Shea, Leo Buring, Dr Henry Lindeman, Audrey Wilkinson and James King.

The ironbark hut built in 1858 still stands today near the
entrance to Tyrrell's cellar door and has been named the Hunter's
first heritage icon by the Hunter Valley Vineyard Association.

The fight for dirt

The dirt floors that Dan Tyrrell was so passionate about are still a feature of Tyrrell's winery, but not without a major fight with bureaucracy. In 1977, eighteen years after Dan's death, health inspectors arrived and insisted that the floors be concreted in the name of public health. His nephew, Murray Tyrrell, was furious and with the help of his son Bruce (the current managing director) undertook a scientific investigation to prove that the dirt floors posed no risk.

To the disbelief of the bureaucrats the bacterial counts with the dirt floor and wooden casks were much less than where there were stainless steel vats and concrete floors. Despite this evidence they continued to demand the winery change its practices, but they had to give up when they discovered that the winery had been classified by the National Trust.

Dan learnt much from these winemakers and later, with the help of his brother Avery, who was almost twenty years his junior, produced some of the best wines in the Hunter Valley.

Dan and Avery were a formidable team, with Dan managing the winery and Avery managing the vineyards. Apart from Avery's service in World War I and some time spent in Queensland with their brother, Frederick, before enlisting, the pair spent their entire lives living and working at Ashmans.

Avery was meticulous with his viticulture and would often redo work done in the vineyards by others — including Dan— if it wasn't 'just right'. Dan thrived on hard work. His remedy whenever he felt ill was to go out into the vineyard with a hoe to 'shake his liver up'. Dan worked up until the day he died in 1959 at the age of eighty-seven.

Although the wine made by the Tyrrell brothers was reputedly among the best in the Hunter Valley, the Tyrrell name was not well recognised. Most of the wine was sold in bulk to wine merchants and many of the best vintages were sold to Maurice O'Shea for his Mount Pleasant winery and bottled under his own label.

When Dan fell from a ladder in the winery in 1955 he began to gradually hand the management of Tyrrell's to Avery's oldest son, Murray. Avery died of a heart attack at the age of sixty-four in 1956. Three years later Dan also passed away following a heart attack, having presided over a remarkable seventy consecutive vintages. Regretfully, very few of them were bottled under a Tyrrell's label.

Dan never married, so it was Murray who was destined to take the Tyrrell family into its third generation of winemaking. The impact he eventually had on the Australian wine industry was surprising because after completing high school he went to work on a cattle station as a jackeroo. After serving in the army in World War II, Murray settled on a Hunter Valley cattle property called 'Vioka', which became the site of the Rothbury Estate winery in 1968. However, when Dan died Murray was able to step into the role of winemaker armed with the knowledge and experience he had gained over the years helping his father and uncle on the property.

Retaining the dirt floors in the winery required a major fight with bureaucracy.

Murray Davey Tyrrell took over the family business at a difficult time. The land under vine had declined from 130 to sixty-eight acres following the economic downturn of the 1930s. To make matters worse, hailstorms buffeted the Hunter Valley in 1958, 1960 and 1962, devastating the vines. However, Murray was not about to let Mother Nature win without a fight. After the first hailstorm of 1958, he imported one-metre-long rockets from France in an attempt to save his vines from future hailstorms.

Edward George
(Dan) Tyrrell
(1871–1959).

Dorothy and
Avery Tyrrell.

He fired them into the clouds, transforming some of the hailstones into harmless sleet before they could hit the ground. Despite his best efforts, the degree of success in saving the crops was not clear. The vintages in the years affected by the hail were made from less than 75 per cent of the usual crop.

Despite the setbacks, Murray was determined to build on the success that his Uncle Dan had achieved — and he made sure that this time the wines were sold under the Tyrrell's label so the accolades were directed to where they belonged. Murray also introduced the 'vat' system, where the fruit from the best vineyard blocks was matured in individual oak vats and numbered to identify the wines. Vats 5, 7 and 9 (all Shiraz) were released in 1961 and Vat 1 (Hunter Semillon) was released in 1963. The vat system proved to be very successful. By 1969 more than twenty red vat numbers were released as the Tyrrell's Private Bin range. Vat 47, one of Australia's first commercial Chardonnays, was released in 1971, and by 1972 there were nine white vat numbers.

> ‘Why muck around wasting time reading thermometers? You test a baby's bottle with your arm, so why not wine?’
>
> Murray Tyrrell

Described variously as 'larger than life', 'King of the Hunter Valley' and, most famously, 'the Mouth of the Hunter', Murray Tyrrell was always ready to share his opinions forcefully when he thought it necessary. Murray favoured traditional methods of winemaking and was very selective about using new technology. He even rejected the humble thermometer, preferring to plunge his arm into open vats to check the temperature, just as his Uncle Dan did.

In 1968, together with renowned winemaker Len Evans and eight others, Murray founded the Rothbury Estate winery. Expansion of Tyrrell's within the Hunter Valley was also taking place, as the demand for its wines increased with the purchase of Penfolds HVD vineyard and both the Glenbawn Estate winery and the Brokenback vineyard (from Rothbury Estate) in 1987.

Murray Davey Tyrrell AM (1921–2000).

In 1986, Murray's services to the wine industry were recognised when he was made a Member of the Order of Australia (AM) for services to the wine industry. Not only had he set a new benchmark for quality wine production with his vat system and built a market for new wines like the Vat 47 Chardonnay, but he had made significant contributions to growth in tourism in the Hunter Valley. Murray was one of the pioneers of wine tours, and allowed visitors to the winery to taste wines directly from the vats so that they could pre-order for delivery when the wine was bottled. Wine lovers flocked to Tyrrell's to taste and buy wines direct from the winery, sales boomed and the Hunter Valley became a favourite destination for tourists.

Preparing rockets to launch into a hailstorm, circa 1960.

Murray's son, Murray Bruce Tyrrell, known as Bruce, was born in 1951 while his Great Uncle Dan Tyrrell was still in charge at Ashmans. Bruce was always interested in the business side of winemaking, and was the first member of the Tyrrell family to go to university, studying Agricultural Economics at the University of New England in Armidale, New South Wales. He joined the company full-time in 1974 at the age of twenty-three. It was during this time that Bruce fell in love with Semillon, eventually creating one of Tyrrell's most acclaimed white wines. He assisted his father as a winemaker and played a role in establishing distribution in major cities, setting up a direct-mail system and developing export markets in the United Kingdom, United States and Canada. Bruce took over the leadership of Tyrrell's Wines from the then seventy-three-year-old Murray in 1994.

Since 1858, when Edward began clearing the land at Ashmans, sport has been a feature at Tyrrell's. Edward and his neighbours spent their days off on the property playing cricket,

Alf King and Ivy Taff in 1962 working the hand press built for Edward Tyrrell in 1863. This press is an ongoing part of the Tyrrell's winemaking tradition.

tennis and Australian Rules Football. Murray was an opening batsman in the New South Wales schoolboys cricket team, but his cricketing career stalled when World War II broke out. The young Bruce Tyrrell was a talented rugby player until injury forced him out of the game. His wife, Pauline, worked in the ABC's sports department in Queensland in the early 1970s, and it was a common interest in sport and wine that laid the foundation for their partnership after they met at the 1975 Brisbane Wine Show.

Today Tyrrell's continues its association with sport through sponsorships. Between 1991 and 2001 Tyrrell's was the wine sponsor of Cricket Australia. In true Tyrrell's character, being a sponsor meant more than providing financial support and wine for the Australian cricket team and officials — Bruce became the unofficial wine educator for the team.

After moving into the top job Bruce took the expansion of Tyrrell's Wines outside the Hunter Valley for the first time. During his first two years as chief executive he purchased a McLaren Vale vineyard in South Australia (growing mainly Cabernet and Shiraz), a Heathcote vineyard in Victoria (growing Shiraz) and a share of St Mary's vineyard on South Australia's Limestone

Coast (growing mainly Cabernet Sauvignon, Merlot and Shiraz). Although expansion into new and unproven regions is risky — it took fifteen years before he was convinced that the purchase of the Heathcote vineyard was the right decision — Bruce was determined to succeed. In 1997 the super premium all red Rufus Stone wine range made from McLaren Vale and Heathcote fruit was released to acclaim from wine critics.

In 2006 Bruce Tyrrell was honoured as his father was with appointment as a Member of the Order of Australia (AM) for his contribution to the Australian wine industry, improving grape quality, research, tourism and export opportunities.

The motto at Tyrrell's — introduced by its founder more than 150 years ago — is 'Nothing is great unless it is good'. The 'good' starts in the vineyard. Each vineyard site is run differently according to its meso-climate, soil and topography. Bruce explains: 'There is an amazing variety of soil types in the Hunter Valley. We experiment with different patches of dirt to match varieties to the best-suited soil. There are some great little patches, such as the great old vineyards, but there are also some that are useless'.

The preservation of Tyrrell's premium vineyards is crucial to the future of the business. Bruce explains: 'We believe in minimal

A standout red

Tyrrell's Vat 9 Hunter Shiraz is Tyrrell's flagship red wine. Since its first release in 1961 it has won numerous awards, the standout being a trophy win at the International Wine and Spirit competition in London in 1995 for the 1992 Vat 9 Hunter Shiraz.

The fruit for this elegant red is hand-picked from Shiraz vines dating back to the 1879 vines planted by Edward Tyrrell. The influence of these older vines results in a unique fruit-driven wine with distinctive characteristics of polished leather and spice.

interference in the vineyard. We try to use the least possible amount of chemicals, and make our own mulch and fertiliser'.

At Ashmans, until recently there had never been water for irrigation and most of the vineyard is dry grown. Tyrrell's has also improved its irrigation systems in other vineyards to make more efficient use of water and reduce wastage. The result is that the amount and quality of grapes has improved significantly. At the Glenbawn vineyard at the top of the Hunter Valley, the crop has doubled in size and is of higher quality. Bruce's philosophy on sustainability is simple. 'We just want to be good farmers', he says. 'We have to be sustainable or we wouldn't have lasted 150 years and certainly couldn't last another 150.'

Former Australian cricket team wicketkeeper Ian Healy and captain Mark Taylor spreading the word about Tyrrell's during a tour of India.

Until 1971 no-one outside the family had been given a winemaking role at Tyrrell's. Since then only three non–family members have taken on the position of chief winemaker — Ralph Fowler, Mike DeGaris and incumbent Andrew 'Spin' Spinaze. Ralph admits that when he set up his own winery, Ralph Fowler Wines on South Australia's Limestone Coast, he was trying to re-create the passion, enthusiasm and excitement that permeates Tyrrell's Wines. Everyone who works, or has worked, at Tyrrell's absorbs part of its unique heritage, heart and soul.

Being chief winemaker at Tyrrell's is no easy task. Expectations are high and any errors are pointed out in no uncertain terms. The role was quite frightening when Murray Tyrrell — ever one to call a spade a bloody shovel — was in charge. Bruce recalls, 'I remember the meeting where the old man called in Mike DeGaris and told him he was the new chief winemaker. I'll never forget the look on Mike's face. It said "Oh, shit!"'

The midnight leap

During the late 1960s white wine production became a higher priority at Tyrrell's. Semillon had always been grown at Ashmans, but Murray Tyrrell was convinced that there was a market for Chardonnay. He knew that the nearby Penfolds HVD (Hunter Valley Distillery) vineyard had some varieties of Chardonnay because as a young boy he picked bunches of them to eat. When the Penfolds manager refused him permission to take some cuttings for his own property in 1967, Murray decided to take the matter into his own hands. Late one night he jumped over a barbed wire fence to 'liberate' a variety of Chardonnay cuttings. The vines that grew from these cuttings were used to make Tyrrell's first release of the hugely successful Vat 47 Chardonnay in 1971.

Ironically, fifteen years later, in 1982, Tyrrell's purchased the HVD vineyard from Penfolds and it is now one of only three vineyards used for Vat 47 Chardonnay.

Tyrrell's Wines' Hunter Valley vineyard
and the Brokenback Ranges.

'It's a bloody obsession'

Since Edward Tyrrell first planted vines at Ashmans, each subsequent generation has championed a different variety. For Dan it was Shiraz, for Murray it was Chardonnay and for Bruce it is Semillon. When Bruce was asked by international wine judge and author Jancis Robinson whether his passion for Semillon was still as strong, his response was, 'It's not a passion — it's a bloody obsession'.

Murray, however, did not approve of Bruce's faith in the aging of Semillon. He was convinced it would never work. Determined to prove his father wrong, Bruce secretly put away 1000 cases of 1989 Vat 1 Semillon to age and wrote them off on the stock sheet. He disguised his secret cache by surrounding it with cases of red. Seven years later Bruce began to sneak the aged Semillon into wine shows and tastings with excellent results. At one of the tastings Murray Tyrrell was heard to remark, 'Bloody younger generation — they'd never have thought to put this wine away'.

Andrew 'Spin' Spinaze has been chief winemaker since 1989. He served his apprenticeship at Tyrrell's and after completing his studies at Roseworthy Agricultural College in Adelaide he travelled to France to finetune his winemaking skills. Andrew oversees all of the winemaking operations in the Hunter Valley and has been instrumental in the company's investments outside the Valley. In 2004 he was named Winemaker of the Year by the two most important wine magazines in Australia — *Winestate* and *Gourmet Traveller WINE*. Since Andrew's appointment, Tyrrell's Wines has been awarded numerous trophies and medals. In 2008 the winery received fourteen of the nineteen trophies presented at the Hunter Valley Wine Show. The accolades continued in 2009, including the award for Best Semillon at the Decanter World Wine Awards in London for Vat 1 Semillon 1998, and in 2010 leading Australian wine authority

James Halliday named Tyrrell's Wines the Winery of the Year in his annual *Wine Companion*.

Chris Tyrrell, part of the fifth generation, works as an assistant winemaker. His sister, Jane, and brother, John, also work at the winery. Growing up in the vineyard and winery, Chris has been involved with wine for as long as he can remember. He began making wine under the guidance of grandfather Murray and completed his first vintage in 2001 while he was studying Wine Science at Charles Sturt University. Since then, Chris has travelled extensively and worked in some of the world's greatest wine regions, including Burgundy, the Rhone Valley and Bordeaux in France, and in Spain.

> **'In my mind, inviting people to the winery is the single most important thing Murray Tyrrell did. He was the father of wine tourism.'**
>
> Bruce Tyrrell

Red winemaker Mark 'Richo' Richardson, born and bred in the Hunter Valley, is in charge of red wine production and is credited with giving Tyrrell's reds a new lease of life since his appointment in 1994. Mark was awarded Winemaker of the Year by Campbell Mattinson and Gary Walsh in *The Big Red Wine Book 2009/10*.

Winning prestigious awards is nothing new at Tyrrell's. In 1979 Murray demonstrated that Australian winemakers could compete with the world's best when he won the Gault Milleau Award for the World's Finest Pinot Noir at the Wine Olympiad in Paris for his 1976 Vat 6 Pinot Noir. Another Murray Tyrrell creation (thanks to the 'midnight leap' into the Penfolds HVD vineyard), his Vat 47 Chardonnay, has won countless trophies and medals since its release in 1971. Vat 1 Semillon has also been a prolific award winner ever since the cases that Bruce hid from his father were released. At the time of writing, its tally stood at 118 trophies and 364 gold medals, no doubt with many more to come.

✦   ✦   ✦

Working the grape press.

Testing the reds. From left: Chris Tyrrell, Bruce Tyrrell and Mark Richardson.

A grape picker completing the last of the handpicking for the single vineyard 2008 Belford Chardonnay. The vines were planted in 1933.

The Hunter Valley and many other Australian wine regions were spared the devastation of the phylloxera louse epidemic that wiped out the great vineyards of Europe during the nineteenth century. As a result, some of the vineyards in the Hunter Valley are among the oldest in the world. Bruce Tyrrell has identified a selection of the oldest of his own Hunter Valley vineyards as 'sacred sites' for their ability to produce fruit that is 'so good and so different' that it warrants individual bottling. Individual vineyard wines from sacred sites are only bottled if they meet the highest standards of regional and varietal expression. Among them are Stevens Shiraz, Stevens Semillon, HVD Semillon and Belford Semillon.

> ❛They are passionate, proud and involved wine people, and that rubs off on anyone who's lucky enough to pass through. I'm proud to have learned my trade here.❜
>
> Ralph Fowler, former chief winemaker

The integrity of Tyrrell's Wines is vital to its future as a family business. Any vintage that doesn't meet Tyrrell's standard of excellence is withheld and written off. 'Family [wine] businesses can't afford to disappoint the drinking public', Bruce explains. To ensure future success, Bruce and his team are always keen to try something new and make selective use of new technology. However, when times are tough the winery prefers to concentrate on what it is already doing well.

Export markets are also important for future success. Tyrrell's has been exporting to the United Kingdom since the

The old and the new at Tyrrell's.

Cliffy's lost block

Not one to completely hand over the reins to any part of the winery, it was not unusual for Murray Tyrrell to arbitrarily direct grape pickers from one block to another without telling the vineyard manager. When Murray moved pickers out of the HVD vineyard and into another block one day in 1993, vineyard manager Cliff Currie was surprised and impressed that picking in the HVD block had been completed so quickly. However, much to his embarrassment, a week later he discovered that a whole block of grapes meant for HVD Semillon had been left unpicked. He enlisted a nightshift gang of pickers to retrieve the approximately thirty-five tonnes of grapes.

Some time later, one anonymous employee with a healthy sense of humour wrote on the side of the tank in which the grapes were fermented 'Cliffy's Lost Block Semillon'. Subsequently, the wine made from these grapes was labelled 'Lost Block Semillon'.

The Lost Block label has expanded to an annual portfolio of wines that are deliberately crafted in the same style that made the original Lost Block Semillon such a success—fruit laden, fresh, vibrant and easy to drink. The portfolio now includes Cabernet Sauvignon, Chardonnay, Merlot, Sauvignon Blanc, Shiraz Viognier and Semillon.

1950s, and to the United States and Canada since 1983. World-wide exports currently account for approximately 20 per cent of Tyrrell's sales, with China the largest single export market.

The continuation of Tyrrell's Wines as a family business for at least another 150 years is Bruce Tyrrell's dream. He believes strongly that the innovation and leadership required by the wine industry, nationally and locally, will come from family businesses.

Bruce and Pauline's three children, Jane, John and Chris, all grew up around the winery, just as their father and grandfather did. As children they earned money by working in the business and as adults they are well entrenched there. Jane worked her way up from assistant to the business development manager to New South Wales sales manager. John is a winery assistant, helping to keep things in line and ensuring that crew members always have a smile on their face. Chris, as mentioned, is an assistant winemaker, and is already establishing his own identity in the wine industry.

> 'Wine is forever in our blood and in our dreams. With an eye towards the future, we will continue to create individual wines of character, flavour and, above all, integrity.'
>
> Bruce Tyrrell

The sixth generation — alongside members of the fourth and fifth generations — will play an important role in taking Tyrrell's into the future and maintaining its integrity. For all, it is 'a bloody obsession'. Without doubt, this 150-year-old family-owned winemaking company will continue on, producing rich, elegant wines crafted with care and dedication for another 150 years.

Left: The Tyrrell family. From left: Chris, John, Jane, Pauline and Bruce.

Overleaf: Tyrrell's Wines' Four and Eight Acres vineyard in the Hunter Valley at sunset.

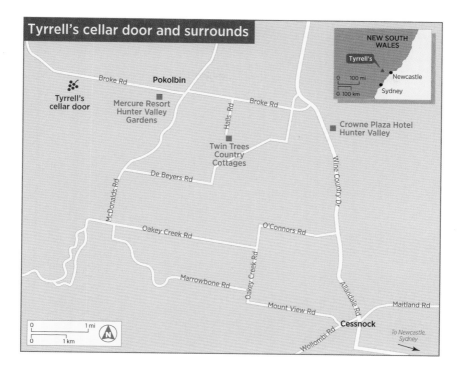

Cellar door

1838 Broke Rd
Pokolbin NSW 2320
t: 02 4993 7000
w: www.tyrrells.com.au
e: cellardoor@tyrrells.com.au

Opening hours
Monday to Saturday: 9 am to 5 pm
Sunday: 10 am to 4 pm

Accommodation options

Crowne Plaza Hotel Hunter Valley
430 Wine Country Dr
Lovedale NSW 2325
t: 02 4991 0900
w: www.crowneplazahuntervalley.com.au
e: reservations.hunter@ihg.com

Mercure Resort Hunter Valley Gardens
2090 Broke Rd
Pokolbin NSW 2320
t: 02 4998 2000
w: www.mercurehuntervalley.com.au
e: reservations@mercurehunter
    valley.com.au

Twin Trees Country Cottages
Halls Rd
Pokolbin NSW 2320
t: 02 4998 7311
w: www.twintrees.com.au
e: stay@twintrees.com.au

Tahbilk
Priceless heritage

'For my grandfather, Eric Purbrick, Tahbilk was not just everything, it was the only thing, and for successive generations that passion for all things Tahbilk has become part of our family fabric.'

Alister Purbrick, chief winemaker and CEO, Tahbilk

Surrounded by a network of lakes, billabongs and lagoons near the Victorian town of Nagambie lies the historical Tahbilk winery and vineyards. The wetlands and waterways are linked by the Goulburn River, which flows from the Victorian Alps to the mighty Murray River. Nagambie Lakes is the only wine region in Australia (and one of only six in the world) in which the meso-climate is dramatically and positively influenced by an inland water mass.

At first glance, the winery and underground cellars don't look a great deal different from the way they were 150 years ago. In fact, if there were no cars or trucks on the site, you could easily believe that you had been transported back to the nineteenth century.

Much of the
Tahbilk property
looks just the
way it did
150 years ago.

One of Australia's oldest and most beautiful wineries, Tahbilk
is also one of the most successful, having been recognised with
numerous awards for its wines at the world's principal exhibitions
and wine shows. The first awards date back to the early 1860s, and
were won at exhibitions in Bordeaux, Paris, Brussels and London.
The accolades and awards of the past fifty years have been no less
impressive, with Tahbilk winning an array of trophies and medals
in major Australian and international wine shows.

Tahbilk was founded in 1860 by a group of Melbourne
businessmen, including John Pinney Bear, whose family later took
control of the estate, and French-born surveyor and winemaker
Ludovic Marie. They selected a site known to the local Aboriginal
people as *tabilk-tabilk*, meaning 'place of many waterholes', and
named their company Tabilk Vineyard Proprietary.

Ludovic Marie was appointed manager of the property and
during 1860 he oversaw the construction of the winery. The
walls were built using mudstone quarried on the property and
handmade bricks sundried on site. The supporting beams and
pillars were cut by hand from red gum and ironbark. Marie also
planted just over sixty acres of vines in the same year, with a

further 140 acres planted during the following twelve months. His first vintage was completed in 1861.

Marie left Tabilk in October 1862 and was replaced with former Hunter Valley winemaker and new director James Blake. Excavation and building on the property continued and by 1865 the cottages, sheds, stables, blacksmith's shop and underground cellar, all of which still exist, were completed.

In 1869, with Tabilk struggling to sell its wine and in financial difficulty, James Blake departed, apparently after being blamed for Tabilk's decline. His successor was Leopold Quinton de Soyres, who was of French and Swiss origin. He left after only two years as winemaker to plant his own vineyard and was replaced by director and chemist William Ford, whose term was cut short by his sudden death in 1875. Despite the 'passing parade' of winemakers, by 1875 Tabilk had recovered from its financial woes. Each winemaker had left his mark on the property and the Swiss–French influence was clearly visible in the architecture of the buildings.

A further underground cellar, which became known as the 'new cellar', was completed in 1876. Yet another manager and winemaker, Dr James S Adams, oversaw the construction. John Pinney Bear, one of the founding directors, and his family took full ownership of the company during 1876.

This advertisement from illustrated newspaper *The Australasian Sketcher*, 22 April 1882, highlights some of the awards won by Chateau Tahbilk in the late nineteenth century.

CHATEAU TAHBILK VINEYARD WINES.

These wines obtained prize medals at Philadelphia, 1876 ; Paris, 1878 ; Melbourne International Exhibition, 1880-81 Eleven awards out of twelve samples submitted, including SECOND ORDER OF MERIT (the highest award obtained by any Colonial Wine), for Hermitage. Adelaide, 1881, Gold Medal. Bordeaux, 1882, Highest Award, Gold Medal

Shiraz	Pedro Ximenes
Port	Hock
Hermitage	Verdeilho
Claret	Reisling
Muscat	Chassela
Hermitage	Chablis

The LARGEST STOCK OF PURE NATURAL WINES IN THE COLONY TO SELECT FROM. In bulk or bottle, at prices which will compare favourably with any other house in the trade, at the

TOWN DEPOT MELBOURNE, 131 COLLINS-STREET WEST.

WHERE THE WINES CAN BE SAMPLED.   The Chateau Tahbilk Wines Only Sold.

The site of Tahbilk was known to the local Aboriginal people as *tabilk-tabilk*, meaning 'place of many waterholes'.

Liquid history

Since its first release in 1979 Tahbilk 1860 Vines Shiraz has become one of the most sought-after and collectable wines in the world. This flagship wine is produced from one-and-a-quarter acres of the original vineyard planted in 1860. The vines are some of the oldest Shiraz vines in the world, having escaped the ravages of the phylloxera louse that devastated so many other vineyards in Europe and Australia. In 2002, influential US magazine *Wine & Spirits* nominated Tahbilk's 1860 vineyard as one of the twenty-five great vineyards of the world.

The fruit is hand-picked and fermented in century-old oak vats. It is then transferred to French oak barrels to mature for eighteen months before bottling. The wine is then aged in the bottle a further four years before being released. The wine is only released, however, if it meets the strict quality standards set by chief winemaker Alister Purbrick.

The European influence at Tabilk continued when progressive French winemaker François Coueslant was appointed manager and winemaker in 1877. Within eight months of Coueslant's appointment, with Bear's approval, he changed the name Tabilk to Chateau Tahbilk. There is no record of the reason for the change, but one theory is that the new name was more sophisticated, softer sounding and more appealing to export markets in the United Kingdom and Europe. By this time Bear had moved to London and was keen to promote and sell wine from his Australian vineyards.

Coueslant was responsible for the construction of the distinctive tower, which was completed in 1882. The tower has four levels: the first and second were used for winemaking until the 1940s, the third to store oats for the horses and the fourth was described by Coueslant as an observation room or deck that allowed management to view the whole vineyard, 'which in fact may help the work a little'.

The cellar yard and tower, circa 1896.

The new cellar as it was in the 1970s. The earthen
floor had been replaced with concrete.

The tenure of Coueslant coincided with a period of innovation and consolidation, described by some as the 'first golden age' of Tahbilk. But the success was tempered by the disparity between the motives of Coueslant and his employer. Coueslant was a creative, driven viticulturist and winemaker. He was passionate about making the best wine from the best fruit. Bear ran the business from a distance in London, and, as he saw it, the best way to fund his lifestyle in England was to export 'acceptable' Australian wine to the United Kingdom.

Coueslant left Chateau Tahbilk in disgust in 1886, his vision for excellence unattainable because of Bear's refusal to invest in improvements to the vineyards and winery. Prior to his departure, despite the constraints, Coueslant had produced wines that won awards at prestigious world exhibitions in Bordeaux, Amsterdam, Calcutta and London.

Three years later John Pinney Bear died suddenly, which left his only son, John, in control of Chateau Tahbilk on behalf of his mother, Annette, and sisters, who remained in London. After what was reportedly a major family disagreement, John relinquished

This postcard, circa 1896, shows a view of the Tahbilk cellars and tower from the Goulburn River.

CHATEAU TAHBILK VINEYARD CELLARS
GOULBURN RIVER, VICTORIA

managerial control and departed, leaving his mother and sisters in control of the company from thousands of kilometres away.

Although the vine louse phylloxera was discovered in Victoria in the 1870s, it was not detected at Chateau Tahbilk until twenty years later. Phylloxera attacks the roots of vines, causing them to shrivel and die. Of the 300 acres of vines at Chateau Tahbilk, 200 acres resisted louse attack, including the Shiraz vines planted in 1860. The affected vines were pulled out and replaced with healthy vines grafted onto imported American rootstock.

> 'The winery's future success and destiny will be determined solely by the family and, as such, Tahbilk and the Purbricks are inextricably linked forever.'
>
> Alister Purbrick

The phylloxera infection at Chateau Tahbilk occurred just as the depression of the 1890s began. Export markets collapsed, unemployment soared to more than 25 per cent, and with a population of fewer than four million that was spread across a vast continent and showed little consumer interest in wine, the domestic market was limited. The hope of a resurgence in exports dissipated when World War I broke out. In addition, with proprietors Annette Bear and her daughters in London giving directions to male viticulturists and winemakers by mail, communication was slow and full of tension and distrust. The condition of the vineyards, quality of the wine and income all declined. The London proprietors refused to provide the necessary funding to reverse the slide and in 1925 Chateau Tahbilk was listed for sale.

When retired businessman Reginald (Reg) Purbrick purchased Chateau Tahbilk in June 1925, he had no experience in or knowledge of winemaking and intended to pull out the vines and subdivide the property into dairy farms. Reg had moved to England after selling his milk-processing company in Melbourne, Victoria, to Nestlé.

Reg Purbrick, who purchased Chateau Tahbilk from the Bear family, later became a member of the British House of Commons.

After some time reflecting on his purchase, Reg became convinced that the winery was viable and offered it to his son, Eric Stevens Purbrick, who had already gained honours in law and was studying accountancy at Cambridge University.

The future of the winery appeared to be in even greater jeopardy than when owned by the Bear family — an Australian businessman living in London with no experience in vineyards or winemaking had purchased a rundown vineyard overgrown with weeds and overrun by rabbits. His son, who later agreed to manage it and undertake winemaking responsibilities, had a degree in law, played tennis and skied very well, but had never set foot in a vineyard. However, an exciting new chapter in the history of Tahbilk was about to begin.

When Eric Purbrick joined his father to inspect the newly acquired property in 1925, he remained in Melbourne for a few months but spent most of his weekends at Chateau Tahbilk. On returning to England he completed his accountancy studies, earning a Master of Arts degree, and in 1929 was called to the Bar of the Inner Temple (an association for barristers and judges) in London. Within twelve months of working in the courts Eric decided against practising law. He wanted a challenge and began to search for a rundown business that he could resuscitate.

His father's offer to manage the winery still stood, but it wasn't until Eric was on a holiday in Germany with his new wife, Marjory, that he made the decision to embark on a challenge in Australia instead of England. He was attracted to a sign hanging outside a 200-year-old tavern in the Black Forest. Eric persuaded the local blacksmith to make a replica with the name 'Chateau Tahbilk' and his initials 'EP' on it. The sign was a symbol of the fine, light table wine that he had thought of one day making during his earlier visits to the vineyards near Nagambie.

Eric, Marjory and their one-year-old-son, Reginald John Stevens Purbrick (always known as John), arrived at Chateau Tahbilk in February 1931. Although well educated, intelligent and energetic, the twenty-eight-year-old Eric knew little about winemaking. Despite this, he had a fine palate, a love of wine and a new sign made in Germany for his cellar.

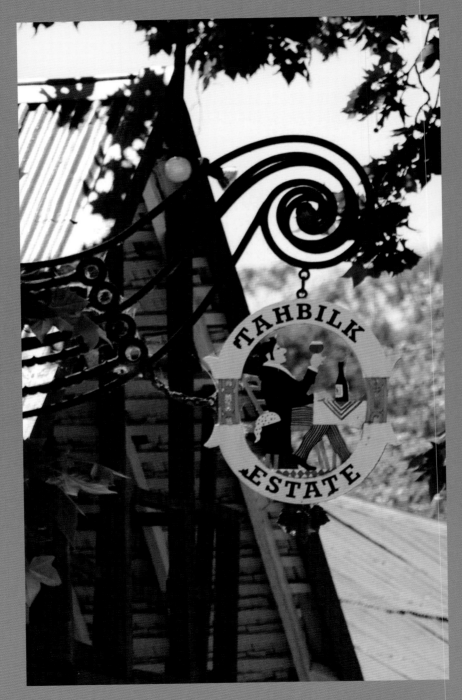

The sign that Eric Purbrick had made in Germany.
The name Chateau Tahbilk has been replaced with Tahbilk Estate.

Chateau Tahbilk's new owner expected to be taking a purely managerial role on the property. A winemaker, Jim Hindhaugh, had been employed since 1927. However, Eric was advised by Victoria's chief viticulturist, François de Castella, that even though the property was ideal for growing grapes for table wines, there were shortcomings in the winemaker's methods. Some of the wines stored in the cellars had spoiled and were unsellable. To make matters worse Eric had arrived in the midst of the Great Depression and Chateau Tahbilk's once fine reputation was in tatters. Jim Hindhaugh resigned as winemaker at the end of 1931 and Eric assumed the role.

With the help of friends, neighbouring winemakers and de Castella, who became his mentor, Eric learnt as much as he could about winemaking, cellaring and marketing. He immersed himself in the dual roles of manager and winemaker, embarking on a massive clean-up operation that was to take several years — restoring the mouldy cellars, replacing ancient equipment and planting phylloxera-resistant vines. He cleared the cellars of unsellable wine, retained vats of quality for maturing, and sold the rest by driving around the countryside, selling from the back of his old Model T Ford.

In 1934 the company's name was changed from The Chateau Tahbilk Propriety Limited to Tahbilk Propriety Limited to avoid confusion about the origin of the wine, and Eric was made

Pickers and drays, circa 1940.

sole owner by his father. It wasn't until 2000 that 'Chateau' was dropped from the wine labels.

Although yields were modest, they had almost doubled by the 1934 vintage. Tahbilk's wines won awards at agricultural shows in Sydney and Melbourne, and at regional wine shows. The recovery seemed to be going well until Mother Nature intervened. In late November 1934 torrential rain fell over much of southern Victoria, and the Goulburn River broke its banks, flooding the vineyards after budburst. The vines were ruined and took several years to recover.

In 1935 Eric became a wine judge at the Royal Melbourne Show, which was an acknowledgement by his peers of his winemaking knowledge and skills, and confirmation that he had learnt a great deal in a very short time.

Several months after World War II broke out in 1939, Eric enlisted as a private in the Australian Army, leaving winemaker Donald McDonald in charge.

Tahbilk Marsanne

Marsanne is one of the world's rarest grape varieties. Originating in the Northern Rhone and Hermitage regions of France, Tahbilk has the largest single holding of the variety in the world.

Marsanne was first planted at Tahbilk in 1860 as 'White Hermitage' from cuttings purchased from St Hubert's vineyard in Victoria's Yarra Valley. None of the original vines still exist; however, cuttings from them were grafted onto phylloxera-resistant rootstock in 1927 on the advice of government viticulturist François de Castella. These plantings are used to produce the exceptional 1927 Vines Marsanne.

Tahbilk Marsanne has a long and distinguished wine show pedigree, winning numerous trophies and medals. Today this rare white wine has a dedicated worldwide following and is renowned for character, complexity and its ability to age in the bottle. Tahbilk Marsanne is by far the winery's biggest selling wine. Alister Purbrick describes it as the 'engine room' of Tahbilk.

Eric Purbrick corking bottles, circa 1940.

Eric served in the Northern Territory with the North Australia Observer Unit (NAOU) for four years before spending a year in Greece as honorary assistant commissioner in the Australian Red Cross. He was awarded the Medal of the Royal Greek Red Cross in 1946 before returning home. Unfortunately, Eric's long absence had taken a toll on his marriage and he and Marjory divorced in 1947.

When Eric arrived back at Tahbilk in 1946 he developed a new marketing program for bottled wine labelled according to variety. He believed that table wine should be marketed under the varietal name, such as Semillon and Shiraz, rather than generic names such as claret, chablis, burgundy and hock.

He appointed agents in each state to market the wine and made his focus the production of high-quality wine. In 1951, on a visit to the UK with his new bride, Phyllis, a chance meeting with Sydney Fells allowed Tahbilk to edge into the UK market, exporting two hogsheads (a little less than 600 litres) of white wine per year. Modest exports of red wine soon followed.

A year later Eric commissioned a new label for his vineyards, incorporating the Chateau Tahbilk crest and the varietal name. The new labels and the rest of Eric's marketing plan paid off quickly at home and abroad, with exports to New Zealand, Hong Kong, Japan and Fiji, swiftly followed by exports to the US and Canada. Chateau Tahbilk wine was served to Queen Elizabeth II at a Commonwealth Heads of Government luncheon in London in 1953 and on her first visit to Australia in 1954.

The first Chateau Tahbilk varietal labels. The generic names were also included until 1956.

Eric's passion for winemaking extended well beyond his own winery and vineyards. He became increasingly active in the Australian wine industry, serving as vice president of the Federal Wine and Brandy Producers Council, deputy member of the Australian Wine Board, president of the Wine and Brandy Producers Association of Victoria and president of the Viticultural Society of Victoria.

When Eric's second wife, Phyllis, died of tuberculosis in 1955, his son, John, returned from the Riverina in New South Wales, where he had been managing his mother Marjory's rice farm, to take over the management of the estate's farm. George Comi, who first started work on the property as a farmhand in 1931 at the age of fourteen and worked his way up to manager of the vineyards and winemaker, had developed a close friendship with Eric and was an invaluable companion.

When Tahbilk celebrated its centenary with a gala luncheon in September 1960, its reputation had been well and truly re-established. Australia's then prime minister Sir Robert Menzies officiated, choosing to attend the luncheon rather than one of Victoria's most important events, the Victorian Football League's

A formidable gentleman and formidable wines

Renowned Australian wine authority and writer James Halliday once described Eric Purbrick as 'a formidable gentleman'—the same could be said of the wines named in his honour. One of Eric's greatest contributions to Tahbilk was the creation of the 'Special Bin' flagship range in 1948, produced from the best vats of each vintage. The name was changed from 'Special Bin' to 'Reserve' in 1985. In recognition of Eric's contribution to Tahbilk and the Australian wine industry in general, in 2002 the name was changed again to 'Eric Stevens Purbrick'.

Only the most outstanding fruit from a vintage makes its way into these wines. The fruit for the Cabernet Sauvignon is primarily sourced from vines planted in 1949, while the Shiraz is mainly sourced from vines dating back to 1933. Both wines have the fruit intensity and flavour characteristic of older vines.

Eric Stevens
Purbrick,
circa 1975.

grand final at the Melbourne Cricket Ground. Such was the
esteem in which Tahbilk was held.

Following the luncheon, at the request of Eric Purbrick the
prime minister placed one bottle of red and one bottle of white
from the 1960 vintage in a cavity in the cellar wall, sealed the
cavity and declared that the wine was not to be disturbed until
2060. He then addressed the owner: 'Why, Purbrick, you would
wish to deprive the people of Australia of two bottles of your wine
for 100 years I cannot conceive, when none of you will be here,
and, what is far worse, I shan't be here, to enjoy it!'

While the Beatles and the Rolling Stones were revolutionising
popular music, the Purbricks were making changes of their own
at Tahbilk. The acreage under vines was increasing and exports
were expanding to new markets including Singapore, Bahrain
and Abu Dhabi. The company was also receiving excellent
publicity at home, but the domestic market was limited by the
small proportion of the population that enjoyed drinking table
wine. As a result of the publicity, Eric was invited to speak about
wine to a range of clubs and organisations, joining the campaign
by other winemaking companies, distributors, retailers and the
Australian Wine Board to educate an increasingly affluent public
about wine.

The campaign worked — sales more than doubled between 1960 and 1975, despite some difficult years from 1969 when heavy rain and over-planting of vines produced a glut of inferior wine. However, the low-quality wine eventually had an impact, with sales falling after 1975.

As part of the push to entice the public to buy table wine, the wine industry began promoting the cellar door experience. Like many of his contemporaries, Eric saw the value of attracting more visitors to the cellar door. In 1971 he established a biannual newsletter, which included information about the winery, vineyards and new releases. Eric staffed the cellar door, engaging visitors in discussions about the winery, its history and the wines. This personal touch was appreciated by visitors, and kept them coming back to the winery.

> ‘Nothing really threatened us financially. The old man ran it very tightly. We never felt like we struggled. Things like floods just made life awkward for a while.’
>
> John Purbrick

Eric retired as general manager and chief executive in 1974 at the age of seventy-one, handing both roles over to John. Eric continued working alongside his good friend George Comi as winemaker until 1978, when his grandson, Alister, took his place. Comi eventually retired in 1982, having completed more than thirty vintages as winemaker.

In late 1977 John Purbrick invited Alister to take on winemaking responsibilities at Tahbilk. Alister, a graduate of Roseworthy Agricultural College, had worked two vintages at the Mildara Wine Company in the Coonawarra wine region of South Australia before completing a third vintage at the Hungerford Hill Winery near Mildura in north-western Victoria. Alister accepted the challenge and arrived at Tahbilk in time to finish the 1978 vintage with his father, his grandfather and Comi.

There were some interesting parallels between the arrival of Eric at Chateau Tahbilk in 1931 at the age of twenty-eight and Alister's arrival as a twenty-four year old nearly fifty years later. Both men arrived when the company's sales and reputation were in decline and both were determined to reverse the slide. There were also some differences. Alister was the family's first fully qualified winemaker, with three years' experience at other wineries. Eric had arrived at Chateau Tahbilk with no qualifications or experience and was largely self-taught.

Eric Purbrick was thrilled when his eldest grandson returned to Tahbilk. Alister idolised his grandfather and the pair spent countless hours together in the cellar tasting, comparing and discussing wines. They worked closely together and Eric became Alister's teacher and mentor.

Enthusiastic and with an abundance of new ideas, Alister was keen to convince his grandfather and father to update the style of both red and white wines. Everyone agreed that the white wines could be improved, and Alister was able to persuade Eric and John to invest in new winery equipment and a new white wine fermentation cellar. The equipment was ready for the 1979 vintage and Alister's skills, in his first year as white wine maker, were affirmed when both his Semillon and Riesling won gold medals at major Australian wine shows.

Persuading his elders to update their method for making red wine proved somewhat more difficult. Alister and his grandfather continued to debate the change over a number of years, always with a drink in hand. As they shared a glass of Eric's beloved Cabernet Sauvignon or Shiraz, Eric would ask for Alister's opinion of the wine. Each time Alister would reply that it was magnificent. A few years later, thoroughly frustrated by his grandfather's resistance to changing the process, Alister went to Eric again to present his case. Realising just how determined his grandson was, Eric decided it was time to pull out his 'pièce de résistance' — a 1962 Tahbilk Special Bin 26 Cabernet Sauvignon — over which to discuss the proposal. After finishing the bottle Eric once again asked Alister what he thought of the wine. Alister replied that it was exceptional — the best wine he had ever tasted. The elder Purbrick looked him squarely in the eye and asked, 'Well, why would you want to change it?' Alister finally agreed that Tahbilk reds should continue being made as they always had been.

✤   ✤   ✤

A cuppa in the cellar, circa 1955. John is on the far left, Eric is on the far right.

George Comi worked as winemaker at Tahbilk with three generations of the Purbrick family.

Some Tahbilk reds maturing nicely.

John Purbrick moved to Sydney in 1979 to set up and run the distribution of Tahbilk wines in New South Wales, where sales had been disappointing for many years. The move was highly successful. John remained chief executive until 1980, when Alister assumed the role at the age of twenty-six. A new Australian national distribution arrangement for Tahbilk's wines was established in 1982 with Rhinecastle Wines, and domestic sales have continued to grow since that time. John remained in Sydney, remarried and worked as a sommelier at a leading hotel.

John moved back to Nagambie some years later after separating from his wife. He met and married his third wife, Kay Crawford, in 1992 and together they established a small company, Purbrick & Crawford, which produces relishes, jams and pickles. John's recipes are now published in Tahbilk's Wine Club newsletter. John remains at Tahbilk as chairman of the board and maintains a keen interest in the winery. Each Sunday he can be found chatting to visitors at the cellar door about the history of Tahbilk. 'Some people are gobsmacked with the living history — especially young people', he says.

Eric and Alister Purbrick sharing a glass of wine and discussing its merits.

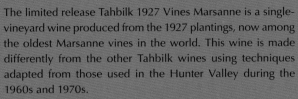

From ugly duckling to beautiful swan

The limited release Tahbilk 1927 Vines Marsanne is a single-vineyard wine produced from the 1927 plantings, now among the oldest Marsanne vines in the world. This wine is made differently from the other Tahbilk wines using techniques adapted from those used in the Hunter Valley during the 1960s and 1970s.

Alister Purbrick explains, 'We pick the fruit greener and allow the wine to age in the bottle, where it is transformed from an ugly ducking into a beautiful swan'. It will be the future generations who are able to boast about and enjoy this exceptional Marsanne when it reaches its best as a thirty-, forty- or fifty-year-old wine.

Responsible environmental management and sustainability are also an important part of Tahbilk's agenda. The use of chemicals is kept to a minimum and mulching under the vines has reduced water consumption. The aim is for Tahbilk to be carbon neutral by 2012. Part of this environmental agenda also included a long-term project to reinvigorate the surrounding wetlands.

John is extremely proud of what Alister has achieved since returning to Tahbilk as winemaker. 'Alister came in as a twenty-four year old and just absorbed and absorbed. He never stops working — he thrives on it. And he has never ceased learning.'

Like his grandfather, Alister has served as an executive member of wine industry bodies, including time as president of the Winemakers Federation of Australia and of the Australian Regional Winemakers Forum. Alister was also elected inaugural chairman of Australia's First Families of Wine in 2007.

Before Eric Purbrick passed away in 1991, it was agreed that Tahbilk was to remain in Purbrick family hands forever. The company's constitution was revised to restrict the sale or exchange of shares to anyone except Purbrick family members related by blood. A family council was established in 2010, which includes the youngest generation when they reach the age of eighteen.

At the same time, it was decided to cap production to maintain the integrity of the wines produced under the Tahbilk label. This did not preclude expansion through acquisitions and joint ventures, which can be sold off if necessary. The decision led to the formation of the 'Tahbilk Group' of companies in 1992, which as a whole, is now substantially larger than Tahbilk.

The fifth generation of Purbricks is now represented in the family business. Alister's daughter Hayley joined Tahbilk as an accountant in 2009. She has also taken on the role of project manager, involving her in acquisitions, environmental

A new dimension

Alister Purbrick added a whole new dimension to Tahbilk's cellar door activities with the establishment of the Tahbilk Wetlands and Wildlife Reserve. Occupying about 1000 acres of the estate—300 acres of which is water mass—the reserve opened in 2005 after ten years of development.

The family's aim was to merge ecotourism with the rest of its heritage, and to restore the wetlands to the way they were before European settlement. Many of the shallow wetlands, fed from the Goulburn River, had dried up because water could not flow into them. The original watercourse had been 'plugged up' after years of stock grazing. Excavators were brought in and the entrances to the wetlands were opened up to let the water back in. Once the water began flowing again much of the original native aquatic flora grew back. The land surrounding the restored wetlands was also revegetated with native species.

Today visitors to Tahbilk can cruise the wetlands, walk through the reserve, tour the old underground cellars and explore the cellar yard, which contains old farming and vineyard machinery dating back to the nineteenth century. The ironbark and stone Wetlands Cafe overlooks part of the wetlands and the original 1880s-constructed bridge. Since the opening of the wetlands, wildlife reserve and cafe, the number of visitors has doubled and wine sales from the cellar door have increased dramatically.

The regenerated wetlands area
attracts a large number of birds.

John, Hayley and Alister Purbrick, representing three generations of the Purbrick family.

management and wetlands development on the property. In 2010 she was appointed wine club and cellar door manager.

Growing up at a winery offered plenty of opportunities for fun. Hayley remembers getting into all sorts of trouble for playing in the cellars: 'The cellars were dark and eerie, and sometimes we'd hide behind the barrels and suddenly jump out and scare the tourists'. Initially, however, Hayley had no interest in joining the family business, admitting that she didn't enjoy the viticulture component of the Agricultural Science course she undertook at the University of Melbourne.

The turning point came after completing a Diploma of Applied Commerce and 'doing the hard yards' at accounting firm Ernst and Young for a few years. During this time she came to appreciate the importance and significance of being passionate about her career and the opportunities that a small, privately owned business could offer. Hayley realised that as an accountant she could make a significant contribution to Tahbilk and keep the family heritage alive. Since joining the business Hayley has become a fully qualified chartered accountant. Her younger brother and cousins are beginning to show interest in the wine industry and, from the Purbrick family's perspective, it will be exciting to see who joins the company in the future.

Although not directly involved in wine production at Tahbilk, Alister's younger siblings Debbie and Mark are directors of Tahbilk Pty Ltd. Debbie is a primary school principal and is married to Alan George, who has been chief winemaker of the Tahbilk Group since 1999. Mark is a qualified winemaker, but has chosen to work in managerial roles in the wine, mail order, hospitality and human resource industries. Mark is currently a board member of the Australian Wine and Brandy Corporation and has served on a number of other wine industry organisations.

> ❛I'm proud of our heritage, our contributions to sustainability and ecotourism. And coming here as a young person I'm very proud that my father and grandfather are open to change.❜
>
> Hayley Purbrick

The history and heritage of Tahbilk are an important part of the winery's tourism strategy. Visitors don't just come to purchase wine — they want to view the old underground cellars and the tower, and talk to John Purbrick when he's at the cellar door.

Having received worldwide recognition of his company's Marsanne, red wines and historic vineyards, Alister Purbrick is not inclined to venture into experimenting with new varieties. Yet, he also recognises that striving for improvement is essential.

The Purbrick family, 2010.

'We'll stick to what we do best', he comments. 'All of our wine has been produced from vineyards on the same patch of dirt for 150 years. Our red wines have a recognised pedigree and have been stylistically pure for fifty or sixty years. We have no intention of changing, but every intention of continually improving the style.' With this resolve and determination for the company to remain in family hands, the future of Tahbilk is surely assured.

The influence of oak on wine

Oak barrels have traditionally been used to ferment and age wine. In more recent times most white wines have been fermented and aged in stainless steel tanks. Oak imparts tannin structure, texture and enhances the flavour of wines, particularly red wines. It can add desirable characteristics, including vanilla, coconut, cloves and black pepper. The influence of the oak on wine depends on its origin, how it is treated and how the barrels are coopered.

French oak barrels originate from forests that were planted to supply timber for shipbuilding during the time of Napoleon. They are very expensive but deliver subtle flavours and characteristics to wine. American oak barrels are much less expensive and impart bolder characteristics, dominated by vanilla and robust tannins.

Oak barrels only impart oak flavour to wine for three to four years, so need to be replaced regularly. The characteristics imparted by new oak can sometimes overpower the fruit flavours of the wine, so some winemakers use a combination of new and old oak to ensure that the oak and fruit flavours are in balance.

Chardonnay can be fermented in stainless steel tanks, but is usually aged in oak, which gives it more prominent vanilla characteristics. However, many consumers prefer unoaked Chardonnay, as the fruit flavours and aromas are more dominant.

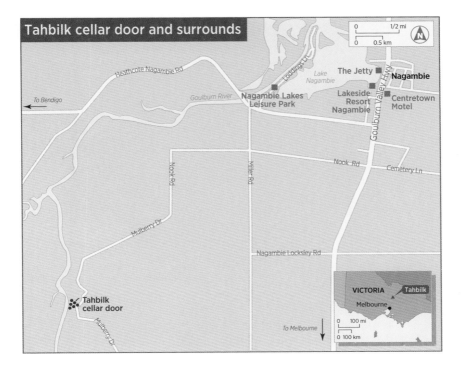

Cellar door

254 O'Neils Rd
Tabilk via Nagambie Vic. 3608
t: 03 5794 2555
w: www.tahbilk.com.au
e: admin@tahbilk.com.au

Opening hours
Monday to Friday: 9 am to 5 pm
Weekends and public holidays:
10 am to 5 pm
Closed: Christmas Day

Accommodation options

Centretown Motel
266 High St
Nagambie Vic. 3608
t: 03 5794 2511
w: www.centretownmotel.com
e: reservations@centretownmotel.com

Lakeside Resort Nagambie
277 High St
Nagambie Vic. 3608
t: 03 5794 1410
w: www.lakesideresortnagambie.com.au
e: stay@lakesideresortnagambie.com.au

Nagambie Lakes Leisure Park
Loddings Ln
Nagambie Vic. 3608
t: 03 5794 2373
w: www.nagambielakespark.com.au
e: info@nagambielakespark.com.au

The Jetty
317 High St
Nagambie Vic. 3608
t: 03 5794 1964
w: www.thejetty.com.au
e: nagambiejetty@bigpond.com

Henschke
The gardens of Eden

❝Prue and I are the current "keepers of the flame". Just as earlier generations have done, we want to manage the vineyards and winery so they can be passed on to the next generation in a better condition than we found them.❞

Stephen Henschke, managing director, CA Henschke & Co.

The Henschke family has been making wine in the tranquil, undulating landscape of the Eden Valley, in South Australia's Barossa zone, for more than 140 years. During that time Henschke has established a reputation for quality, with a focus on ultra-premium single-vineyard wines. Along with the iconic Hill of Grace Shiraz, which has captured the imaginations of red wine lovers around the world, the Henschke portfolio contains an enviable collection of historic single-vineyard wines, such as the Mount Edelstone Shiraz and the Cyril Henschke Cabernet Sauvignon. It also includes some exciting white wines, such as the Julius Eden Valley Riesling and the Louis Semillon.

Fifth-generation winemaker Stephen Henschke and his viti-culturist wife, Prue, make an extraordinary team. In addition to being custodians of some of the oldest vineyards in Australia — and producing wines that are some of the most revered in Australia —the Henschkes are constantly improving the quality of their wines through viticultural research and experimentation with winemaking techniques.

The original two-storey wine cellar was built into the side of a hill in 1868. It has since been added to by each generation. Now covered with ivy, it retains an old-world charm, drawing visitors in with its rustic, cosy feel.

The Eden Valley was first settled in the mid nineteenth century by Lutherans from Silesia who had fled their homeland to escape religious persecution. Silesia, a region now mainly located in Poland, was part of Germany at the time. The Silesians brought with them traditional, self-sufficient farming methods, and German language and culture. Many raised livestock and poultry, and planted their properties with fruit orchards, vegetables and small vineyards, which they called gardens.

The Henschke winemaking heritage began with Johann Christian Henschke. In 1841, at the age of thirty-seven, he, his

Prue and Stephen Henschke in their Mount Edelstone vineyard.

wife, Appolonia, and their four children travelled from their home in Silesia to Hamburg to board the *Skjold*, a ship bound for South Australia. Tragedy struck the family even before the ship departed in July 1841, when their youngest daughter, nine-month-old Johanne Luise, died in Hamburg. Sadly, Appolonia and their six-year-old-son, Johann Friedrich Wilhelm, died during the ninety-eight-day voyage and were buried at sea.

Johann Christian and Dorothea Elisabeth Henschke, circa 1870.

After settling at Lobethal in the Adelaide Hills with his two surviving children, Johann Christian worked as a wheelwright. In 1843 he married Dorothea Elisabeth Schmidt, with whom he was to have eight more children. Four years later the family moved to Krondorf in the Barossa Valley, where their house still stands today.

In 1862 Johann Christian purchased land in what is now the Keyneton district of the Eden Valley. It was thought that the area was capable of producing wines that would match Germany's best. A farmer and mason by trade, he built the small two-storey cellar that still stands today and, with the help of his third son from his second marriage, Paul Gotthard Henschke, planted a small vineyard. The Henschke family continued to live in Krondorf, so Johann Christian would often walk the twenty kilometres to Keyneton with a wheelbarrow while he developed the property. His original intent was to make enough wine for consumption by family and friends. The first commercial vintage, believed to be principally Riesling and Shiraz, was completed in 1868.

The year before Johann Christian Henschke's death in 1873, he transferred the property to Paul Gotthard, who took over the running of the farm and vineyard. Paul Gotthard continued the winemaking tradition of his father and increased production after planting more vineyards. He had married Johanne Mathilde Schulz in 1871 and they would eventually have seven children.

Like his father, Paul Gotthard Henschke was actively involved in the local community. In 1874 he became one of the first constables of the Keyneton district. He was also the organist of the Gnadenberg Church for many years, and went on to form the district's first brass band, the Henschke Family Brass Band. Most of the instruments were brought from Germany and three of them — a euphonium, a clarinet and a cornet — are still in the family's possession. The Keyneton Euphonium, a blend of Shiraz Cabernet Sauvignon and Merlot, is so named as a tribute to the village's early musical culture.

> ‘I'm proud of our heritage and our history. I'm mindful of the blood, sweat and tears that previous generations endured.’
>
> Stephen Henschke

Following Paul Gotthard's death in 1914, his son, Paul Alfred Henschke, took charge of the family property. Paul Alfred was in his mid thirties at the time and had worked on the family farm and winery, as well as on other farms further to the north as a shearer. In 1907 he had married Johanne Ida Selma Stanitzki (known as Selma), who was also from a family of viticulturists and winemakers. Her grandfather, Nicholaus Stanitzki, was one of the earliest settlers in the district and had planted the first Shiraz vines in about 1860. His vineyard later became known as the Hill of Grace. The property was later purchased by Paul Alfred's son, Louis Edmund Henschke, who extended the vineyard in the 1950s.

Paul Gotthard Henschke and Johanne Mathilde.

Paul Alfred extended the original cellars, and built brick and cement fermenting vats and underground storage tanks by hand. In response to rising demand for fortified wine, he planted more vineyards on the property. He also purchased farming land near the neighbouring towns of Angaston and Moculta, and further away in Loxton to provide his sons with the opportunity to be independent. Paul Alfred continued the tradition of the Henschke Family Brass Band and was the organist for the Gnadenberg Lutheran Church for many years.

Of Paul Alfred and Selma Henschke's eleven children, only one of them, their youngest son, Cyril Alfred, born in 1924, was destined to become a winemaker. Cyril went straight to work in the winery after leaving school at the age of fifteen. During the Great Depression farming took precedence over winemaking on the Henschke property due to falling demand for wine, but with Cyril's youthful enthusiasm winemaking regained its importance during the 1940s.

A true masterpiece

The Henschke's Hill of Grace vineyard is one of the oldest Shiraz vineyards in the world. The original vines were planted about 150 years ago, and today the vines are gnarled, twisted and low-yielding, yet produce exceptional Shiraz fruit. The vineyard is unirrigated, dry grown and has managed to survive several long droughts, including the Federation- and Depression-era droughts. The variations within this single vineyard are intriguing — some pockets perform better in wet years, while others cope better in dry years. Despite what the name suggests, the vineyard is not located on a hill. In fact, it is in a valley, and takes its name from the Gnadenberg Church, which is adjacent to the vineyard — 'gnadenberg' meaning 'hill of grace'.

Henschke Hill of Grace Shiraz was first created in 1958 by fourth-generation winemaker and Paul Alfred's son, Cyril Alfred Henschke. This iconic and much-lauded single-vineyard wine has been made every year since, except in 1974 and 2000 due to unfavourable seasonal conditions. The grapes are hand-picked and, following traditional open fermentation, the wine is matured in new oak to build greater complexity before bottling.

He spent about two years working at Hardy's Siegersdorf winery in Tanunda, where he was able to augment the skills he had learned from his father, or simply through trial and error, with some of the finer points of winemaking. Although the Henschkes drank unfortified wine at home, Paul Alfred had concentrated on producing fortified wines in response to consumer demand. Cyril, however, was convinced that the quality of the fruit in the Eden Valley was better suited to the production of fine dry table wines.

In 1949, with the help of his brother Louis, Cyril made several additions to the winery and built a fermentation cellar that incorporated the old stable area. Three years later his father retired, and Cyril took charge of the winery. He experimented with different varieties — including Frontignac, Semillon, Sercial, Ugni Blanc and Riesling — and soon became one of the pioneers of varietal table wine. He began phasing out the production of fortified wine in 1952, the same year in which he created the magnificent Mount Edlestone Shiraz.

The transition from fortifieds to dry table wines was slow and the Australian market was still dominated by the traditional fortified wines. In 1956, fortified wines still made up 65 per cent of total production by volume, but by 1959 fortified wines had

Left: The Henshcke Family Brass Band, circa 1888. The boy beside the drum is Paul Alfred Henschke.

Opposite: Hand-picking in the Lenswood vineyard.

Cyril Henschke
at work in
the winery,
circa 1950.

been completely phased out of Henschke's production, paving the way for even greater acclaim for its dry table wines. Cyril focused on restaurant sales, recognising that the change in the food and wine culture, with increased demand for table wine, was predominantly driven by the Italian and Greek families who settled in Australia after World War II.

By the mid 1950s Cyril Henschke was acknowledged as one of the pioneers of Australian table wine, having recognised the emerging demand for this product and being one of the first Australian winemakers to successfully produce single-vineyard wines. He was also among the first winemakers to realise the Eden Valley's potential to produce exceptional wines from varieties such as Riesling and Shiraz.

Cyril was the first Australian winemaker to be awarded a prestigious Churchill Fellowship, which funded a study tour in 1970 of many winemaking regions of Germany, the United States and South Africa. He was also one of the wine industry identities who founded the Barons of the Barossa wine fraternity in 1974. Other founders included Wyndham Hill Smith (of Yalumba), Colin Gramp (of Orlando Wines), Bill Seppelt (of Seppelt Wines) and Peter Lehmann (of Peter Lehmann Wines). The objective of the Barons of the Barossa was, and still is, the promotion of the Barossa and Eden valleys, and their viticultural and winemaking cultures. It also aims to preserve and maintain the heritage, gastronomy, lifestyle and traditions of the Barossa.

One of the greatest

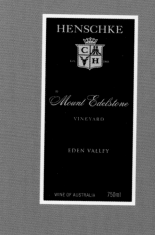

Henschke Mount Edelstone is recognised as one of Australia's greatest Shiraz wines. The Mount Edelstone vineyard was planted in 1912 by Ronald Angas, great-grandson of George Fife Angas, one of the founders of South Australia. The east-facing hillside on which it is planted was named Mount Edelstein, meaning gemstone. Unusual for the time, it was planted solely with Shiraz.

The grapes were contracted from Colin Angas, son of Ronald, by Cyril Henschke until 1974 when Cyril purchased the vineyard. Cyril's 1956 Mount Edelstone Shiraz took out first prizes in all major Australian wine shows and has subsequently won awards for Best Shiraz (or Syrah) three times at the International Wine and Spirit Competition in London. Henschke Mount Edelstone Shiraz is a true expression of its origins — the Eden Valley and, in particular, the Mount Edelstone vineyard.

Cyril's son, Stephen, is currently the Grand Master of the Barons of the Barossa.

Cyril married Doris Elvira Klemm in 1947 and they had three children — Paul, Stephen and Christine. Paul is the principal research microbiologist at The Australian Wine Research Institute and Christine is a lawyer. When Cyril died in 1979, twenty-nine-year-old Stephen took over the running of the winery.

Stephen Henschke, born in 1950, was certainly well qualified to take on the roles of owner and winemaker. After completing a Bachelor of Science degree at the University of Adelaide with majors in biochemistry and botany, he gained winemaking experience at Rothbury Estate winery in the New South Wales Hunter Valley. He and his wife, Prue (also a University of Adelaide Science graduate), then spent two years studying at the Geisenheim Institute of Viticulture and Wine Technology in Germany. During their stay Stephen undertook work experience at two wineries, Winzerverein Oberrotweil in Baden and the Institut für Rebenzüchtung und Rebenveredlung (the Institute for Special Crop Cultivation) in Geisenheim.

On their return to Australia, Stephen and Prue enrolled in a wine science distance education course at the Riverina College of Advanced Education in Wagga Wagga, in southern New South Wales, to catch up on the changes in the Australian wine industry. During this time, Stephen worked with his father while Prue embarked on a career as a technical research assistant at Roseworthy Agricultural College in South Australia. She was researching top-grafting of grape vines as a tool to change varieties in the vineyard.

In 1981 Prue and Stephen purchased an apple orchard in Lenswood, in the Adelaide Hills, with the intention of eventually redeveloping it as a vineyard. This would allow them to experiment with different varieties in a cool-climate situation. Prue spent two years operating the orchard before some of the worst bushfires the country had ever seen — known as the Ash Wednesday bushfires — engulfed the property in flames, leaving nothing but blackened stumps. As a result, the Henschkes brought forward their plans to redevelop the property.

The Adelaide Hills stood out as a region with exciting potential. Pinot Noir, Merlot, Chardonnay, Riesling and Cabernet Sauvignon were planted in response to theories about cool-climate viticulture, site selection and canopy management. The Lenswood vineyard became a research and development project that was to have a positive influence on the quality of the fruit from the older Henschke vineyards in the Eden Valley.

While Prue was operating the apple orchard at Lenswood and redeveloping it, Stephen began incorporating barrel fermentation as a component of red wine production. The poor quality of the oak at the time led him to introduce an oak timber purchase program, seasoning it in the Barossa Valley and using the local cooper AP John to make the barrels, to obtain better quality seasoned oak flavours.

A lasting tribute

The Cyril Henschke Cabernet Sauvignon was created by Stephen with the 1978 vintage as a tribute to his father. The Cabernet Sauvignon vines first planted by Cyril on the Eden Valley property in 1969 were on contour—that is, curving around the hill—to reduce water run-off and erosion. Stephen and Prue replanted the entire vineyard, called the Cyril Henschke Cabernet vineyard, on a north-facing slope, which allows for exceptional fruit maturity to produce one of Australia's best Cabernets. The Cabernet Sauvignon is blended with small amounts of Merlot and Cabernet Franc from the same vineyard to add depth and complexity.

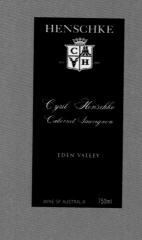

It is fitting that this acclaimed Eden Valley red bears Cyril's name because it was he who created the wine that has so captured the hearts and minds of red wine drinkers throughout the world—the Hill of Grace Shiraz. The Cyril Henschke Cabernet Sauvignon has won many awards since its first release, including the London International Red Wine Challenge Trophy and the Tucker Seabrook Perpetual Trophy, which is given to the best wine exhibited at major state wine shows over a twelve-month period.

Stephen also brought in more flexible state-of-the-art refrigeration to improve the quality of their white wines. For his red wine making he maintained traditional methods — such as open fermentation, minimal handling and no fining — to ensure that the Henschke reds remained a true expression of the fruit in the vineyards.

In 1986 Prue embarked on a project to select the best genetic material from the Hill of Grace and Mount Edelstone vineyards. She conducted grape and wine quality trials involving varying trellis types, crop density and leaf area. The aim of this project, which is still ongoing, is to ensure that the unique flavours of the fruit from these iconic Shiraz vineyards are preserved and even enhanced.

Prue Henschke has been a pioneer and innovator in a number of areas of vineyard management and soil health. Her research now revolves around organic and biodynamic vineyard management using minimal chemical input. Her work also includes seeding native grasses between the vine rows, trials with native flowering plant species to provide a food source for predator insects and trials with a foliage lifting system.

The protection and revegetation of the original native grasses, woodlands and forests on 30 per cent of their properties has restored an ecological balance. Prue has also used mulching and biodynamic compost to preserve soil moisture and soil structure in the vineyards. Her beliefs go further than just sustainability —her aim is for the vineyards to be part of a completely integrated healthy carbon-neutral ecosystem.

> ‘Running the Lenswood vineyard can't be done from a textbook. It takes a lot of clever thinking and fine adjustment to make it work.’
>
> Prue Henschke

In 1988 and 1989 Stephen and Prue travelled to France to work on vintages in Burgundy and Bordeaux, researching viticulture and winemaking. Since returning, they have forged their own styles for the Lenswood vineyard wines.

The focus at Lenswood is on producing the best possible quality regardless of the cost of production. Due to the steep and slippery slopes, using mechanical processes is difficult, so tasks in the vineyard such as shoot placement, crop thinning, pruning and harvesting are labour intensive. However, the quality of the fruit makes up for the costs involved.

Stephen's innovations have extended to bottle closures. In 1996, frustrated by the amount of wine ruined by tainted cork, he became one of the first Australian winemakers to introduce screw caps to replace the cork.

He was also the first winemaker in Australia to trial and use the German glass closure, the Vino-Lok, launched in Europe in 2004.

Prue assessing composted cow manure.

The Henschke family. From left: Andreas, Stephen, Prue, Justine and Johann.

After conducting due diligence on the closure with an independently assessed five-year trial, Stephen now uses it for top-end reds.

Among the numerous awards won by Stephen and Prue are the Advance Australia Award for Outstanding Contribution to the Wine Industry in 1995, the International Wine and Spirit Competition's 1995 International Red Winemaker of the Year award and the 2006 *Gourmet Traveller WINE* magazine Winemaker of the Year. In 2005 Stephen and Prue were inducted into *Wine & Spirits* magazine's hall of fame. In addition to these honours, both have served on various wine industry, land conservation and community bodies.

❛It makes me feel proud when I'm somewhere in the world and someone tells me that they love Henschke wines. It reminds me how hard the previous generations have worked to develop the family business.❜

Justine Henschke

Stephen and Prue, together with their three children Johann, Justine and Andreas, quietly continue the proud Henschke heritage. Johann, Justine and Andreas have fond memories of growing up at the winery — playing in the winery and riding bikes around the property. Justine recalls sitting on the open-top fermenters with her brothers and tasting the fermenting berries. Eager to be part of the family business, the three children would pretend to run the company, using the winery paging system to call each other in their parents' offices.

Johann expects that his generation will face numerous challenges in managing a family wine business in the twenty-first century. However, he is focused on ensuring that it is passed on to future generations. 'What it means to me to be part of the sixth generation is to continue the legacy that my parents have carried on so successfully', he says. 'My parents didn't pressure me into studying wine. I had thought I would like to study something else, but after looking into wine courses a little more, I realised that becoming a winemaker was something I really wanted to do.'

The Lenswood collection

At an altitude of more than 500 metres, the Lenswood vineyard sits high in a mountainous region, surrounded by stringybark forests, apple orchards and creeks, with a commanding view over traditional vine lands. It is cooler, wetter, more humid and botanically richer than the rest of South Australia. When Prue and Stephen were searching for a new site for growing earlier ripening, subtle varieties — such as Pinot Noir, Chardonnay and Merlot — the Adelaide Hills seemed the perfect choice. To reduce the threat of frost they chose a steeply sloped site, which at the time was covered in apple, cherry and pear trees.

More than twenty years after the site was discovered the Lenswood vineyard is the source of an enviable collection of wines, which are the result of the rich knowledge, experience and passion of the fifth-generation Henschkes. The acclaimed collection includes Lenswood Coralinga Sauvignon Blanc, Lenswood Green's Hill Riesling, Lenswood Croft Chardonnay, Lenswood Giles Pinot Noir, Lenswood Abbott's Prayer Cabernet Sauvignon and Lenswood NV Blanc de Noir.

The Lenswood vineyard sits at an altitude
of 550 metres in the Adelaide Hills.

Honouring a proud heritage

Several of Henschke's Eden Valley wines are named to honour the heritage and culture dating back to the migration of Johann Christian Henschke and other Silesians who fled their homeland in the 1830s and 1840s in search of religious freedom.

Johann's Garden Grenache is so named as a tribute to the early Lutheran settlers, many of whom were named Johann and who traditionally referred to their vineyard as their garden. The traditions and culture of these Barossa pioneers have survived to this day, including the techniques used to make this vibrant red wine.

Keyneton Euphonium is a blend of old-vine Eden Valley Shiraz, Cabernet Sauvignon and Merlot. It is named in tribute to the musical heritage of the settlers. The Henschke Family Brass Band, which included a B-flat euphonium that is still in the family, was a musical focus for the village.

Julius Riesling, a reserve selection from Eden Valley vines up to fifty years old, is named in honour of ancestor Julius Henschke (1888–1954), an acclaimed sculptor and renowned euphonium soloist.

At the time of writing, he is undertaking a masters degree in viticulture and oenology in Europe, following on from his studies in oenology at the University of Adelaide. He has also spent time working in various wine regions around the world, gaining insights into differing styles of wine production. This has assisted his contribution to the family business, where he has had roles in winemaking, vineyard work and marketing.

Justine is taking a more roundabout route to the family business. After completing an Advanced Diploma of Arts (Acting) at the Adelaide College of the Arts and performing in several arts festivals, she spent six months working with Henschke's distributors in London. Since then she has commenced a double degree in law and marketing at the University of Adelaide. Working in the winery during breaks from study — in particular, working during the vintage period — has improved her wine knowledge. Justine's current plan is to work interstate for a few years in a

Left: Justine and Johann Henschke.

Below: Andreas after shovelling out his first fermenter in the Henschke cellar during the 2005 vintage.

marketing role, and then return to the family business. 'I want to see how other companies operate — bigger or smaller', she explains. 'I want to return to Keyneton with a mind full of ideas.'

Andreas is currently studying for a degree in mechanical engineering at the University of Adelaide. During his time away from study, he returns home to help out in the winery and to build his knowledge of wine and viticulture. He also applies his engineering knowledge to assist Prue with her experiments in the vineyard. While Andreas is still at the beginning of his tertiary studies, he has his mind set on venturing into the family business.

As for the future, the Henschkes have no desire to be the biggest winery.

Stephen explains: 'Our focus is on the long term and because it's also a family business, there is a responsibility to hand the vineyards and winery down in the best possible condition. Our motto says it all: "exceptional wines from outstanding vineyards"'.

For Stephen the true value of a five-generation family business is much more than its financial value. 'What we've got is something with unimaginable value — a truly beautiful historic property full of family tradition and heritage.'

Cellaring wine

At Henschke we recommend cellaring your wine in ideal conditions, as the most important factor affecting the ageing of wine is the conditions in which it is stored.

Bottles sealed with a cork should be stored on their side so that the cork remains moist. This minimises the amount of air entering the wine, which will cause it to become oxidised. Storage in very dry areas and air-conditioned areas can cause rapid drying of the cork. Bottles sealed with a screw cap or glass stopper can be stored upright, lying down or upside down.

The storage area should be cool, preferably with a constant temperature. Warmer conditions will increase the rate at which a wine ages. For example, wine stored in a cupboard in a centrally heated or air-conditioned apartment with an average temperature of twenty-two degrees Celsius will age much more quickly than wine matured in an underground cellar with an average temperature of fourteen degrees Celsius.

Extreme temperatures can cause rapid maturation and/or spoilage of wine. For example, a few minutes in a shop window or hot car at forty-five degrees Celsius can cause a wine to mature rapidly; an hour could spoil it totally.

Light can also increase the rate of ageing in wine, and can spoil it over time, so we recommend storing wine in a dark place. As such, we recommend drinking wines sooner if stored outside the ideal conditions.

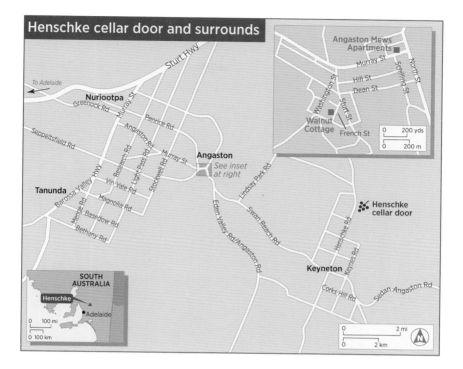

Cellar door

Henschke Rd
Keyneton SA 5353
t: 08 8564 8223
w: www.henschke.com.au
e: info@henschke.com.au

Opening hours
Monday to Friday: 9 am to 4.30 pm
Saturday: 9 am to 12 noon
Public holidays: 10 am to 3 pm
Closed: Sunday, New Year's Day,
Good Friday and Christmas Day

Accommodation options

Angaston Mews Apartments
8 Murray St
Angaston SA 5353
t: 08 8563 1000
w: www.angastonmewsapartments.
     com.au
e: getaway@grs.com.au

Walnut Cottage
8 French St
Angaston SA 5353
t: 08 8562 4556
w: www.walnut-cottage.com.au

Campbells

It's in our blood

‘A family winery is not just the wine in the bottle; it's the soil under your fingernails, it's storms and spring sunshine, tears and laughter, and customers who become family friends.’

Isabel Campbell, widow of third-generation
winemaker Allen Campbell

*I*n north-eastern Victoria lies the historic wine region of Rutherglen. It is here in Australia's premier fortified wine–producing area that the Campbell family has been making its distinctive wines since 1870. The region's reliable climate, with good soaking rains in winter and hot, dry summers that extend well into autumn, provides ideal conditions for the slow ripening that delivers the true varietal flavours so desirable in red and white table wines. The climate is especially kind to Shiraz and Durif, which thrive in conditions similar to those in the Rhone region of France. Grapes can be left to linger on the vines to develop the high sugar levels and complexity needed to produce the unique Muscats and Topaques (formerly known as Tokays) of Rutherglen.

Colin and
Malcolm
Campbell in the
Bobbie Burns
vineyard.

Add 140 years of winemaking experience and it's not
surprising that Campbells has received international acclaim
for both its fortified wines and its table wines. As one of the
pioneering wine families of Rutherglen, the Campbells remain
at the centre of wine production, tourism and wine education
in the region. The public face of Campbells is its warm and
welcoming cellar door, which was constructed in 1972. The cellar
door is integrated with the winery to allow visitors to explore the
sights, sounds and aromas of the winemaking process. Visitors
can wander through the cellars and stacks of new oak barrels,
as well as the old cellars, at the heart of which are rows of huge
ancient casks that house the precious Muscats and Topaques of
Campbell generations past.

The founder of this renowned winery was John Campbell,
who in 1857 left his home in St Andrews, Scotland, to board a

ship bound for Australia. The twenty-four-year-old had gold on his mind, and on arrival in Victoria made his way to the small town of Beechworth in the state's north-east with the hope of striking it rich. He did some prospecting amid the frenzy of the gold rush, where he met Jessie Robb, who was later to become his wife.

By 1860 gold fever had lured him further north-east to Rutherglen, home of the rich Bobbie Burns goldmine, where some miners made their fortune while others gave up in frustration. There is little doubt that the name of the goldfield was inspired by Scotland's beloved eighteenth-century poet Robert Burns.

> ❝You may arrive a stranger, but you will leave a family friend when you join us in celebrating the pleasures of good wine, food and family fellowship.❞
>
> Prue Campbell

In 1866 James Lindsay Brown, who had followed the advice of German settlers and planted Rutherglen's first vines in the 1850s, questioned the wisdom of continuing to dig for gold. He knew from experience that Rutherglen's soil was ideal for the establishment of vineyards, famously saying, 'Dig, gentlemen, dig, but not deeper than six inches, for there is more gold in the first six inches than there is lower down'.

When it became apparent that the gold had been mined out, some of the miners looked to the land and the various forms of agriculture to make a living. In 1868 John Campbell took Brown's advice and purchased seventy-nine acres of land. He named the property 'Bobbie Burns' after the nearby goldmine, and set about clearing the land and planting wheat, oats, fruit trees and two acres of vines. John built a timber slab hut with a shingle roof in 1869, and after completing his first vintage in 1870 established Campbells winery.

John Campbell joined the gold rush before establishing Campbells.

By 1886 John had acquired a further twenty-four acres and the Bobbie Burns vineyard occupied thirty-eight acres of the entire property, with plantings of Shiraz, Pedro Ximenez, Malbec, Riesling and Brown Muscat. He had also built a small timber-beamed cellar with an iron roof and replaced his hut with a homestead built from bricks that were made and fired on the property. The homestead, which John named Bobbie Burns, still stands beside the winery.

> ❛Could John Campbell have foreseen that 140 years later his descendants would be shipping wine from Rutherglen, Australia to Rutherglen, Scotland? We would like to think so.❜
>
> Malcolm Campbell

In 1891 Campbells won its first prize for wine at the Rutherglen Show for its dry, full-bodied red. Two years later it won the same prize for the second time and the prize for 'Best Riesling, sweet and full bodied, two years and over'.

Although the small root-sucking insect phylloxera, responsible for wiping out millions of acres of vineyards in Europe, arrived in Victoria in 1877, it was not detected in the Rutherglen wine region until twenty years later. Its presence was confirmed

The Bobbie Burns homestead, built in 1885, still stands beside the winery.

Liquid gold

Isabella Rare Rutherglen Topaque is Campbells' most famous and acclaimed Topaque. It is named in honour of David Campbell's wife, Isabella, who stood by him during the long process of replanting and nurturing the devastated vineyard, the financial hardship of the Great Depression and his health problems in the final years of his life. Isabella also provided invaluable support to their son, Allen, who was forced to diversity the family business so they could survive the remaining years of the Depression.

Topaque is made from a white grape and is much lighter in colour than Ports or Muscats of the same age. Long maturation in oak gradually transforms it from a pale gold into a rich amber. The base wine used to make Isabella is more than sixty years old. Isabella Rare Rutherglen Topaque has helped establish Rutherglen's reputation as the world's pre-eminent region for fortified wine.

in the Bobbie Burns vineyard in 1898, causing a slow decline in production at the Campbells winery.

When John Campbell died in 1909 at the age of seventy-six, the eighty-seven-acre vineyard was in serious decline. Phylloxera had reduced his precious vines to withered branches and dead twigs. Jessie Campbell had also died some years earlier, so their son, David, and his wife, Isabella, decided to take over and began a twenty-year task of replanting most of the Bobbie Burns vineyard with American phylloxera-resistant rootstock.

David Campbell was a popular and well-respected figure in the Rutherglen community. He was a member of the local band, football club, rowing club, agricultural society, winegrowers' association, Masonic Lodge and Presbyterian Church.

When David's eyesight was affected by an accident in 1931, his only son, Allen, then aged seventeen, returned from his studies at Dookie Agricultural College in Victoria's Goulburn Valley to assist in the business.

Isabella and David on
their wedding day.

In response to the plunging wine sales during the early years of the Depression the family began raising sheep in an attempt to generate income. Two years later David stumbled while carrying a ladder from the cellar, breaking three ribs. Shortly afterwards pneumonia set in and he died at the age of fifty-eight. At the time of his death, David was in despair — financially devastated by the Depression, he had given up any hope of saving the vineyards and winery for his descendants. He was survived by his wife, their three daughters and their son.

The tragic loss left twenty-year-old Allen struggling at the helm of the heavily mortgaged Bobbie Burns vineyard. The future of Campbells looked uncertain with 15 000 litres of wine in the cellar and no buyers.

Determined to continue the family heritage, Allen set about diversifying the business and steering it through the remainder of the Depression. In 1940 Allen married Isabel Diffey and together they continued rebuilding the business, growing crops and raising livestock, including dairy cows, sheep, pigs and chickens. They sold milk, cream, eggs, wool and meat to survive the difficult times. They also began selling wine in kegs and jars — a change from the usual practice of selling wine by the barrel — largely to Italian tobacco growers in Cobram and at the Queen Victoria Market in Melbourne. Revenue was increased by selling small lots of wine to private customers by rail delivery, instead of loading up trucks and selling in bulk to distributors.

Allen and Isabel were slowly building a solid foundation for the consolidation and future expansion of Campbells. Expansion began in 1943 with the purchase of thirty-nine acres of nearby land, which included ten acres of vines that had been planted in 1912. Also in 1943 Allen and Isabel's first son, Malcolm, was born. Two years later the Campbells had a second son, Colin. Their daughter, Jeanette, was born in 1950.

Three further purchases of land within the Rutherglen wine region were to provide the springboard for Campbells' future success. In 1948 the Campbells bought a twenty-four acre vineyard adjacent to the Bobbie Burns vineyard, which comprised vines that had been sent from France between 1910 and 1912 using the first form of cold storage. Four years later the Campbells family purchased the adjoining 200-acre Silverburn property, part of which was eventually replanted with vines that would produce a string of very successful white wines.

The third purchase that proved successful was 200 acres of land from Graham Brothers (once part of Rutherglen's largest wine estate) in 1960. The availability of irrigation made this land suitable for grazing and growing crops that could be used to feed the livestock. A further 140 acres of adjacent land was purchased in 1965, including a patch of fifty-year-old bush vines, which were used to produce a much sought-after aged white wine, Pedro Ximenez.

Not long after buying the Graham Brothers' property Allen Campbell fell ill. Malcolm returned home to assist his father in the running of the vineyard and farm in 1961 after completing high school as a boarder at Scotch College in Melbourne. Colin returned to Rutherglen in 1968 after completing a Diploma of Agriculture at Dookie Agricultural College and a Diploma of Oenology at Roseworthy Agricultural College in South Australia.

KEEP THIS FOR REFERENCE

"BOBBIE BURNS" RUTHERGLEN WINES

In Jar Lots up to Five Gallons
LARGER ORDERS ACCEPTED

NEW PRICE LIST

White Port	15/- per gal.
Red Port	15/- ,, ,,
Tawny Port	15/- ,, ,,
Muscat . . 15/- &	17/6 ,, ,,
Madeira	15/- ,, ,,
Frontignac	20/- ,, ,,
Reserve Port . . .	17/6 ,, ,,
Aged Tokay	20/- ,, ,,
Aged Muscat . . .	20/- ,, ,,
Sweet Sherry 15/- &	17/6 ,, ,,
Dry Sherry	15/- ,, ,,
Claret	8/- ,, ,,
Chablis	8/- ,, ,,

All Prices F.O.R. Rutherglen

Jars will be supplied but MUST be returned, freight paid, by first available train.

A. D. CAMPBELL

'Phone 58. Box 44
RUTHERGLEN

The cellar door price list in the 1950s.

In 1968, almost 100 years after John Campbell completed his first vintage, Campbells began to sell its first labelled wine in bottles. This included Pedro Ximenez (which was given the generic label 'Chablis'), and Shiraz (which was given the generic label 'Claret'). Previously, Campbells had produced only fortified wines in significant quantities.

Allen Campbell riding a dray
in the vineyard, circa 1940.

Isabel Campbell (on the right) helped out with the grape
harvest through the war years when labour was short.

Malcolm, Colin
and Allen
Campbell
working in the
cellar in the
late 1960s.

A year later Malcolm and Colin embarked on a new program
to expand the winery, raising the curtain on a new age for
Campbells — and for white wines in the Rutherglen wine region —
by pioneering sophisticated cooling methods. With wines of
flavour and finesse, the family very soon gained a reputation as
the premier white wine producer of the region. Following on from

this success a massive replanting program began. The vineyards were converted to a 'T' trellis to enable better air circulation, disease control and ease of picking, and a further fifteen acres of new vineyard were planted.

Still aged in their twenties, Malcolm and Colin demonstrated extraordinary foresight and vision when in 1969 they established a nursery block in a search for new varieties that would do well in the Rutherglen wine region. They compiled a list of varieties that they thought might have potential, and then obtained cuttings from the Victorian Department of Agriculture and imported some from California, planting just fifty vines of each variety. The nursery block was instrumental in developing varieties such as Viognier and Roussanne for release, both of which were launched in 2005. A unique blend produced from the 2008 vintage of Shiraz, Cabernet Sauvignon and up to ten obscure varieties originating from the nursery block was launched in 2010 as 'The Sixties Block'.

Malcolm and Colin Campbell with their mother Isabel in front of the newly constructed cellar door in 1973.

Colin and Prue
at their home,
Bobbie Burns,
in 1975.

Colin Campbell
drawing a
sample of
Muscat from a
cask in 1976.

Malcolm and Colin training young vines in 1970.

Colin Campbell carefully testing the juice of a new variety.

Colin Campbell sampling grapes prior to picking in 1974.

The 1970s marked the beginning of a cavalcade of trophies, medals and other awards that recognised the excellence of Campbells table and fortified wines. Among the award-winning wines were Trebbiano, Chablis, Cabernet Malbec, Vintage Port, Topaque and Muscat. Expansion and innovation continued with the construction of the cellar door, a new fermenting house and a warehouse, and the installation of an irrigation system in the vineyards.

Amid the triumphs, the 1970s also saw the passing of Allen Campbell at the age of sixty. With the same passion and vigour as their father, Malcolm and Colin took Campbells winery and vineyards into a fourth generation. Malcolm's enjoyment of, and skill in, the grape-growing process had led to him managing the viticultural and other aspects of the business with Allen for thirteen years. Colin, on the other hand, preferred winemaking, and after completing his Diploma of Oenology gained experience in the cellars of two of Australia's largest and most prestigious winemakers, Seppelts and Lindemans. Together, the Campbell brothers would make a prodigious team of viticulturalist and winemaker, taking the family business into the twenty-first century with an enviable reputation for innovation and wine of uncompromising character and quality.

> 'Quality, even at the expense of quantity, is our sole aim. We assist nature, we do not seek to dominate her.'
>
> Malcolm Campbell

During the 1980s the accolades continued to flow. Campbells Rhine Riesling won the trophy for Best Victorian Dry White Wine for three successive years at the Royal Melbourne Show. Merchant Prince Muscat won gold in the Open Muscat classes at the Rutherglen Wine Show and was named Top Muscat and Best Victorian Wine by *Winestate* magazine.

The 1980s were also a decade of self-education for the Campbells. In 1981 Colin and his wife, Prue, travelled to California on a study tour and to establish an agent there. The results were quick and rewarding — the company's first export

Opposite:
The best way to clean tartare from the cask!

Bobbie Burns Shiraz

Launched in 1970, Bobbie Burns Shiraz has become a Campbells and Rutherglen icon. It bears the name of the goldfield in which founder John Campbell worked, the property he selected and the homestead he built in 1886. The release of each new vintage is celebrated with the popular annual black tie (and more than a few kilts) Bobbie Burns Dinner in the cellars.

At the time of writing, Bobbie Burns Shiraz is Campbells' biggest selling wine. With its proven ageing ability it is hailed as a benchmark Rutherglen Shiraz. Well known for its consistent style, complexity and balance, Bobbie Burns has won numerous awards and other accolades in Australia and internationally.

order, for shipment to San Francisco, was dispatched in 1982, marking the beginning of global exports and recognition for Campbells wines. Malcolm undertook a six-week study tour of European vineyards in 1983, while Colin embarked on an in-depth winemaking study tour across France. In 1989 Andrew Campbell, son of Malcolm and Jenny, became the first member of the fifth generation to join the business when he returned to Rutherglen after completing his schooling to manage the Campbell farming operations.

In the twenty years since then, Malcolm and Colin, with the support of their wives, Jenny and Prue, and an increasing number of fifth-generation Campbells, have transformed the family business into an internationally respected wine producer. The list of international awards is long, with Bobbie Burns Shiraz, Campbells Rutherglen Muscat and Merchant Prince Rare Rutherglen Muscat all winning gold medals at the International Wine Challenge in London, the world's largest wine exhibition.

Malcolm Campbell celebrating his Scottish
heritage at the Bobbie Burns dinner.

Colin Campbell taking a sample in the winery.

Campbells is the only winery to win gold medals for both table and fortified wines in a single year at the London exhibition; that remarkable feat occurred in 1998. Campbell's Rutherglen Muscat has won several trophies in London and double gold at the San Francisco International Wine Competition for two consecutive years in 2003 and 2004, and again in 2010. Seeing their wines take on the world's best and come out on top has meant a great deal to all involved in this small winery.

International recognition by wine critics and at wine shows and competitions has propelled the export of Campbells wines. Export markets spread from San Francisco to the rest of the United States and beyond, including Canada, the United Kingdom, China, Denmark and Sweden.

> ❛We have a fond saying that a good Muscat or Topaque is a unique blend of the wisdom of age and the exuberance of youth, much like life.❜
>
> Colin Campbell

Malcolm Campbell's desire for constant improvement and appetite for learning took him and Jenny on study tours to vineyards in New Zealand, Chile and Argentina. With his son, Andrew, Malcolm travelled to Israel and the United States to study drip irrigation, and within a year of that trip the original Bobbie Burns vineyard and the Silverburn vineyard had been converted from spray irrigation to drip irrigation. Colin and Prue, meanwhile, sought to promote Campbells and the whole Rutherglen wine region internationally, exploring export opportunities in Ireland, the United States and China.

The perfect Muscat?

Campbells Merchant Prince Rare Rutherglen Muscat was the first Australian wine to be awarded a perfect score of 100 by legendary wine columnist Harvey Steiman of *Wine Spectator* magazine, the most authoritative and widely read wine journal in the world.

Named after the ship on which founder John Campbell sailed to Australia in 1857, Merchant Prince Rare Rutherglen Muscat was launched in 1983. Colin gives credit to his grandfather and father for producing the old and unique stocks of Muscat from which Merchant Prince is crafted. Colin explains: 'This Muscat displays the extraordinary qualities that result from the blending of selected parcels of only the very richest and most complete wines in the cellar. Our Rare Rutherglen Muscats are only bottled in tiny quantities each year'.

Like all of Campbells' fortified wines, Merchant Prince Rare Rutherglen Muscat is drawn from a solera containing wines that go back to David Campbell's era. Campbells' solero system is a series of five stages, each containing wine at successive stages of maturation. From the final stage the finished mature wine is drawn for sale and each stage is progressively filled from the preceding stage with the youngest wine introduced at the earliest stage. This blends the individuality and variances of different vintages. The wine moves slowly over the years through the casks until it reaches optimum maturity in the final stage. Wine is only withdrawn from the final stage and in small quantities when it matches exactly the previous withdrawal, assuring its consistency.

The Campbell brothers have made numerous improvements and innovations in the vineyards and the winery, some of them influenced by their study tours and wine industry networks. Colin Campbell also recognised the similarities in climate between the Rhone region in France and Rutherglen, and selectively adopted some of the Rhone winemakers' techniques, including using fully ripe fruit and subtle oak fermentation. In 1990 Colin initiated a series of open fermentation trials, seeking to integrate modern fermentation technology with the best aspects of traditional winemaking. The following year Malcolm introduced a non-cultivation system in the vineyards, allowing the vines to grow without human interference. Further enhancements have been made at every

> ❛I see my task as winemaker to maximise and protect the natural fruit flavours and craft our wines to a harmonious balance.❜
>
> Colin Campbell

A red with attitude

Durif has been described as a 'red variety with attitude' and has been grown in Rutherglen for more than 100 years. However, The Barkly Durif, first released in 1992, is something extra special. Colin Campbell describes it as 'Durif at its finest'. He adds, 'We spent a long time getting it right. We had to tame the tannins to make it approachable in its youth without taking away the longevity'. The Barkly is only released in years in which vintage conditions are exceptional for Durif.

Barkly was the original name of the Rutherglen township when it was a mining settlement. According to local folklore the name was changed in 1860 when developer John Wallace was challenged: 'If you're prepared to shout the bar when you open the Star Hotel you can rename Barkly after your native town in Scotland'. Wallace replied, 'Right you are, Rutherglen it shall be!'

stage of the wine production process, from the vineyard all the way through to bottling. They have also reduced the winery's environmental footprint, conserving water and minimising the need for chemical intervention.

The improvements made by Malcolm and Colin have had a significant impact on the complexity of Campbells traditional portfolio of fortified and table wines. They have paved the way for the rollout of some exciting new wines, including The Barkly Durif, Viognier, Roussanne, Tempranillo, The Brothers Shiraz, The Sixties Block and Campbells '1870' Sparkling Shiraz, which was released in 2010 to commemorate the company's 140th year of family winemaking in Rutherglen. For the Campbell brothers, such changes and developments are an adventure, and satisfaction comes from knowing they are getting the best out of their vineyards.

Walking through the century-old cellars, dwarfed by the towering casks containing muscats and topaques, Colin is reminded daily of his responsibility to past Campbell generations. He remains unwavering in his commitment to quality, and likens his wines to children. 'They need to be watched carefully and handled lovingly as they mature', he says.

✤   ✤   ✤

The Campbell family is active in its support of the Rutherglen community and the Australian wine industry. Dinners at the winery and events on its extensive grounds, shaded by tall old oak trees, are used to boost tourism in Rutherglen and provide a showcase for regional produce.

Malcolm's deep-rooted commitment to ensuring the future of the industry led him to establish the not-for-profit Rutherglen Vine Grafting facility, which provides vines for the district. He has been involved in several other wine industry groups, including the

The Campbell family has a long tradition of community involvement. In 2004, at the age of eighty-five, Isabel Campbell was awarded a medal recognising her fifty years of service to the Red Cross.

Three generations of the Campbell family. Standing, from left: Colin, Donna, Roger and Jane Campbell. Seated, from left: Susie, Isabel, Malcolm, Jenny and Prue.

Victorian Murray Valley Vine Improvement Association and the National Vine Health Committee.

Colin Campbell is determined to see Rutherglen Muscat recognised worldwide as a unique Australian wine and the 'world's richest wine'. To that end, he drove the formation of the Muscat of Rutherglen Network, which he now chairs. The network comprises a group of Rutherglen Muscat producers and has developed a classification system for these wines to ensure quality

Oh, brother ... what a Shiraz!

Campbells flagship wine 'The Brothers' Shiraz was first released in 2002 and subsequent vintages have all been created with the same goal: 'To produce an astounding expression of Rutherglen Shiraz, structured and complex with layer upon layer of rich Rutherglen Shiraz fruit'. It is fitting that the pride of Campbells' table wines is named in honour of the Campbell brothers. Malcolm and Colin have worked side by side for almost fifty years. Colin Campbell proudly points out, 'This wine is the pinnacle of our endeavours and the ultimate expression of Rutherglen Shiraz'.

and reliability. Colin also established the Durif of Rutherglen Network to promote this special wine. He has chaired the Fortified Sustainability Project — which was charged with a relaunch strategy for Australian fortified wines, including the development of new names for Tokay and sherry in the Australian market — and is a board member of the Winemakers' Federation of Australia.

Colin and Prue's daughter, Susie, founded the Rutherglen Young Bloods, a group of the new generation of the Rutherglen winemaking families. This exciting group of young winemakers and marketers has come together with the aim of holding functions to engage with younger wine consumers. They also form a powerful alliance with their parents, combining 'the wisdom of age and the exuberance of youth' — a powerful blend indeed.

Jenny Campbell describes Rutherglen wineries as 'a brotherhood'. 'We share our knowledge and we work together to attract visitors to the region.' Susie adds, 'Uncle Malcolm and Dad have been at the forefront of tourism and bringing people together to contribute to the greater good'.

Malcolm and Colin Campbell have each been honoured with a Distinguished Service Award for 'outstanding service to the development of the Victorian wine industry'. In 2001 Malcolm was awarded the Order of Australia Medal (OAM) for services to viticulture and to the community.

Julie, Jane and Susie playing in the basket press, 1979.

The first fifth-generation Campbell to join the company, Andrew, died tragically in a car accident. All five of the remaining fifth generation are now working in the family business, adding their skills and enthusiasm. Colin and Prue's youngest daughter, Julie, became the first female winemaker to craft wines under the Campbells label in 2001. Julie has since married Cameron Ashmead of Elderton Wines in the Barossa Valley, where she is actively involved in the wine industry. However, she returns to the family winery at key decision-making times throughout

The 'Young Bloods' — fifth generation Roger, Susie, Jane and Donna.

the year to assist her father and the winemaking team, bringing another perspective to the wines.

Julie's older sister Susie joined the family business in 2003 as marketing manager and has also 'inherited' the role of brand custodian. The eldest of Colin and Prue's daughters, Jane, was manager of the cellar door and special events. For the moment, with a young family to keep her busy, she is a keen member of the cellar door sales team. Malcolm and Jenny's daughter, Donna, joined the cellar door team in 2006 and her younger brother, Roger, works closely with Malcolm on the farm and in the vineyards. Jenny and Prue are both actively involved in the business.

> 'Wine is in our blood. We've grown up with it; we live it, breathe it and love it.'
>
> Susie Campbell

These younger Campbells have grown up in the winery and vineyards. Susie remembers sitting around the dinner table as a child listening to conversations about cellar doors, expansion and export markets. She has fond memories of 'sitting on dad's knee and being asked to describe the smell of the wine in his glass'.

Opposite:
Muscat grapes.

She recalls seeing her younger sister Julie stretch up for the glass of grape juice during communion in their Uniting Church. 'She sniffed it, screwed up her nose and said "Ugh, that's not Daddy's wine!" and gave it to our grandmother.'

After more than 140 years of family winemaking, the wines of the Campbell family of Rutherglen are recognised as some of the best in the world. Even after the devastation of phylloxera, the Great Depression and the early deaths of David, Allen and Andrew, the spirit of a Scottish immigrant, gold prospector and pioneering winemaker lives on through the fourth and fifth generations of the Campbell family.

How to serve and enjoy Muscat

Rutherglen Muscat is blended for optimum flavour and balance at the time of bottling. It will not improve with further cellaring, so should be enjoyed ideally soon after opening.

It is a versatile accompaniment to food, and the many styles of Muscat produced in the region allow innovative combinations of wine and food. The lighter Rutherglen Muscats are superb aperitifs—the perfect way to prepare for a hearty meal. In the warmer months they can be served chilled straight from the fridge.

The richer Classic Rutherglen Muscats are excellent accompaniments to both savoury meals (such as pâtés, terrines, soups, stews and spicy Asian cuisine) and desserts (in particular, dishes that contain caramel, toffee and chocolate, as well as marinated fruits and ice-cream). Richer Rutherglen Muscats also match well with strong cheeses such as vintage cheddar or blue-vein.

A glass of Grand or Rare Rutherglen Muscat can be enjoyed with freshly brewed coffee and petit fours—and it is the only wine that is not overpowered by even the richest dark chocolate.

The wine and food combinations possible with Rutherglen Muscats are almost limitless. Whenever richly flavoured dishes are offered, the world's richest wines will prove perfect partners.

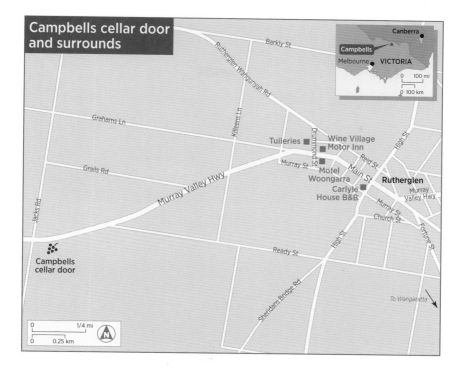

Cellar door

Murray Valley Hwy
Rutherglen Vic. 3685
t: 02 6033 6000
w: www.campbellswines.com.au
e: sales@campbellswines.com.au

Opening hours
Monday to Saturday: 9 am to 5 pm
Sunday: 10 am to 5 pm
Closed: Christmas Day and Good Friday

Accommodation options

Carlyle House B&B
147 High St
Rutherglen Vic. 3685
t: 02 6032 8444
w: www.carlylehouse.com.au
e: carlylehouse@optusnet.com.au

Motel Woongarra
Cnr Main and Drummond Sts
Rutherglen Vic. 3685
t: 02 6032 9588
w: www.motelwoongarra.com.au
e: stay@motelwoongarra.com.au

Tuileries
13–35 Drummond St
Rutherglen Vic. 3685
t: 02 6032 9033
w: www.tuileriesrutherglen.com.au
e: info@tuileriesrutherglen.com.au

Wine Village Motor Inn
217 Main St
Rutherglen Vic. 3685
t: 1800 028 365
w: www.winevillagemotorinn.com.au

LIGHT DRY RED
VINTAGE 1946
K.S. HERMITAGE
PLEASANT WINES PTY. LTD.
NEWCASTLE.

McWilliam's
Morning light

'Talk to any winemaker, and you embark on
a journey that goes beyond the boundaries
of vine and blend, vintage and region.
You'll find yourself on an excursion into the
myriad complexities of human nature.'

Don McWilliam AM, former chairman, McWilliam's

Founded in Hanwood, near Griffith in the Murrumbidgee
Irrigation Area of southern New South Wales, more
than 130 years ago, McWilliam's has grown into a thriving
business with an array of vineyards across Australia. Even
with its own diverse vineyards, McWilliam's obtains about
two-thirds of its fruit from other premium growers, with whom
the company has developed long-standing relationships. This
enables McWilliam's to source the best fruit for its wineries
at Hanwood Estate in the Riverina region and McWilliam's
Mount Pleasant Estate in the Hunter Valley.

Always innovative, McWilliam's has set up its wineries with
some of the world's most advanced equipment and laboratories.

It has recently created a new winemaking facility at the Hanwood winery that can handle small quantities of premium fruit and develop new wine styles.

Some of the best known of McWilliam's table wines come from the Mount Pleasant vineyards. They include the Lovedale Semillon, a single-vineyard wine, and the Maurice O'Shea Shiraz, made from 120-year-old Shiraz vines and named in honour of the legendary Australian winemaker from whom McWilliam's purchased Mount Pleasant. The Hanwood winery also produces an enviable range of fortified wines, including ports and sherries.

The McWilliam's story began in 1857 when Samuel McWilliam, a twenty-seven-year-old labourer from Northern Ireland, joined hundreds of other young adventurers aboard the clipper *Morning Light*, for the long voyage to Melbourne, Australia. Many were headed for the goldfields, but the bustling city of Melbourne provided other opportunities. Samuel moved to the Bellarine Peninsula, south-west of Melbourne, where he was able to find work on newly settled farms. In 1863 he married Martha Steel, the daughter of a pardoned convict who had become a farmer. Shortly afterwards Samuel and Martha followed the gold rush to the east in Gippsland and bought a parcel of land near the town of Sale. Samuel saw an ideal opportunity to use his farming experience to provide food for the growing number of miners. He built a homestead on the property, grew cereal crops and ran livestock.

After a number of setbacks in Gippsland, including droughts, floods and an infestation of caterpillars, Samuel McWilliam decided there were better opportunities for his family elsewhere.

> ❝ I believe that wine consumers enjoy learning. They like a wine or even a label that gives them an extra bit of knowledge. They enjoy trying different varieties and styles from different regions. Our diversity gives us a competitive advantage. ❞
>
> Scott McWilliam, sixth-generation winemaker

In 1877, he and Martha sold their land and moved their growing family to a newly acquired 480-acre property near the town of Corowa in New South Wales. He immediately set about planting an eighty-acre vineyard, which he named Sunnyside, eventually making table wine in a galvanised iron shed. He also ran sheep and cattle on the property. Just as he had been in Sale, Samuel was active in the small community, becoming involved in the Presbyterian Church and the Corowa Agricultural Society.

Martha McWilliam died of cancer in 1889 at the age of forty-eight, and Samuel was left to raise their five sons and four daughters. All five boys worked on the farm and in the vineyard, and in their spare time revelled in the surrounding bushland, trying their hand at mining and developing a love of nature.

Founder of McWilliam's, Samuel McWilliam.

Two years later Samuel sold part of the property and moved to Sydney with his daughters, leaving his third son, Lawrence John Roy (known as JJ), in charge of Sunnyside. Shortly after taking over, JJ obtained a colonial wine licence and opened a wine shop on the property. JJ was resourceful, ambitious and perceptive, and after leaving school at the age of thirteen he had built up ten years of both farming and winemaking experience, under the watchful eye of Dr Henry Lindeman, who had a well-established winery in Corowa. With this knowledge and experience he was able to drive the property forward while the rest of the country was reeling from the depression of the early 1890s.

JJ married a Scottish immigrant, Elizabeth Aitken Dewar, in 1892, and the couple had two children before moving north to Junee, in what is now known as the Riverina wine region of New South Wales. JJ successfully applied for a liquor licence

The Mark View
Cellars at Junee,
circa 1910.

and opened The Wine Vaults in the small settlement, where he was able to sell his own wine. Junee was a major rail depot for the Riverina and the increasing number of itinerant workers passing through the town provided a market for his wines. JJ took a lease on vineyards near the town and quickly gained a reputation for growing high-quality fruit. He later purchased the vineyards and constructed a winery, which he named Mark View. Like many wineries of that period, Mark View was built into the side of a hill to allow gravity-feeding of grapes, juice and wine. Underground vats kept the ageing wines cool during hot weather.

JJ's younger brother Thomas and two of his sisters had been left to manage Sunnyside, but it was JJ who was mainly responsible for driving the growth of the family business in Corowa and Junee, along with the family's merchandising business in Sydney, which was established several years later. In 1896 Sunnyside won its first wine award — second prize for a full-bodied dry white. Several first prizes followed in subsequent years at the Corowa and Junee Agricultural Shows for wines crafted by both JJ and Thomas. When Thomas left in 1899 to fight in the Boer War, JJ was once again solely in charge of Sunnyside.

Samuel McWilliam died in 1902 at the age of seventy-two. He bequeathed shares of his property at Corowa to his four daughters and four of his five sons. JJ and his brother Crawford were left smaller portions because of the financial assistance they had already received from their father. It is believed that eldest son, William, wasn't included at all for the same reason. Three of the four daughters bought all of the equipment used in the vineyards and winery, including casks, vats and the crusher; however, less than five years later, without the ability to raise capital to keep Sunnyside afloat, they sold their shares in the property and their equipment to JJ. Following on from this purchase, JJ bought the remaining shares in the property from his brothers Crawford, Thomas and Edmond.

After gaining complete control of Sunnyside in 1907, JJ was faced with several large problems. The Federation of Australia in 1901 had freed up trade between the former six colonies, increasing competition from the many larger vineyards in South Australia, particularly in the Barossa Valley. Like most of the vineyards in the area, Sunnyside's yields were relatively small. To make matters worse, the detection of phylloxera in local vineyards in 1909 threatened to devastate the vines. Two years later, JJ made the difficult decision to sell his beloved Sunnyside.

In 1913 JJ successfully applied for two fifty-acre farms in the Murrumbidgee Irrigation Area, which had been established in 1912 by the New South Wales government to enable the growth of crops in what was previously unsuitable semi-arid land. The rule was that each person could only hold one lease, so JJ leased one farm in his name and the other in his eldest son's name, Lawrence John Roy (known as Jack).

Jack McWilliam was the first born of JJ and Elizabeth's eight children. He had three younger brothers — Doug, Keith and Glen — all of whom were later to be influential in the development and expansion of the family business. Jack was more than nineteen years older than his youngest brother, Glen. Jack also had four younger sisters — Jessie, Maude, Dorothy and Joyce.

JJ McWilliam was a large, good-humoured man with a booming voice and an uncompromising work ethic.

JJ and Jack worked together to clear, plough and grade the land on both farms. They planted a cash crop of fruit and nut trees, as well as about 35 000 vine cuttings of Shiraz, Malbec and Doradillo from Junee in a nursery from which a vineyard was planted in 1914. JJ also sold cuttings to other local settlers. Theirs was the first commercial vineyard in the Murrumbidgee Irrigation Area. Indeed, so anxious were they to get started that they planted the vineyard a few weeks before water was flowing in the irrigation channels, using a water cart and watering the vines by hand from a nearby dam.

Three years after planting the first vineyard, and at about the same time as the establishment of the nearby town of Griffith, construction began on the Hanwood winery. Doug joined his father and brother in 1922 when construction began on a second winery in Yenda to process the grapes grown by local settlers. His success in producing both fortified and table wines inspired many other settlers in the Riverina area to plant vineyards. Some time later the McWilliams bought a third winery and storage facility from a failed Cooperative at Beelbangera, also near Griffith.

> ‘This soil is so fertile that you could plant a six-inch nail, water it and grow a crowbar.’
>
> JJ McWilliam

As the leading purchaser of local grapes during the 1920s, JJ was able to dictate terms. He was a shrewd businessman and negotiated grape prices annually instead of entering into long-term contracts. His wine was being sold directly from family-owned cellars in Sydney, Goulburn, Bathurst, Brisbane and New Zealand.

The business was exceptionally profitable. Keith joined in 1924 and within four years had been promoted to manager of the Sydney cellars. By 1935 the company had twenty-seven outlets. The successful expansion of McWilliam's during the economically difficult times of the Great Depression was largely due to sound viticultural practices, the use of technology and JJ's building skills. With the help of his sons, JJ constructed storage vats, small fermenting vats and other winery facilities.

McWilliam's went into partnership with legendary Hunter Valley winemaker Maurice O'Shea in 1932 when it purchased a 50 per cent share in his winery at Mount Pleasant and established Mount Pleasant Wines Pty Ltd. O'Shea had founded his Mount Pleasant vineyards and winery in the foothills of the Brokenback Ranges at Pokolbin in 1921.

The McWilliam family gave O'Shea free rein to work his magic as chief winemaker, even after purchasing his 50 per cent share in 1941, but took control of the business affairs. The Mount Pleasant vineyards later expanded with the purchase of the Lovedale and Rosehill properties, which were selected and planted by O'Shea. Maurice O'Shea died of lung cancer in 1956 at the age of fifty-nine. Since his death there have only been two other chief winemakers at Mount Pleasant — Brian Walsh, between 1956 and 1978, and Phil Ryan, who still holds the position today.

McWilliam's first entry into the export market was in 1935 when it began selling into the United Kingdom. However, when World War II broke out in Europe, wine exports to the UK declined. The war also caused other issues for wineries: men enlisting to fight resulted in a labour shortage, grape surpluses

JJ McWilliam and his family, circa 1936. Standing, from left: Dorothy, Maude, Jessie, Jack, Doug and Keith. Seated, from left: Joyce, Elizabeth, JJ and Glen.

Maurice O'Shea founded Mount Pleasant and changed the way Australian wine was made.

grew and the importation of viticultural and winemaking equipment became impossible. All of this fuelled predictions of disaster for the Australian wine industry. In fact, the opposite happened — as the war continued, unemployment fell and wine sales grew. McWilliam's was also able to add to its profits in another, rather unusual, way. The company had the facilities to produce alcohol to fuel motor vehicles by fermenting molasses brought in by rail.

Elizabeth McWilliam died in 1943 after a painful illness, believed to be cancer. JJ was deeply affected by the death of his wife of fifty years and gradually withdrew from company activities. Ten years earlier he had stopped participating in the day-to-day running of the vineyards, wineries and wine outlets, but had maintained his positions of managing director and chairman of the board.

Meanwhile, the company continued to prosper. By 1945, what had begun with Samuel McWilliam's eighty-acre Sunnyside vineyard near Corowa had grown into vineyards in the Riverina and Hunter Valley, and numerous wine outlets throughout Australia. By 1947 vineyards, wineries and outlets had also been established across the Tasman Sea in New Zealand.

In 1945 JJ decided to sell all of his shares in the company to his four sons, thereby avoiding substantial death taxes when he died. His plan was to make substantial cash payments to his daughters with the proceeds. This decision sparked a bitter family feud that was to last for more than twenty years. When JJ and his four sons failed to agree on the distribution ratio, JJ decided to sell and apportion his shares to ensure that Jack, Doug, Keith and Glen had equal shareholdings.

Jack was furious that his father had distributed the shares in this fashion. He had undeniably put more work into the company, having started working there much earlier than his brothers, and felt that he had earned the right to be his father's successor and have

The vineyard speaks

McWilliam's Mount Pleasant Lovedale Semillon is a single-vineyard wine sourced exclusively from the Lovedale vineyard, which was planted by Maurice O'Shea in 1946 as part of the expansion at Mount Pleasant. Since its inaugural vintage in 1950 it has been widely acclaimed, winning numerous trophies and gold medals. In 2006 UK wine critic Matthew Jukes described it as 'the finest single-vineyard Semillon in the world'.

With the potential for cellaring for up to thirty years, this wine captures the very essence of the vineyard's character, and the skill and personality of its creator.

a controlling influence in the company. His brothers, however, believed that Jack had already been well rewarded for his efforts, and had doubts about his corporate and financial judgement.

By 1946 Jack and Glen were not on speaking terms. Jack appealed to his father to reconsider the distribution, reminding him of his pioneering work at Hanwood and pointing out that he had trained his younger brothers. When JJ refused to change his mind, Jack stopped attending board meetings and rejected the opportunity to take up his portion of the share allotment.

The dispute escalated when Jack made unauthorised sales of wine to a company in Griffith. Locks had been broken and replaced to gain access to the wine. Glen accused Jack of robbery and the two brothers eventually came to blows. When Jack refused to give full disclosure of the Hanwood and Yenda wineries' accounts in 1949, he was suspended from the company and removed as a director.

Doug had been appointed chairman of McWilliam's Wines Ltd in 1947. A year later Keith became managing director and Glen was given sole control of the Hanwood winery. There was a slight problem, though. Jack's home and the Hanwood

McWilliam's
Mount Pleasant
Estate and
winery.

winery were both on the original Murrumbidgee Irrigation Area property and were in his name. The solution devised by the three younger brothers was to erect a wire fence between Jack's home and the winery, preventing his access and allowing them to work the vineyards on the property. Not surprisingly, Jack was furious. Shotguns were produced in the vineyard in 1950 and a shot was fired in Glen's direction. Glen subsequently issued an apprehended violence order against Jack.

Jack initiated legal proceedings, accusing his brothers and the company of fraud in an attempt to restore what he believed to be his rightful equity in the company. While the resentment and verbal, and sometimes physical, recriminations continued at Hanwood, the legal battle moved all the way to the High Court of Australia, which in 1964 ruled against Jack. The effects of the bitter feud left Jack's family without equal shares in the company, and left both Jack and Keith in ill health. Jack continued to live on the Hanwood farm with his brothers' approval until his death in 1973.

JJ McWilliam died in May 1951 at the age of eighty-two while the legal battles were continuing. JJ had taken the company from a small family business into a large, complex, but still family-owned enterprise.

With Glen McWilliam as production director, the company demonstrated that irrigated vineyards such as those at Hanwood could produce premium table wines, not just wines suitable for selling in bulk. Better control of irrigation, investments in stainless-steel tanks, state-of-the-art temperature control and other new technology used during the 1960s and 1970s resulted in the quality of the table wines improving dramatically. During the same two decades, Australian wine consumption increased almost four-fold and McWilliam's enjoyed a large share of the growing market, averaging about 10 per cent market share during that twenty-year period.

Doug McWilliam retired as chairman in 1982 after thirty-five years in the role and was replaced by Keith, who held the position until retiring in 1988. Keith's son, Don, was then appointed chairman.

From rot to Morning Light

During Glen McWilliam's time at the helm of the Hanwood winery he often travelled overseas to sharpen his winemaking skills and broaden his knowledge. On one occasion in 1958 he returned from France to a very wet summer and a damp vineyard. The Pedro Ximenez grapes were rotting on the vines. In the past he would have picked them quickly and put them through the still to use in the company's traditional fortified wines. However, because of what he had recently observed in Sauterne, Glen recognised that it was worth letting them go and picking them even later.

The result was the 1958 Pedro Sauterne, the first Botrytis wine made commercially in Australia. Similar wine styles later became known as McWilliam's Botrytis Semillon and are now labelled Morning Light Botrytis Semillon to commemorate the name of the ship on which founder Samuel McWilliam sailed to Australia. Having received many accolades since it was created in 1958, McWilliam's Morning Light Botrytis Semillon is now one of the company's flagship wines.

Don was born in Sydney in 1934, where his father was managing the McWilliam's distribution centre and cellars. Like his predecessors, Don left school early, joining McWilliam's as a bottle-line hand in 1950. As a managerial trainee from the age of eighteen, he worked in the company's wineries, vineyards and cellars. His most cherished memories of that period are of working on the 1954 and 1955 vintages at McWilliam's Mount Pleasant with Maurice O'Shea.

Don was appointed a director in 1957, chief executive in 1970 and chairman in 1988. He was inspired by Maurice O'Shea's brilliance to establish the McWilliam's Maurice O'Shea Award in 1990. The award is presented annually to an industry leader recognised by his or her peers for excellence and service to the industry. The inaugural Maurice O'Shea Award was presented to Max Schubert, creator of Penfolds Grange Hermitage.

Opposite:
Vintage
McWilliam's.

Don acknowledges his uncle Glen as a gifted winemaker. 'Glen took a huge risk when he planted Cabernet Sauvignon in the Riverina vineyards, which were thought only suitable for growing grapes for fortified wines', he says. 'In 1966 the Cabernet ripped the wine shows apart!' Glen's other successes include developing the Botrytis Semillon and Cream Sherry.

Don retired from the position of chief executive in 1993 and was replaced by Kevin McLintock, a South African and graduate of Harvard Business School. Kevin later became deputy chairman of McWilliam's and played a major role in the continued expansion of the company. As chairman, Don steered the company into premium segments of the table wine market and into new export markets, including the United States, Japan and Germany.

The McWilliam's winery at Hanwood was redeveloped and expanded to accept production and storage from the Yenda and

A tribute to a legend

In 1987, three years before the Maurice O'Shea award was established, McWilliam's launched its Maurice O'Shea Shiraz. This iconic wine is made in limited quantities and showcases the skills of today's winemaking team. Maurice O'Shea Shiraz is made from the very best of the Shiraz crop grown at Mount Pleasant as a tribute to O'Shea. Most of the fruit comes from the vines planted by the property's original owner, Charles King, in 1880. The remainder is from the Old Paddock, planted by O'Shea in the 1920s.

Maurice O'Shea had a remarkable palate and was a master blender. His techniques and sophisticated use of oak were credited with producing table wines of enormous flavour, intensity and longevity. O'Shea's achievements were all the more remarkable because they occurred in an era without electricity or automated cooling systems, and when fortified wines dominated the Australian market.

Maurice O'Shea
(on the left)
weighing barrels
during vintage
in 1950.

Robinvale wineries, which had been sold. The new Hanwood
winery opened in 2008 with a laboratory and winemaking areas
equipped with state-of-the-art technology. It allows greater flexibil-
ity and opportunities for wine style development and innovation.

A prolific and active participant in the Australian wine
industry, Don served on the boards of the Australian Wine and
Brandy Producers' Association, the Australian Wine Board,
the Australian Wine Research Institute and the Winemakers
Federation of Australia. In 2003 Don was appointed a Member
of the Order of Australia (AM) for services to the wine industry.

The McWilliam's Mount Pleasant
vineyard in the Hunter Valley.

The redeveloped
and expanded
Hanwood winery.

When Don announced his retirement as chairman in
December 2009 (he remains a director), he was succeeded by
Doug, son of Jim McWilliam, grandson of third-generation Doug
and great-grandson of JJ. Doug had a very different background
from his predecessors. After completing an honours degree in
science at the Australian National University in Canberra,
he worked in the mining industry for two years. He joined
McWilliam's as a wine chemist and winemaker in 1972, and then
travelled overseas to complete a masters degree in oenology at
the University of California. In 1983 he accepted the position
of production director at McWilliam's and joined the board
of directors.

Doug grew up among vineyards and a winery. He recalls
that as a seven or eight year old he decided to make his own wine.
He put some grapes into a meat mincer and fermented them in
an old kerosene can. One of the workshop staff fitted a valve
onto the bottom of the can to draw out the liquid. According
to Doug, the wine was 'bloody awful'. Like most of the young
McWilliam boys he worked in the winery to earn pocket money

during school holidays, washing bottles, cleaning tanks and filling tankers.

Like his predecessor Don, Doug has been actively engaged in advancing the Australian wine industry. He served as chairman of the Australian Wine Research Institute for ten years, was a director of the Cooperative Research Centre for Viticulture and has served as president of the Riverina Winemakers Association. He has also served on the Winemakers Federation Research and Development Subcommittee.

Sustainability is an important part of the agenda at McWilliam's. Doug is committed to ensuring that the company minimises any detrimental effects to the environment through its activities and contributes to environmental improvement. For example, mulching and planting selected grasses between rows in the vineyards has resulted in soil enrichment, a reduction in soil erosion and an increase in water retention.

A fabulous celebration

McWilliam's 1877 Cabernet Sauvignon Shiraz commemorates the year in which Samuel McWilliam planted his first vines at Corowa. Launched with the 1998 vintage, it celebrates the passion and work ethic of the six generations of Samuel's family who have followed in his footsteps and pursued a dream to make McWilliam's one of Australia's most diverse, innovative, exciting and largest wine producers.

This flagship wine is crafted from premium fruit sourced mainly from old vines at the Brand's Laira vineyard in the Coonawarra wine region and the Barwang vineyard in the Hilltops wine region. Smaller parcels of fruit now come from other regions, including Margaret River in Western Australia and Heathcote in Victoria. 'What's exciting about this wine', says current chairman Doug McWilliam, 'is that we're not restricting ourselves to a particular vineyard or region. We are just trying to make a fabulous wine'.

Don and Louise McWilliam at McWilliam's Maurice O'Shea Award Dinner.

Don McWilliam, Stephen McWilliam, Doug McWilliam and Phil Ryan.

The company participates in the New South Wales government's Sustainability Advantage Program, which is charged with developing a sustainability 'roadmap' for the state. McWilliam's has also sought to minimise the environmental impact of its packaging, signing the National Packaging Covenant. McWilliam's was recognised for its environmental initiatives in 2008 when it was awarded the Harden Murrumburrah Landcare Award for development of environmentally sensitive viticultural practices.

In another initiative, the company has converted its vineyard supplementary water system into a high-tech drip system to reduce water usage. The company has also worked closely with scientific research organisation CSIRO to trial Tyrian, a new grape variety that requires up to 20 per cent less water than mainstream varietals. After initially planting a small test block in 1995, there are now more than 120 acres in full production. According to Doug McWilliam, the quality of Tyrian is similar to Shiraz but the grape is less susceptible to mildew disease and produces a bigger crop.

> ʿIt was drummed into me that, as a family member, I had to earn my position in the business and that there is no room for passengers. You have extra responsibility as a family member, but on the other hand there is extra satisfaction. ʾ
>
> Scott McWilliam

In the semi-arid Riverina wine region, reducing water use is an important issue for the Hanwood vineyards. Doug points out, 'Our main goal is to reduce evaporation. All of the water at the Hanwood vineyards comes through pipes at pressure. There are no more open channels. But pressure pumping increases our carbon footprint, so we are looking at possibly using bio-generated power from our wine effluent. There is also lots of potential in the future for solar energy in this sun-drenched region'.

The current winemaking team at McWilliam's includes sixth-generation Scott McWilliam, son of Doug. Scott is currently senior winemaker at Mount Pleasant. He joined the family company in 2000 as a winemaker after completing vintages in Bordeaux and Beaujolais in France, and in the Napa and Sonoma valleys in California. Chief winemaker Corey Ryan oversees the development and management of McWilliam's entire portfolio. He was appointed in 2008 following six years' experience with Henschke in South Australia's Eden Valley and time spent at wineries in France's Rhone Valley and in Spain. His predecessor, Jim Brayne, was appointed production director after spending eighteen years as chief winemaker.

> ❛ I'm proud that after six generations we are still here and moving forward. ❜
>
> Doug McWilliam

The winemaking team takes great pride in its success at wine shows and exhibitions. McWilliam's sixteenth consecutive award at the Sydney Wine Show for Most Successful Exhibitor in 2010 is a measure of consistency of quality. Doug McWilliam believes that this success 'celebrates all family wineries and our commitment to making the very best wine, in the same way my great-great-grandfather did many years ago'. However, while such wins

Doug McWilliam and family at McWilliam's Maurice O'Shea Award Dinner.

Cream of the crop

In the late 1950s Glen McWilliam developed McWilliam's Cream Sherry in response to his brother Keith's vision for a light, sweet sherry, and since then it has been the company's most popular fortified wine. It was first produced at the Hanwood and Yenda wineries near Griffith from Gordo grapes grown in the Sunraysia district of the Murray-Darling region, about 300 kilometres to the west.

The grapes had to be transported over poorly maintained and sometimes impassable roads in hot weather, arriving at Hanwood or Yenda in less than ideal condition. Glen and Doug searched for a site closer to the source of the fruit on which to build a new winery. Construction on a winery in Robinvale, built exclusively to produce Cream Sherry, began in 1962 and the first grapes were crushed in April 1963. The Robinvale winery operated until 2009 when it was sold and production moved to the Hanwood winery.

are satisfying, this winery doesn't simply enter shows for the trophies. 'The shows provide opportunity for valuable feedback from industry peers and allow us to get out and taste everyone else's wines', says Scott. He is especially proud of the gold medal awarded to Hanwood Estate Chardonnay at the 2008 Chardonnay du Monde show in France, where his wine was competing with wines valued at ten times its price.

A McWilliam's family reunion in 2002.

McWilliam's Hanwood vineyard.

Over six generations and more than 130 years, the McWilliam family has witnessed and embraced changes from human labour and horsepower to mechanisation and petrol power and, more recently, to computerised automation. Adding to all that, the family business has endured two depressions and world wars, and survived a bitter twenty-year family feud. McWilliam's has transformed itself into one of Australia's largest and most respected family-owned wine companies and, with the fifth and sixth generation at the helm, is determined to remain a family-owned wine company for generations to come.

Decanting wine

There are two reasons for decanting red wine before serving. The first is to remove the natural sediment from a bottle of wine, and the second is to let the wine breathe.

The decanting process allows a well-cellared wine to be served without suspended particles and presented at its best. The selected wine should be taken from the cellar twenty-four hours prior to opening and rested in a cool place to enable all sediment to settle on the bottom of the bottle. Just before serving, open the bottle and taste the wine for faults. In one single movement, pour the wine steadily from the bottle into the decanter until sediment can be seen to flow into the neck of the bottle. Stop pouring at this point. (A small amount of wine and sediment will remain in the original bottle.) Pour wine for guests from the decanter.

We recommend wines less than five years old be decanted up to two hours prior to serving. At this stage there will probably be no sediment and the process is purely one of allowing air to mix with the wine. This softens harsh tannins and allows a gentle oxidative process to occur, making the wine softer and more harmonious with food.

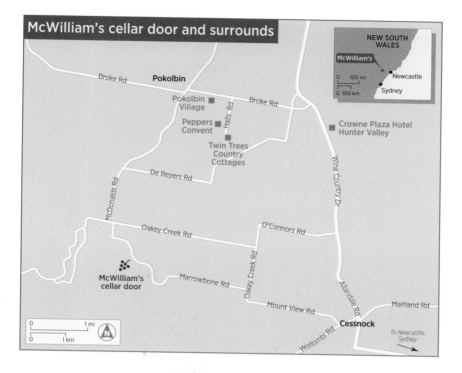

McWilliam's cellar door and surrounds

Cellar door

401 Marrowbone Rd
Pokolbin NSW 2320
t: 02 4998 7505
w: www.mcwilliams.com.au
e: mtpleasant@mcwilliams.com.au

Opening hours
Monday to Sunday: 10 am to 4.30 pm

Accommodation options

Crowne Plaza Hotel Hunter Valley
430 Wine Country Dr
Lovedale NSW 2325
t: 02 4991 0900
w: www.crowneplazahuntervalley.com.au
e: reservations.hunter@ihg.com

Peppers Convent
Halls Rd
Pokolbin NSW 2320
t: 02 4998 4999
w: www.peppers.com.au/convent
e: convent@peppers.com.au

Pokolbin Village
2188 Broke Rd
Pokolbin NSW 2320
t: 02 4998 7670
w: www.pokolbinvillage.com.au
e: relax@pokolbinvillage.com.au

Twin Trees Country Cottages
Halls Rd
Pokolbin NSW 2320
t: 02 4998 7311
w: www.twintrees.com.au
e: stay@twintrees.com.au

Brown Brothers

Celebrating diversity

6 Wines are as different as the people who drink
them, which is why we have developed such a
comprehensive range of wine styles and blends. 9

John Charles Brown (1915–2004)

*T*he small town of Milawa in north-eastern Victoria is home
to one of the most successful family-owned wineries in
Australia. It is here in the thriving King Valley wine region that
Brown Brothers has been making its distinctive wines for more
than 120 years. Renowned for the diversity of its wine styles, the
company has vineyards in five locations across the state. Climatic
conditions are as varied as the wine styles, ranging from cool
alpine areas to lush temperate valleys to sun-drenched plains.
And each site has been selected on the basis of its suitability for
the variety of grape planted.

Their first vineyard was planted at Milawa in 1885, and since then the Brown family has championed the development of varietal table wines in Australia. Today, third-generation brothers Ross Brown and John Graham Brown are keeping the family tradition of innovative winemaking alive, with about forty varietals produced and sold at their cellar door.

The Milawa property that was to become the heart of Brown Brothers was purchased at a land auction in 1857 by Scottish migrant John Graham. After initially settling in Canada with his parents, John had sailed to Australia in 1853 with his wife, Hannah, and their two children, eight-year-old Rebecca and five-year-old James. They initially settled in the small Victorian town of Beechworth, where Hannah passed away in 1856.

John Graham moved to Milawa in 1858 with his sister, Jane, and his son, leaving Rebecca with her uncle in Beechworth so that she could attend school. He bought a property and planted an orchard and a vineyard, and built a Canadian-style barn in which to store hay and grain. The steep pitch of the roof was designed to prevent the build up of snow during the freezing Canadian winters — not in any way necessary at Milawa, which would have received less than a couple of centimetres of snow

Ross and John Graham Brown.

in the years since the barn was built. It still stands today and has become known as the Canadian Barn.

The connection between the Brown family and the property at Milawa began when George Harry Brown married John Graham's daughter, Rebecca, in 1864. George was a Scottish migrant who had turned to farming after failing to strike it rich in the goldfields. When John Graham died in 1873 his property was transferred to George and Rebecca Brown.

During the 1880s many of the men who had earlier made their way to Victoria in the search for gold turned to farming to make a living, in particular through the cultivation of vineyards. Wine was the talk of the north-east and Rutherglen was on its way to becoming Victoria's premier wine-producing district.

In 1886, eighteen-year-old John Francis Brown, the ambitious and imaginative second son of George and Rebecca, persuaded his father to follow the lead of others who had gone into the wine business. They went into partnership and planted ten acres of vines, mostly Riesling, Muscat and Shiraz. Most of the property was used to grow fruit and grain, which they sold by the roadside to the passing gold miners travelling to and from Beechworth.

The Canadian Barn has been the home of Brown Brothers' ageing fortified wines for more than a century.

John Francis had no experience in winemaking. What he did have, however, were ambition and plenty of people in the district to whom he could turn for advice and guidance. He was aware of the success at Rutherglen and was convinced that the soil in the King Valley was more suited to vineyards than grazing or cereal crops.

The hay and grain in the barn was cleared out and in 1889 the barn was used as the winery for the production of their first vintage. In 1891, Victorian government viticulturist François de Castella visited Milawa and proclaimed, 'Mr Brown has about ten acres, principally Hermitage and Riesling, in addition to which he has several other sorts. The wines I tasted were of excellent quality'.

During the depression of the 1890s winemakers in the district began going out of business. Using a combination of business acumen, ingenuity and determination, John Francis was able not only to save his winery and vineyards from failure, but to expand them. Early in the same decade the government offered land cheaply to anyone who would plant approved grapevines — the theory was that the future of exporting wine was unlimited. John Francis and his father took advantage of this offer and bought another ten acres.

John Francis named the vineyard 'Brown Brothers' in the hope that his three brothers would join the business, but they had other interests and never did. In 1898 he built a weatherboard winery and cellar, and he was able to purchase some of the much sought-after hand-crafted oak O'Sullivan barrels and other equipment from wineries that had been forced to sell up. Four years later he added a brick distillery for the production of fortifying spirit, which was used to make Muscat and port.

In 1909 John Francis had a total of forty acres under vines, growing Shiraz, Malbec, Pedro Ximenez, Brown Muscat, Riesling, Tokay and Golden Chasselas. Although the demand for Muscat and port was high, John Francis was influenced by François de Castella who advocated the planting of table wine varieties. Business was booming — so much so that in 1916 John Francis was able to purchase a Model T Ford, at a time when any sort of automobile was a rare site in rural Victoria.

In that same year the dreaded phylloxera louse came to Milawa, devastating many acres of vines. Over the following four years John Francis ripped up his beloved vineyard, found a suitable 'clean' site elsewhere on the property and, once again following the advice of François de Castella, ordered

The view across the Mystic Park vineyard to Kangaroo Lake.

enough phylloxera-resistant rootstock to replant thirty-five acres. To the surprise of other winegrowers in the area, John Francis grafted varieties for table wines rather than the fortified wines favoured by most Australian wine consumers. He

replanted Riesling, Tokay, Chasselas and Shiraz, and included new plantings of Muscat, Mondeuse, Semillon, Graciano and Cabernet Sauvignon.

John Francis Brown was elegant and energetic, as well as ambitious. He was active in the local community throughout his life, serving as shire secretary and treasurer of the Shire of Oxley, honorary secretary of the Free Library, secretary of the Cemetery Trust and several other local organisations. During each of the two World Wars he served as treasurer of the Milawa and District Patriotic Society. John Francis also served as president of the Rutherglen Wine Growers' Association.

In 1899 John Francis married Ida Peady, and they had four chil-

John Francis Brown, founder of Brown Brothers.

dren: Bertha, Clarice, Ida and John Charles. As the only son, John Charles was destined to take Brown Brothers (again without brothers) into its second generation. John Charles completed his secondary education as a boarder at the prestigious private school Scotch College in Melbourne and returned home to Milawa at the end of 1933. He was immediately set to work by his father. The winery was buzzing with a massive order of Tawny Port from London and a growing market for table wines among the newly arrived Italian migrants in the nearby Ovens Valley.

Over the following ten years the softly spoken and quietly ambitious John Charles Brown took on a succession of roles, including delivery man, farm hand, accountant, salesman, vigneron and winemaker. In 1934, during the Great Depression, he persuaded his father to open a cellar door. The cost of transporting wine and dealing through distributors was becoming prohibitive and John Charles believed a cellar door would attract customers to the winery, reducing the dependence on external sales. The success of the cellar door was well beyond expectations, largely because of the growing population of Italian migrants in north-eastern Victoria and their tradition of drinking table wine with meals. Sales rose so much that the size of the vineyards had to be doubled and grapes had to be purchased from other growers. New varieties — including Grenache, White Grenache, White Hermitage and Palomino — were planted at Milawa.

John Francis passed away in 1943 at the age of seventy-six. John Charles had been effectively managing the vineyard and farm for several years, so he was well able to take on the roles officially. From the late 1930s John Charles was faced with a number of setbacks that tested his determination and could have stopped a lesser man in his tracks. A plague of grasshoppers completely destroyed the 1938 vintage, which had already been ravaged by a two-year drought. Following the outbreak of World War II, many of the regular pickers enlisted and there was a shortage of labour. In addition, during the war, interstate sales of liquor were prohibited. For wineries such as Brown Brothers, situated not far from the New South Wales border, this ban resulted in a significant drop in sales. To make matters worse, in 1943 another drought set in. John Charles took it all in his stride, however, his determination and spirit unbroken.

John Charles married Patricia Matthews in 1939, forming what was to become one of the most enduring and influential partnerships in the Australian wine industry.

John Francis Brown with his only son, John Charles, aged ten.

Working in
the vineyard,
circa 1926.
Initially, Patricia took no role in running the family business —
she was otherwise engaged running the household, especially
after the couple's four sons, John Graham, Peter, Ross and Roger,
came along. There were always visitors and they were hosted
around the kitchen table. 'Mum had a natural flair for making
simple food taste great, and most of the ingredients came from
the home garden', Ross recalls. 'She also milked at least two cows
every morning and evening. That's what you did on a family farm
post-Depression.'

As the boys grew up the conversation around the dinner table
was dominated by the subjects of vineyards and wine varieties,
inspiring in Patricia what she called a 'slowly developing interest'
in wine. This interest was fostered as she helped serve customers
at the cellar door. In particular, Patricia enjoyed matching wine
with food, and in later years, she joined forces with her daughters-
in-law, Judy and Jan, to provide regular catering at the cellar door
(the precursor to the renowned Epicurean Centre).

John Charles had been taught how to make wine by his
father, and, like his father, had a good business sense and
followed the technical advice of François de Castella. He was
an innovator — and was even more progressive than his father.

John Charles and Patricia Brown
on their wedding day in 1939.

John Charles experimented with uncommon grape varieties, and derived a great deal of pleasure from seeing so many make their mark and be accepted by consumers.

> ❛As kids there was always a glass of wine on the table for us and we were required to taste it, comment on the flavours we experienced, and talk about its history and background.❜
>
> John Graham Brown

In 1950 Brown Brothers purchased a 117-acre property at Everton in the hills north-east of Milawa. More elevated than the Milawa property, cooler and free of frost in winter, it was already planted with orchards and a small vineyard. One-third of the property was cleared and planted, bringing the total area of vines, mostly Cabernet Sauvignon and Shiraz, to about thirty acres. Yields were small due to poor soil and little rainfall, but the quality of the grapes led to wines of great richness, depth and ageing potential.

At the time, sacrificing yield for quality was not well understood by consumers, who preferred lower priced wine from the

A three-year-old John Graham Brown on the family tractor in 1944.

A golden wedding wine

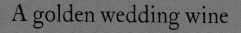

Brown Brothers' unique Shiraz, Mondeuse and Cabernet blend was first produced by John Charles in 1954. Each of the three varieties brings different attributes to the final blend, which is a wonderful marriage of flavours. The varieties came together by chance as one of John Charles's experiments at Milawa. Shiraz can be rich and ripe, and the Mondeuse is high in acid and firm in tannin, but together they are sublime. Cabernet adds the master touch.

The grapes are fermented together, which enhances the integration and balance. François de Castella, who introduced John Francis to Mondeuse, called it a 'golden wedding' wine because of its legendary ageing qualities. Brown family gatherings have often become memorable events once the forty-year-old 'SMC' has been opened.

higher yielding irrigation districts. For the Browns, this made the vineyard uneconomic. Ross recalls that whenever the idea of selling the property was raised, John Charles would host a barbeque on the property, open a few old vintages on a hill overlooking the vines and say, 'How could you sell this? The wine is so good!' Unfortunately, the Everton property was eventually sold in 1977.

With a string of good vintages in the 1950s and rising demand for table wines by consumers, Brown Brothers continued to expand and take advantage of emerging technology. Automation was introduced in the winery in 1961 when the hand presses were replaced with a hydraulic press. Refrigeration was installed in the same year, which rendered unnecessary the regular and tedious trips to the Wangaratta ice works to buy blocks of ice. Prior to refrigeration the young fermenting juice was pumped through ice to reduce fermentation temperatures. John Charles had developed a reputation for producing fine delicate Riesling

when he combined lower fermentation temperature and pre-
draining of juice. Commercial refrigeration allowed him to
increase production, improve quality and develop new aromatic
wine styles. One particularly fragrant style, White Frontignac
from the Muscat grape, was a national success.

John Graham Brown, the eldest son of John Charles and
Patricia, joined the family business in 1958. Educated locally at
first and then at Scotch College in Melbourne, there was never
any doubt that John G would become Brown Brothers' third-
generation winemaker. John G had spent most school holidays

A noble accident

The first commercial vintage of Brown Brothers Botrytised Riesling was
produced by John Charles Brown in 1962. It came about almost by accident.
A few days of constant rain had prevented access to the vineyard to allow
harvesting of the ripened Riesling. 'By the time we picked it', says John G, 'it
was mouldy and I wasn't sure what to do with it. We crushed some of it and
the juice wasn't smelly. It was a beautiful gold and green colour. I got Dad
to come and have a look, and he recognised it as Botrytis.' The juice was
fermented for about five months in a 500 gallon (2270 litre) cask, bottled
and labelled as Milawa Late-Picked Riesling.

To obtain suitable fruit a twelve-acre site of Riesling is
now left until late April to get very ripe. John Graham explains,
'The botrytis needs three or four humid days to really take
off. Some years, perhaps one out of every four, it just doesn't
work'.

In 1978 with another exceptional vintage, the family
decided to label the wines Noble Riesling, and were the
first to use that name. During the 1980s many inferior late-
harvest rieslings began to appear on the market, made from
late-picked fruit, but without the magic of the special botrytis
fungus often referred to as 'noble rot'.

Noble Riesling is a prolific winner of trophies and medals
at wine shows. A flagship wine, it was later renamed Patricia
Noble Riesling in honour of Patricia Brown.

The Brown family, circa 1960.

driving tractors in the vineyard, pumping wine, pressing grapes and washing vats. 'When I first went to primary school I'd already decided that I wanted to be a winemaker', he says.

In 1965 John Graham married local school teacher June Ellis. Three years later, after the birth of his son, John Andrew, he assumed the role of chief winemaker from his father. He followed in his footsteps, experimenting with new grape varieties and innovative winemaking techniques.

John Graham's three younger brothers — Peter, Ross and Roger — also decided early on that they wanted to work in the family business. Growing up, Peter Brown loved the outdoors, and was fascinated with different grape varieties and viticultural experimentation, particularly enjoying time spent in the vineyards during school holidays. His viticultural career began when he took on the role of vineyard manager at Milawa in 1963 after completing high school. Peter also had a passion for all things mechanical and later developed an on-site mechanical maintenance workshop and welding shop, which provided services for the entire company.

Ross Brown followed his older brothers into the family business in 1966 at the age of eighteen as cellar door manager. Like his mother, Ross developed a passion for matching food and wine. Since then he has overseen what has become one of

Peter Brown
and his son
Nicholas
in Peter's
ultralight plane.

Australia's most successful cellar doors, initiated and developed the Milawa Epicurean Centre and successfully steered Brown Brothers wines into export markets around the world. Ross was also instrumental in encouraging investors to build a hotel on land that had been annexed for them, so it would be close to the cellar door and Epicurean Centre.

Roger Brown always wanted to work in the vineyard, eventually becoming a master propagator and breeder of vines. He didn't join the family business after completing school as his brothers had done; instead, he worked in a Melbourne nursery for a year, learning simple techniques that he would later apply in the vineyards. He spent the following year in California and worked in a nursery that specialised in vine grafting. When Roger returned from California in 1976 he set up his own propagation farm, preparing for new plantings at Brown Brothers' expanding vineyards. He also had remarkable mechanical skills and a passion for motorbikes.

In 1985 Roger Brown was diagnosed with a brain tumour. He underwent surgery, which kept the tumour at bay for three years, but tragically lost his battle in 1990. He is survived by his wife, Elu, and daughters, Stephanie and Phillipa.

Opposite:
A luscious
Brown Brothers
vineyard.

According to John Graham, his father was a laissez-faire style of leader. 'He gave us the freedom to do our own thing', John says.

John Graham navigating
the underground cellars
after flooding in 1974.

'We each had different interests and didn't get under each other's feet. I was the winemaker, Peter was the outdoor type and loved the vineyards, Ross has the gift of the gab and is a natural at marketing, and Roger took on the nursery role. He loved machinery, motor bikes and cars. He did some contract harvesting when mechanical harvesters became available.'

The 1968 Milawa vintage was completely destroyed by a severe frost in 1967. The family subsequently purchased its eighty-acre Mystic Park property in the frost-free Murray Valley to the north-west. The property was undeveloped and in a sorry state, but Peter Brown planted several varieties, including Mataro, Carignane, Cinsaut, Grenache, Flora, Orange Muscat and Ruby Cabernet. The Mystic Park vineyard has since expanded to more than four times its original size.

> 'We've had our fair share of setbacks, but each setback has resulted in a giant step forward.'
>
> John Graham Brown.

With a number of vineyards exposed to a range of soils and climates, the potential for varietal diversity was exciting. In European terms, the diversity of Brown Brothers' vineyards could be described 'as cold as Champagne at one end and as hot as Sicily at the other'.

In response to the frost of 1967 the Brown brothers drilled a bore at Milawa, hoping to find underground water. Not only did they find water, but it was of a high enough quality to use for drinking, washing and cleaning the equipment in the winery. It allowed them to defend against frost by installing overhead sprinklers to spray the vines with the tepid water. An irrigation system that negated the effect of drought and protected the vineyard from frost was also developed.

The discovery of underground water at Milawa along with further investment in new technology was followed by a succession of excellent vintages. The dream run was interrupted in 1977 by a mini cyclone and hailstorm that almost destroyed the winery and all but wiped out the vintage at the Milawa vineyard.

The cellar door as it was in 1974 and as it is today.

The network of vineyards continued to grow with the establishment of the Hurdle Creek vineyard, only a few kilometres from Milawa, in 1974. The St Leonard's winery at Wahgunyah in north-east Victoria was purchased in 1980, followed two years later by the purchase of the Whitlands vineyard, 800 metres above the King Valley. The Whitlands vineyard was planted with varieties suited to the cooler climate, including Riesling, Pinot Noir, Chardonnay, Cabernet Franc, Merlot and Pinot Meunier. Roger Brown was instrumental in providing new vines for the family's growing collection of vineyards. Expansion was also continuing at Milawa. The cellar door was redeveloped and the current tasting room was built, which attracts more visitors per year than any other in Australia.

⚜   ⚜   ⚜

Under the leadership of John Charles, Brown Brothers had started exporting its wine during the 1930s and again in the 1970s, mainly to New Zealand. However, exports didn't really become significant until after the Australian dollar was floated in 1983 — at which point the value of the Aussie dollar dropped and all Australian exports became significantly cheaper. Today, Brown Brothers wine is exported to twenty countries, including the United Kingdom, Denmark, Belgium, Germany, Sweden and the Netherlands. New Zealand has become one of the biggest markets, particularly for red wines, and in 2008 the company opened a sales office in Auckland. While Brown Brothers has had strong business relationships in Asia through local agents for more than twenty years, the expansion of the Chinese market has ignited strong interest and focus over the last ten years.

> ❛Wine and food are a passion for the Brown family and have been for as long as I can remember. Many of my childhood memories are of the family and extended family getting together to share good wine, food and company. ❜
>
> Ross Brown

In 1988 John Charles stepped down as managing director at the age of seventy-three and took up the role of chairman of directors. John Graham relinquished his role of chief winemaker to take his father's place, and in turn, Roland Wahlquist became chief winemaker.

John Charles was widely acknowledged as one of Australia's foremost winemaking innovators. A humble man, John Charles was much loved and admired in the wine industry, and generous in his support of new entrants. His efforts were acknowledged in 1989 when he was appointed a Member of the Order of Australia (AM) for services to the wine industry. John Charles was further honoured in 2003 with a Lifetime Achievement Award from Restaurant and Catering Australia, in recognition of his outstanding achievements as a winemaker, developer of regional tourism and supporter of the industry.

The expansion and innovation at Brown Brothers, under the leadership of John Graham, continued from the time of his appointment and throughout the 1990s. At the forefront of the innovations is a miniature winery, known as the Kindergarten Winery, which was designed as a research and development facility. Established in 1989, it allows the winemakers to trial new grape varieties and wine styles in small quantities, and experiment with different viticultural and winemaking practices. Some of the experimental varieties developed in the Kindergarten Winery have since become widely available, including Dolcetto, Cienna, Tempranillo, Prosecco, Pinot Grigio and Moscato.

John Charles Brown and his four sons in the barrel shed. From left: Ross, Roger, John Charles, Peter and John Graham, 1986.

In 1990 a viticultural research and development team was created, extending Brown Brothers' pioneering work to the vineyards. This created the perfect product-development cycle, from growing, making, trialling and marketing through the cellar door. It has been this dynamic process that has seen Brown Brothers leading the industry with new wine styles and varietal flavours.

The year 1994 was a very special one for Brown Brothers on a number of fronts. John Charles celebrated his sixtieth vintage, and his grandson John Andrew joined the company — the fourth generation of family winemakers. The Milawa Epicurean Centre, a restaurant dedicated to matching food with the flavours and complexities of Brown Brothers wines, was opened. The Banksdale vineyard in the western King Valley, with an elevation of 450 metres, was purchased. The site's cooler climate is ideal for many of the classic Italian varieties such as Pinot Grigio, Prosecco and Barbera.

In 1998 Brown Brothers added further to their vineyards with the purchase and development of 500 acres of land in the rolling hills of the Mount Camel range, in Central Victoria's Heathcote wine region. The growth of rich, spicy shiraz and the reputation of the red soils of this region drove the decision to expand the fruit sourcing to this slightly drier and warmer site. This vineyard has become the company's main source of fruit for the classic red varieties Shiraz, Cabernet and Merlot. Further plantings of new varieties have seen richly flavoured Tempranillo, Durif and Petit Verdot as single-vineyard wines.

Although Brown Brothers has access to huge underground reserves of water at Milawa, and sufficient rainfall in the nearby hills, the company is conscious of the need to reduce its use of water, particularly in the Mystic Park and Heathcote vineyards. At Mystic Park, subsurface irrigation allows water to trickle under the vine, reducing weeds and the need for herbicides, as well as cutting water use by 30 per cent. In addition to these measures, Brown Brothers is working on ways to be more energy efficient. One such way was the building of a warehouse without mechanical refrigeration. 'The walls and roof are heavily insulated and we maintain a temperature of less than twenty degrees Celsius by using fans that draw in cool air at night', explains John Graham. 'We've also reduced our use of tractors in the vineyard and have a carbon-reduction team looking for more ways to reduce our carbon footprint.'

✣   ✣   ✣

The new millennium brought with it a number of major changes at Brown Brothers, including some sad farewells. In 2001 at the age of fifty-nine John Graham relinquished his role as chief executive to pursue other interests that a seven-day-a-week job didn't allow. He continued his involvement in the family business as chairman of the board until stepping down in favour of non-executive chairman Sandy Clark in 2007. Being conscious of the need for a smooth transition between generations, in 2010 John Graham encouraged his son, John Andrew, to take on his role as a director of the company. Ross Brown was subsequently appointed the new chief executive.

The man often hailed as the father of the Victorian wine industry, John Charles Brown, passed away in May 2004 at the age of eighty-nine as his seventieth vintage at Milawa was drawing to a close. Patricia passed away only four months later. With the enthusiastic support of Patricia and his four sons, John Charles had transformed Brown Brothers into the most visited winery in Australia.

At his father's funeral, held in a packed Epicurean Centre, John G Brown spoke about a wonderful lesson delivered to him by his father. 'One day, not long after leaving school, Dad and

I were working in the cellar when he commented, "You four boys can really make something out of this place, but only if you all work together". He had a vine cutting in his hand, which he broke in half, saying, "See how easily it's broken when there's only one?" He then put the pieces together, and said, "See how much harder they are to break when there are two?" He then put four pieces together and said, "Now it's almost impossible to break them. This is the strength you and your brothers can have if you work together".'

John Charles was justifiably proud of what his four sons had achieved and would have been equally proud of the achievements of the fourth generation, which continue to take the company from strength to strength. Further expansion took place in 2005 with the purchase of additional land at Mystic Park, allowing the biggest planting of new vineyards ever undertaken by the company. In June 2005 John Graham's efforts were acknowledged when he was appointed an Officer in the Order of Australia (AO) for services to the wine industry, to the community through his service to the Country Fire Authority, and for the promotion of rural and regional economic development initiatives in Victoria.

The Kindergarten Winery, which was designed by John Andrew Brown.

John Charles and
Patricia Brown,
circa 1995.

Later that same year the Brown family lost another member when Peter was killed in a motorcycle accident. He had managed the St Leonards and All Saints vineyards, both in the Rutherglen wine region, since they had been purchased by Brown Brothers in 1980 and 1992, respectively. He had bought them outright from the family company in 1999.

Peter's children, Eliza, Angela and Nicholas, are all involved in the wine industry. Eliza, after working with her father as sales and marketing manager, is now director and CEO of All Saints Estate and St Leonards vineyard. Angela's expertise lies in brand management, export and graphic design. Nicholas completed a Bachelor of Oenlogy at The University of Adelaide in 2006 and has since followed in his father footsteps, developing the vineyard and working in the winery at All Saints Estate and St Leonards. All three have interests as partners and ambassadors in the Brown Brothers business. Eliza was elected to the Brown Brothers board after Peter's death.

John Andrew Brown, the only son of John Graham and June Brown, had joined the family business in 1994 after working at BHP as an engineer, where he gained invaluable experience in project management. His first task at Brown Brothers was to develop a computer-based management information system, which took the company to the forefront of business systems. John Andrew also spent time in the winery and won a trophy for one of his fortified wines. John and his wife, Anneshka, have two sons, John Yeo and Christopher.

Mum's the word

The flagship 'Patricia' range of wines was named in recognition of Patricia Brown's passion for the family business, and the love and inspiration that she gave her family. During the years of massive growth in the 1970s and 1980s, the family's daily routine was to meet at their parents' dining table at 10.30 am to discuss the business.

Pat was the tea lady, but she was the one who heard all the discussions and usually had the last say. She even heated the teacups to extend the time spent in discussion. This daily communication with all the stakeholders and business roles around the table might be well the reason for the longevity of the company.

The diversity of the Brown Brothers vineyards allows the very best fruit of each variety to be selected for the wines styles for the Patricia range. The winemaking is undertaken with the utmost care, and is designed to maximise flavour and retain the elegance of the wines. The wines are not released unless they are the very best of the variety that can be produced. The range of Patricia wines includes Cabernet Sauvignon, Shiraz, Pinot Noir and Chardonnay Brut, and Noble Riesling.

Ross Brown recalls, 'I had the job of asking my mother if we could use her name on the label. She was overwhelmed and burst into tears, saying, "They better be bloody good", and adding, "You are on eternal notice"'.

The flagship Patricia range of wines.

Four generations
of John Browns
in 1998.
John Graham
(standing) and
(seated, from left)
John Andrew,
John Yeo and
John Charles.

John Andrew's sister, Cynthia, joined the family business in time for the 1996 vintage, gaining firsthand experience in winemaking. Over the next ten years she had a number of different roles within the company before resigning in 2005 to pursue other business interests.

Ross and Judy Brown have three daughters, Katherine, Caroline and Emma. All three are passionate about the business and regularly support the brand at Milawa events and functions. Caroline and Emma have recently graduated from Bond University with business degrees and are currently working outside of the business. Katherine has recently joined the company's sales and marketing team after seven years of external business experience and completing a degree in business and wine marketing. Judy travels widely with Ross and is actively engaged in supporting Brown Brothers at wine industry and other functions.

After more than 125 years, four generations and a history of innovation, ingenuity and determination, Brown Brothers is well placed to continue on for many years to come. Like several other family-owned wineries, Brown Brothers has a code of practice that defines the employment conditions for family members, including a requirement that after completing their education they work elsewhere for four years before applying for a position in the company. John Graham is keen to point out that family members are employed on merit. 'We want to ensure that family members don't take someone else's job just because they're a Brown.'

John Graham is proud of the esteem in which the Brown Brothers brand is held and the way the company has grown. When he joined the company in 1958 he was one of only six staff. Today Brown Brothers employs more than 230 people and is increasingly recognised throughout the world. His desire is for the company to be known as one of the best family-owned wineries in the world and be renowned for quality, consistency and value for money.

Standing, from left: Caroline, Eliza, Nick and Emma. Seated, from left: John, June, Judy and Ross.

Ross concurs, saying, 'It has been our shared vision that has achieved the sustained drive and energy over more than thirty years. We have worked really well and harmoniously as a family, supported by sensational staff. We have seen the business grow from a family farm into a significant business in a single generation, and we believe the next generation has the energy and passion to take it forward for another generation'.

Matching wine and food

The practice of matching wine and food is one that presents great challenges and potential disasters. The reason for this is that there are so many variables influencing the final results. In addition, the pairing of wine and food is subject to individual likes, preferences and whims, so it is only rarely that a particular combination of wine and food will 'ring everyone's bells'.

The variables include flavours, textures, intensity and delicacy, and the interplay of components such as sugar, acid, tannin and oak. The idea is to try to match these aspects between the wine and the food.

This may sound daunting but in reality, it isn't. With a little information, a lot of enthusiasm and a propensity to explore and experiment, you will find many wine and food combinations that greatly enhance your dining experience. One of the major variables in the wine and food equation is flavour; however, while it is an important component, it's not everything. For example, you wouldn't get a big juicy steak, squeeze some lemon juice over it and match it with a Riesling! You need to take into account textures, balance and sometimes contrast when developing a wine and food match.

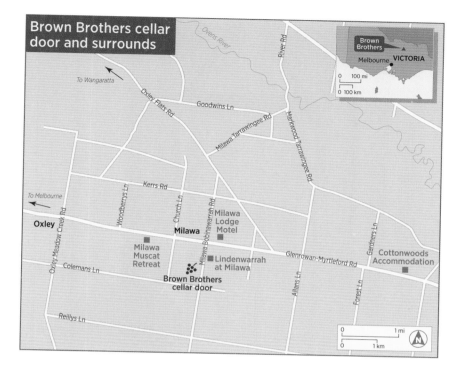

Cellar door

239 Milawa Bobinawarrah Rd
Milawa Vic. 3678
t: 03 5720 5540
w: www.brownbrothers.com.au
e: browns@brownbrothers.com.au

Opening hours
Monday to Sunday: 9 am to 5 pm

Accommodation options

Cottonwoods Accommodation
2139 Glenrowan–Myrtleford Rd
Markwood Vic. 3678
t: 03 5727 0345
w: www.cottonwoods
    accommodation.com.au
e: cottonwoodsaccom@bigpond.com

Lindenwarrah at Milawa
Milawa Bobinawarrah Rd
Milawa Vic. 3678
t: 03 5720 5777
w: www.lancemore.com.au
e: info@lindenwarrah.com.au

Milawa Lodge Motel
Snow Rd
Milawa Vic. 3678
t: 03 5727 3326
w: www.milawagourmet.com/mil_lodge
e: milawalodgemotel@bigpond.com

Milawa Muscat Retreat
1422 Glenrowan–Myrtleford Rd
Milawa Vic. 3678
t: 03 5727 3999
w: www.milawamuscatretreat.com.au
e: info@milawamuscatretreat.com.au

d'Arenberg
Deadly serious fun

'Up until bottling, our winemaking is deadly serious. From then on, it's all about having fun.'

Chester Osborn, fourth-generation chief winemaker

*T*he view from d'Arenberg's historical family homestead is breathtaking. The hills leading down into the valley at McLaren Vale in South Australia are covered in vineyards, some of them containing gnarled vines more than 100 years old. McLaren Vale's climate and fertile soils, influenced by the waters of Gulf St Vincent to the west and the Mount Lofty Ranges to the east, make it the perfect location for growing a wide range of premium-quality red and white grape varieties. d'Arenberg's extensive portfolio of wines, all made from fruit grown in McLaren Vale and the nearby Adelaide Hills, is as incredible as the view. Every wine is hand-crafted by the talented and energetic Chester Osborn, the fourth generation of Osborns to nurture the vines in their expansive vineyards, and his team.

Inside the cellar door, which is housed in the original nineteenth-century homestead, are an array of awards from all

over the world and distinctive cartoons that reveal the unique —
some would say 'larger than life' or even bizarre — personality
of winemaker Chester Osborn. Chester's quietly spoken
octogenarian father, d'Arry, also features in cartoons and photos
on display. From time to time d'Arry strolls unobtrusively into
the room, giving visitors the chance to chat with one of the most
loved and respected winemakers in the Australian wine industry.

The land on which d'Arenberg's McLaren Vale winery
and vineyards now stand was purchased in 1912 by Joseph
Rowe Osborn and his son Francis (Frank) Osborn. Part of their
purchase included the established Milton vineyards, which were
planted in the 1880s. Frank named the property Bundarra, a local
Aboriginal word meaning 'trees on the hill'. Together, Joseph
and Frank set about selling grapes and planting more vineyards.

Although Joseph was a teetotaler, he was also a director of
the successful Thomas Hardy and Sons wine company. Like
many of his winemaking contemporaries, Joseph had a keen
interest in sport. He co-founded the Norwood (Australian Rules)
Football Club with Arthur Diamond and Henry Burnett in 1878.
With Joseph as the club's first captain, Norwood won the South

The d'Arenberg
vineyards with
the Willunga
Hills in the
background.

The always colourfully dressed chief winemaker, Chester Osborn.

Australian Football Association premiership in its inaugural year and in the next five years. Today, Norwood is one of eleven teams that make up the South Australian National Football League (SANFL).

Frank had been studying medicine at the University of Melbourne before dropping out to help his father. He was a heavy smoker but, like Joseph, had pledged never to drink. He broke that pledge, however, after joining the army in 1915. After returning home from the war, Frank renovated and extended the original homestead, which had panoramic views across McLaren Vale to Gulf St Vincent.

Joseph Rowe Osborn, founder of d'Arenberg.

A few years after the war ended Joseph Osborn died, leaving full control of the family business to his son. Frank had married Helena d'Arenberg the previous year, and the couple had three children, Antoinette (Toni), Rowen and d'Arry. Sadly, Helena died shortly after giving birth to d'Arry in 1926. The children were subsequently raised by their father and a nurse fondly known as Mickie.

In 1927 Frank constructed a winery with the help of winemaker Sam Tolley. Frank and Sam had served in the same battalion during

A true thoroughbred

Joseph Osborn was a prolific racehorse owner and was the biggest stake earner in Adelaide for twelve consecutive years. In 1912 he sold all of the horses in his stables to finance the purchase of his share of the McLaren Vale property.

Prior to selling his beloved horses, the pride of his stable was a steed named Footbolt. The Footbolt Shiraz is named to pay homage to the founder of d'Arenberg and his beloved thoroughbred.

The Footbolt Shiraz is sourced from some of the oldest Shiraz vines in McLaren Vale. d'Arenberg has been making this traditional red wine since the winery was built in 1927. First labelled Shiraz and renamed in the 1980s as Old Vine Shiraz, its name changed again to The Footbolt Shiraz in 1996. Chester Osborn describes The Footbolt as, 'a truly regional style, showing the depth, complexity and balance of McLaren Vale Shiraz with great ageing potential, given its modest price'.

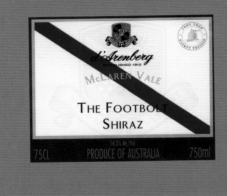

World War I. The following year Frank produced his first modest vintage, comprising a heavy red table wine and a fortified wine. Production increased to allow export to England, but was disrupted by the Great Depression and the outbreak of World War II. Frank was so ill in 1942 that production ceased completely and all of the grapes were sold. Full production resumed in 1943 when d'Arry left school at the age of sixteen to help his ailing father run the business.

It was a demanding job for a teenager, but d'Arry was equal to the challenge and gradually took over the management of the business, known at this stage as Bundarra Vineyards. (In 1953 a partnership was formed and the business was renamed FE Osborn & Sons.) The ownership remained split between himself and his older siblings Toni and Rowen. That family co-ownership continues today, although Toni lives in the United Kingdom and Rowen lives in Canberra. When Frank died in 1957 d'Arry assumed complete control.

d'Arry remembers those early days at the winery when he was still a teenager. It was tough, unforgiving work, but it was a life that he loved. 'We had six Clydesdales for ploughing because there were no tractors', he says. 'I even had to milk the cow, separate the milk and make butter. It wasn't until after World War II that I bought our first tractor. It used to get constantly bogged.'

In 1958, with a number of the vineyards withering, d'Arry embarked on an expansion and replanting program. He soon discovered, however, that many of the original 1890s vines were revitalised by supplementary watering. d'Arry decided to leave many of them in the ground rather than replanting — a decision that proved to be far-sighted. Today these old vines are the backbone of some of the finest d'Arenberg wines of the 1990s and beyond.

Francis (Frank) Osborn, who took the family business from grape-growing to winemaking.

As the interest in and consumption of table wine began to take off in the 1950s, with brands such as Angove's, Lindemans, Seaview, Penfolds, Hardys and Houghton's being well received by consumers, d'Arry could see a healthy future for table wine and wanted to be a part of it. To do this he needed a label.

❛Sometimes I feel like I'm still making mud pies. The ingredients are the same — soil, water and the sun.❜

Chester Osborn

In 1959 d'Arry and his wife, Pauline, who he had married the previous year, set about planning their label. The brand name 'd'Arenberg' was chosen in memory of d'Arry's mother.

The distinctive diagonal red stripe came from d'Arry's memories of his crimson-and-white-striped school tie from his Prince Alfred College days. He thought a striking red stripe would be appropriate for his new label. Red was also his favourite colour. d'Arry then called upon his friend Don Allnut to design the label.

The launch of the new label was both small and humble, involving half-gallon flagons and a small quantity of table wines.

By 1963 the volume was up to hundreds of dozens and d'Arenberg table wines were beginning to gain a cult status among wine consumers. The 1968 Cabernet Sauvignon won the Jimmy Watson Trophy in 1969 and the 1967 Red Burgundy, a Grenache-based wine, went on to be awarded seven trophies and twenty-nine gold medals at Australian capital city wine shows.

> 'The quirky names for the wines never come before about 2 am and after a few, or more, wines.'
>
> Chester Osborn

The late Len Evans, founder of Len Evans Wines and Roth-bury Estate, wine educator, author and internationally renowned wine judge was an influential champion of d'Arenberg in the early days. Evan's observed, '[d'Arry] is knowledgeable and enthusiastic and, I'm told, inclined to formality during vintage. He wears his old dress shirts as winemaking gear and this is said to give elegance to his reds'.

Two-year-old d'Arry Osborn with his siblings Rowen and Toni at a local beach in 1929.

Throughout the 1970s the accolades for d'Arenberg wines increased and spread well beyond Australia's shores. d'Arry became firmly entrenched in serving and promoting McLaren Vale, and the wine industry in general. He has served as a councillor on the South Australian Chamber of Commerce, chair of the McLaren Vale Wine Bushing Festival and chair of the McLaren Vale Winemakers Association. Since joining the Wine and Brandy Producers Association of South Australia in 1958, d'Arry has been treasurer, vice president and president, and has been awarded life membership.

What's in a name?

THE STUMP JUMP

VINTAGE

RIESLING
SAUVIGNON BLANC
MARSANNE
VIOGNIER
CHARDONNAY

McLAREN VALE
ADELAIDE HILLS

d'Arenberg
ESTABLISHED 1912

75CL   750ML

Each d'Arenberg wine is accompanied by a label containing an engaging account of the vineyards, winemaking or history of d'Arenberg. For example, The Stump Jump range of reds and whites is named after the Stump Jump plough, a South Australian invention that was capable of riding over stumps and gnarled roots. The Stump Jump plough was used to clear the land around McLaren Vale and adopted by farmers worldwide.

The fruit for the Feral Fox Pinot Noir is sourced from vineyards in the Adelaide Hills, and the label tells the story of feral foxes that are often found eating low-hanging bunches of grapes during vintage. 'We're not fussed, though,' says Chester, 'as these bushy-tailed critters act as crop thinners and enhance the quality of grapes that are too high for them to reach. It also has the secondary effect of providing a natural source of fertilisation when the laxative nature of the grapes takes effect on the normally carnivorous foxes.'

d'Arenberg
ESTABLISHED 1912

The Feral Fox

PINOT NOIR
ADELAIDE HILLS

750 ml   75 cl

He was also a founding member of the Australian Wine and Brandy Producer's Association, a delegate to the federal council, member of the executive and treasurer. Although in his eighties, d'Arry continues to be active in numerous community and wine industry organisations.

In 1995 d'Arry was appointed a patron of the Australian wine industry in recognition of his outstanding contribution to the affairs of the industry, and in 2004 was awarded a Medal of the Order of Australia (AM) for his contribution to the wine industry and the McLaren Vale region.

Around the World in 80 Years

d'Arry presiding
over the winery.

In December 2006, he celebrated his eightieth birthday and
sixtieth consecutive vintage, and marked the occasion in 2007 by
hosting more than thirty wine industry dinners around the world,
including in the United Kingdom, United States, China and Japan.

d'Arry is quietly proud of the accolades and his remarkable
achievements in turning what was a bulk wine producer in 1928
into the internationally recognised wine brand that d'Arenberg
is today. Yet, nothing has made him prouder than witnessing his
son, Chester, and daughter, Jackie, successfully take the family
business into its fourth generation. Jackie, who has been working
in the wine industry for more than twenty years, lives in Sydney
and sells d'Arenberg wines with its New South Wales distributor,
Ingelwood wines.

Chester d'Arenberg Osborn joined the family business full-
time after graduating from Roseworthy Agricultural College in
South Australia with a Bachelor of Applied Science in Oenology
in 1983. While studying for his degree he worked vintages at
various wineries, including Tullochs in the Hunter Valley and
Hardy's Chateau Reynella. d'Arry allowed him to spend six
months in 1984 touring the vineyards and wineries of France,
Italy, Germany and Spain.

Opposite:
d'Arry's eightieth
birthday in
December 2006
was celebrated
with more than
thirty wine
industry dinners
around the world
and a specially
commissioned
poster.

In honour of d'Arry

In 1992 d'Arenberg proudly released its most well-known wine. First released in 1959 as d'Arenberg Burgundy, this popular red was given the new label 'd'Arry's Original Shiraz Grenache' in honour of d'Arry and half a century of achievements in winemaking.

d'Arry's Original is a blend of 50 per cent Shiraz and 50 per cent Grenache, sourced from d'Arenberg's low-yielding nineteenth-century McLaren Vale vineyards. d'Arenberg Burgundy and d'Arry's Original Shiraz Grenache have enjoyed huge success at wine shows and have been instrumental in building d'Arenberg's reputation.

When Chester returned he took over as chief winemaker from his father, who was confident enough in his son's abilities to allow him have 'the run of the winery' without paternal interference. After all, Chester had been working in the winery during school holidays since the age of seven. Chester reminisces, 'Dad paid me ten cents an hour for picking grapes, pumping wine, filling bottles and sticking labels on them'. He had already decided by then that he was going to be a winemaker, and recalls sitting on Len Evans's knee one night as the grown-ups were discussing the business. On hearing Chester declare that he wanted to be a winemaker, Len asked, 'What sort of wine are you going to make?' Chester replied, 'A yummy one'.

During his secondary school years, Chester also developed an interest in art and photography, for which he won a national award in 1979 at the age of seventeen. His creative flair is apparent in everything he does in the winery and vineyards.

Today Chester holds the dual roles of chief winemaker and viticulturist. He spends a great deal of his time walking d'Arenberg's 500 acres of vineyards and tasting the grapes to determine ripeness, flavour intensity and the ideal picking time.

The Osborns at
a wine function,
circa 1990.
From left:
Chester, Rowan,
Jackie and d'Arry.

Chester on a
tractor and
d'Arry in the
winery, circa
mid 1990s.

After many years of doing this, Chester has developed an exceptional understanding of each individual vineyard's characteristics. Not one to slow down, d'Arry continues in the role of managing director and is still active in the vineyards and winery, and at the cellar door.

Many of d'Arenberg's vineyards are dry grown with no irrigation. Others receive minimal drip irrigation using bore water during the growing period. This makes the vines work hard to produce the kind of intensely flavoured, small-berried grapes that d'Arenberg requires. This stress treatment results in a low yield but, Chester contends, 'In this case less is definitely more, as the quality of the fruit from these low-yielding old vines is tremendous'. This minimal input approach to viticulture also has environmental benefits because no fertilisers are added to the soil and little water is used.

The Dead Arm

In true d'Arenberg style, the most iconic wine in its extensive portfolio, The Dead Arm Shiraz, is named after a disease. *Eutypa lata*, as it is officially known, randomly affects mainly old vines, slowly killing one half, or arm, of the vine. Careful vineyard management can ensure the vines are saved, although yield is severely compromised. However, it is not all bad news for these ancient vines. 'The surviving part of the vine receives all of the nutrients and energy of the extensive root systems that have developed over many decades', Chester explains. 'As a result, the fruit on the surviving arm is incredibly intense and complex.'

The Dead Arm Shiraz is sourced from vineyards up to 130 years old, mainly from the northern parts of McLaren Vale. The 'small batch' winemaking methods used at d'Arenberg allow Chester to select only the very best fruit from each vintage. The tasting process is a rigorous one: as chief winemaker Chester examines all parcels of premium Shiraz—up to 2000 samples—to determine whether they are of The Dead Arm standard. A second tasting occurs to determine the final blend, with a focus on structure, balance of flavour and the wine's ability to age with grace.

Hand-picking Grenache in the dry grown bush vine Hartley vineyard, in north-eastern McLaren Vale.

d'Arenberg sources its fruit from its own vineyards, as well as from about 150 loyal growers in the McLaren Vale region. Viticulturist and growers' relations manager, Giulio Dimasi, and Chester Osborn work with the growers throughout the year to ensure they are producing the style of fruit needed. Growers are not permitted to irrigate or fertilise without approval from d'Arenberg.

To thank their hardworking growers for helping produce their wines, each year in January before vintage begins, Chester and d'Arry host a special dinner at their winery, for all of their growers. 'We've quickly learnt that while our friends' main talent might be growing fantastic grapes, they are also seasoned partygoers', says Chester. The event features a four-course meal prepared by the team at d'Arry's Verandah Restaurant and the full range of d'Arenberg wines. d'Arry recalls the 2006 dinner. The dress code was 'come as your favourite label', and Chester had taken it to the extreme. 'He stopped shaving for a month and ate tuna from a cat food tin to perfect his "Derelict Vineyard" look.'

A diseased vine—while one arm dies, the other survives.

Located in the enclosed verandah of the original homestead, d'Arry's Verandah Restaurant was established in 1996. At a time when the winery was gaining international recognition for its premium red wines, the restaurant was opened to attract more visitors to the cellar door. It has achieved that goal and more, awarded Best Restaurant in a Winery at the South Australian Restaurant and Catering Awards in 2005, 2006 and 2008.

Some fruit (including Viognier, Riesling, Merlot, Chardonnay, Sauvignon Blanc and Pinot Noir) is sourced from the Adelaide Hills wine region because the higher elevation and cooler climate suits these varieties. Occasionally, the fruit is sourced from vineyards further south in the Fleurieu Peninsula. 'This provides us with some excellent cool-climate material, which makes available a great blending component for the McLaren Vale grapes', says Chester.

Chester Osborn setting an example in creativity at the 2006 Growers Dinner as 'The Derelict Vineyard'.

When less is more

The Coppermine Road Cabernet Sauvignon gets its name from a road that runs parallel to d'Arenberg's best Cabernet Sauvignon vineyard. This iconic McLaren Vale vineyard yields less than one tonne of fruit per acre, which is remarkably low, even for ancient vines such as these, grown without fertilisers. However, the quality of the grapes is superb.

d'Arry has long been an advocate of McLaren Vale Cabernet Sauvignon, especially after winning the prestigious Jimmy Watson trophy with one. The Coppermine Road was first made in 1995 using the best parcels of fruit available to make a wine that will cellar for up to twenty years.

An ancient legacy

The soil in most of McLaren Vale's acclaimed and historic vineyards is imbued with an ancient weathered granite-based rock known as ironstone. Its extraordinary rusty red-brown colour is derived from the iron oxides present in the rock. The larger pieces were cleared from the vineyards in the late 1880s and used in many of the buildings at d'Arenberg, most notably the old stables.

The Ironstone Pressings Grenache Shiraz Mourvèdre is sourced from these old vineyards. This flagship wine is described by Chester as 'a very graceful wine with soulful charm and a sophisticated and precise structure that will reward those with the patience to cellar it for up to twenty years'.

Working with individual parcels of fruit with different flavour profiles, which are influenced by the varying soil characteristics and meso-climates of each vineyard, Chester takes great delight in creating wines that highlight the individual characteristics that contribute to the final blend. His aim is to produce exciting wines that have great fragrance, fruit character, length and complexity. Chester explains, 'The art of our winemaking is about great viticulture, extremely gentle handling of the grapes and traditional winemaking processes'. All of the wines that wear the d'Arenberg red stripe label are basket-pressed. The red wines are traditionally fermented in open, wax-lined concrete fermenters and foot-trod by cellar hands wearing fish waders to get the right amount of tannin extraction. Basket-pressing of white wines is rare and in Australia is believed to be unique to d'Arenberg. The label of every d'Arenberg red wine includes a 'foot-trod, basket-pressed' logo, while the white wines bear a 'basket-pressed' logo. Each of these logos is regarded by d'Arry and Chester as a 'badge of honour' that represents the hard work that goes into crafting their wines.

Chester likens his winemaking process to the art of sculpture. It is a process that requires an intimate knowledge and feel for the raw materials used to express the sculptor's artistic vision. He is keen to preserve all of the natural colour and flavour that gives his wines such character, so there is no fining (adding egg whites or chemical agents to reduce cloudiness) or filtration.

> ❛I confess to never having worked a day in my life because I get to do what I love doing every day — this is one of the few things my father and I both agree on.❜
>
> Chester Osborn

Chester has long been recognised by his winemaking peers and wine writers as a talented member of his profession. He is regularly approached by Australian and international wine writers for his comments and insight into the industry, and has been asked to contribute to a number of articles and books about wine. Chester is also a sought-after guest speaker at both wine industry and consumer events.

d'Arenberg has won numerous awards in Australia and overseas for its remarkable portfolio of wines. Some of the most recent accolades include being named a winery of the year by the US magazine *Wine & Spirits* in 2009 and 2010; being named

Third- and fourth-generation winemakers d'Arry and Chester Osborn, and their basket press.

In search of the great white hope

McLaren Vale has long been synonymous with red wine; in particular, Shiraz and Grenache. In the early 1990s Chester went in search of white varieties suited to the McLaren Vale's climate. He looked to the Rhone Valley in France, where the white varieties Viognier, Marsanne and Roussanne thrive. In 1995 he planted these three varieties in d'Arenberg vineyards and, after experimenting with different blends, released the Hermit Crab Viognier Marsanne in 2000. This wine has gone on to become the highest selling white wine in the d'Arenberg portfolio and has helped pave the way for alternative white varieties in McLaren Vale.

Many of McLaren Vale's vineyards are on free-draining soils underlain with limestone, formed by the calcareous remains of the local marine fauna. One such creature was the hermit crab, a reclusive little crustacean that inhabits the cast-off shells of others. The Osborn family thought the name appropriate for this, McLaren Vale's first ever blend of Viognier and Marsanne.

Top All Round Producer at the Houston International Wine Show in 2008, 2009 and 2010; being named Wine Company of the Year in 2008 by *Winestate* magazine; and being named Winery of the Year — Southern Hemisphere at the 2008 Critics Choice International Wine Competition.

Chester has also been recognised for his winemaking prowess. In 2005 he was named Winemaker of the Year at the Australian Wine Selector's Shining Lights Awards, and in 2006 he won the trophy for Red Winemaker of the Year at the Japan International Wine Challenge. Chester was also named one of the world's top forty wine personalities by influential US wine critic and author Robert Parker in 2005. Although he does not make wine to win awards, Chester is certainly proud of his achievements. 'It's always nice to receive industry accolades because it acknowledges that we're on the right path', he says.

Tasting individual barrel
samples is a lengthy process.

d'Arenberg wines are exported to more than sixty countries around the world and are the best-selling premium Australian wine in several of those countries, including France. Chester travels regularly to learn and gain inspiration from other wine regions, as well as to promote the virtues of d'Arenberg wines to the industry, wine writers and consumers.

> ❛I'm excited about tasting wine. Every time I taste a wine I'm tasting the vineyard.❜
>
> Chester Osborn

Chester's lifelong interest in art and architecture has inspired him to design a new, exciting and 'different' building near the existing cellar door and d'Arry's Verandah Restaurant. The design is based on a Rubik's cube with four levels, the third and fourth of which are slightly skewed like a half-finished puzzle. The philosophy of this fourth-generation winemaker is that wine is a puzzle, and for Chester the ultimate puzzle is the Rubik's cube. The building is due to begin construction in 2011.

Chester has three young daughters, Alicia, Ruby and Mia. Like their father, they revel in life at the winery and are beginning to show an interest in the family business. As for the future, Chester continues to experiment with new varieties and explore the different soils and meso-climates of the regions within McLaren Vale. d'Arry and Chester have no desire for d'Arenberg to grow in size, believing that it's about quality, not quantity. 'What's important', says Chester, 'is that we keep improving our wines'.

d'Arry's passion for fishing is as legendary as his passion for winemaking and the Australian wine industry.

This iconic family-owned wine business, which continues to blend tradition with a sense of adventure that often defies convention, will reach its centenary in 2012. With more than twenty-five years' experience as a chief winemaker, Chester confesses to still having a lot left to learn. 'You can never know everything about wine', he admits, 'it's impossible. I am still very much excited about making wine and discovering new varieties and experimenting with how they work in McLaren Vale'.

Serving wine at the right temperature

All wines should be served at a temperature that provides the best possible tasting experience. The correct temperature varies according to variety and style. The rule of thumb is that reds should be served at room temperature and whites should be served chilled, which typically means refrigerated at about four degrees Celsius.

Unfortunately, it's not quite that easy. Room temperature in most modern homes is generally too high, especially in summer, for serving red wine. The solution is simple: if your reds are stored at room temperature in summer, put them into the fridge for half an hour or so before serving. If you are fortunate enough to have your own cellar with a steady temperature of between fourteen and sixteen degrees Celsius, your reds will already be at their ideal serving temperature.

The recommended serving temperatures are as follows:

- between six and ten degrees Celsius for sparkling wine and sweet white wines
- between eight and fourteen degrees Celsius for dry white wines and rosé
- between fourteen and eighteen degrees Celsius for red wines.

It's best to take white wines and rosé out of the fridge for a while before serving. Half an hour is recommended in average indoor temperatures, but less time is needed in hot conditions.

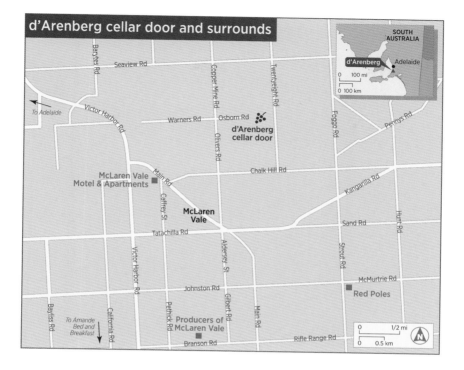

Cellar door

Osborn Rd
McLaren Vale SA 5171
t: 08 8329 4888
w: www.darenberg.com.au

Opening hours
Monday to Sunday: 10 am to 5 pm
Public holidays: 10 am to 5 pm
Closed: Christmas Day, New Year's Day
and Good Friday

Accommodation options

Amande Bed and Breakfast
Lot 13 California Rd
McLaren Vale SA 5171
t: 08 8323 9898
w: www.amandebnb.com
e: innkeeper@amandebnb.com

McLaren Vale Motel & Apartments
Cnr Main Road and Caffrey St
McLaren Vale SA 5171
t: 08 8323 8265
w: www.mclarenvalemotel.com.au
e: info@mclarenvalemotel.com.au

Producers of McLaren Vale
Branson Rd
McLaren Vale SA 5171
t: 08 8323 0060
w: www.producers.net.au
e: tori@producers.net.au

Red Poles
McMurtrie Rd
McLaren Vale SA 5171
t: 08 8323 8994
w: www.redpoles.com.au
e: redpoles@bigpond.net.au

De Bortoli Wines

La tavola lunga

*' It's our life, it's not just a business. So you
put your heart and soul into everything. '*

Emeri De Bortoli, chairperson, De Bortoli Wines

La tavola lunga, the long table, is the focus of a De Bortoli
tradition — a big lunchtime meal with family and workers
from the winery and vineyards. Along with a feast of home-
cooked food and plenty of good wine, there is good conversation,
friendly debate and much laughter. This tradition, which was
brought by Vittorio De Bortoli from Italy to the Riverina wine
region of New South Wales, has been an important factor in
the success of this renowned family wine company, keeping the
lines of communication open and spirits high in both good times
and bad.

De Bortoli Wines is a dynamic and innovative family wine
company now in the hands of its third generation. With vineyards

Lunch at the long table on the verandah at Bilbul, circa 1930.

in the Riverina, Hunter Valley, Yarra Valley and King Valley wine regions, De Bortoli Wines has established a reputation for premium wines and warm hospitality at its three cellar doors. The cellar doors are located at De Bortoli's headquarters at Bilbul in the Riverina, in the Hunter Valley and at Dixons Creek in the Yarra Valley. Since the winery was founded in 1928, De Bortoli has grown into a truly global family company with branches in the United Kingdom, Europe and the United States.

Vittorio De Bortoli, the son of a farmer, left his home in the foothills of the Italian Alps in Northern Italy in 1924 to seek a new life in Australia. There was little work after the devastation of World War I and, like many other young men in the area, he was struggling to put food on the table. He believed Australia would provide him with the opportunity to use his farming skills to grow crops and make wine. So desperate was he to leave that he left his fiancée, Giuseppina, behind, hoping that she would be able to save enough money to join him later.

After arriving in Melbourne with nothing but his clothes and a few coins, he caught a train to Griffith in New South Wales to seek work on a farm. The work was hard, the wages were poor and the flat, sun-drenched, arid land was very different from that of his homeland. But Vittorio, with a seemingly endless capacity for hard work and a gritty determination, had saved enough by 1927 to purchase a fifty-five-acre 'mixed farm', planted with fruit trees, vegetables and grapevines, at Bilbul, near Griffith.

As part of the Murrumbidgee Irrigation Area scheme, established in 1912 by the New South Wales government, semi-arid land had been transformed into fertile land, well suited for growing fruit and vegetables. Vittorio's farm had been one of the soldier settlement farms given to returned soldiers after World War I, but was deserted not long afterwards. Shortly after buying the farm, Vittorio's friend and future brother-in-law, Giovanni, arrived to help.

> ❛My grandfather told me that each pursuit in life should be a noble one.❜
>
> Darren De Bortoli

A grape surplus in 1928 thwarted Vittorio's plans to sell his grapes. As a result he decided to make his own wine to enjoy with family and friends, and De Bortoli Wines was born. This first crush was fifteen tonnes of Shiraz, produced in two 900 gallon (4000 litre) vats. Drinking wine with meals was a European tradition, and with large numbers of Italian migrants settling in the area, his wine proved to be very popular.

By 1929 Giuseppina, who had been working in France, had saved enough money to be able to join Vittorio in Australia.

Lunch at the long table in 2003.

Giuseppina and Vittorio on
their wedding day in 1929.

They married soon after and Giuseppina quickly settled into life at Bilbul, looking after the bookwork while Vittorio managed the farm. Giuseppina eventually became known to workers on the farm as 'the Bossa'. The De Bortolis later had three children, Florrie, Deen and Eola.

Vittorio's mixed farm and those of the other Italian-born farmers who settled in the Murrumbidgee Irrigation Area became known as 'fruit salad farms'. These hard-working Italian immigrants were able to provide enough food for their families, sell the remainder of their crop and save enough money to build and furnish new houses on their farms. Vittorio credited his ability to build an impressive brick house to growing pumpkins, which few others were planting at the time.

While intelligent and good with numbers, Vittorio De Bortoli could not read or write. For him, life was all about working on the land. 'He was progressive, but believed in expanding within his means', says his grandson Darren. 'He was advanced for his time in terms of winemaking.'

In memory of Nellie

The Yarra Valley Melba range of Cabernet blends was created in honour of renowned Australian opera diva Dame Nellie Melba, who for many years resided in the Yarra Valley. In developing this range, Steve Webber has aimed for medium-bodied wines of 'texture, interest and rusticity'.

The Melba Lucia, named after the opera *Lucia Di Lammermoor* performed by Dame Nellie Melba is a blend of Cabernet and Sangiovese. The Melba Mimi is a blend of Cabernet, Shiraz and Nebbiolo, named in honour of Melba's performances from the opera *La Boheme*. The Melba Reserve is a blend of Cabernet sourced from the oldest vines on the estate, planted in 1971, along with a small quantity of Merlot.

Vittorio's winemaking venture grew rapidly, assisted by the demand from Italian immigrants and the lack of good table wine in the Riverina and Rutherglen regions. The De Bortoli family home became a mecca for other Italian migrants. Labourers who worked as cane-cutters in Queensland would come down to pick grapes during vintage, exchanging news of their homeland with old friends and drinking wine. The visitors would always take some of Vittorio's wine home with them and have more freighted up by train. Word soon spread about Vittorio De Bortoli's winemaking skills, and exports to Queensland and northern New South Wales soon followed.

While much of the community struggled through the Great Depression, the more self-sufficient Italian immigrants were able to ride out the storm, including the De Bortolis. By 1936 production was fourteen times that of the first vintage in 1928, mostly Semillon, Trebbiano, Doradillo, Pedro Ximenez, Grenache and Shiraz, and there were up to twenty-five men working at the winery during vintage.

World War II brought new and greater challenges than the Depression. Paranoia took hold and many Australian men of Italian and German descent were interned in camps or had their movements severely restricted. In the Griffith area alone, between sixty and seventy Italian immigrants were interned. Vittorio escaped internment because he was employing people and producing food, but he was forbidden from visiting Griffith without written permission and ordered to report to the police station once a week.

Some Italian-born farmers in the region had their buildings and equipment compulsorily acquired under the Australian government's National Security Act, introduced in 1940 to subdue 'enemy aliens' and 'naturalised Australians of enemy origin'. There was also a strong belief that the fight against Hitler would be helped if the consumption of liquor was reduced. This led to quotas on the sale of wine and other liquor, and interstate sales were banned.

In 1944 Vittorio was fined £16000 and imprisoned for a period of three months for selling wine above his quota.

Grape-picking in the early 1930s. At left
are Giuseppina and daughter Florrie.

Vittorio broke these rocks by hand to
make concrete for the winery tanks.

Barrels of claret ready for transport, circa 1930.

His imprisonment coincided with vintage and the farm and everything that he and Giuseppina had worked so hard for was in danger of being lost. Fortunately, family, friends and workers rallied around Giuseppina, keeping the farm running and completing the vintage.

Following the end of the war the quota system on liquor was withdrawn. Interstate sales resumed under a strict licensing system that limited Vittorio's sales; however, a boom in wine sales erupted, triggered by a new wave of European immigrants and De Bortoli Wines was able to expand in earnest.

In 1952, fifteen-year-old Deen joined the family business.

A receipt for part of Vittorio's fine for selling wine above his quota.

Deen had already developed a keen interest in machinery and embraced the new technology that was rapidly becoming available to winemakers. He saw the potential of table wine as a popular beverage and worked tirelessly to increase production, sometimes with fierce resistance from his father, who regarded his son's ambition as reckless and extravagant. Deen, on the other hand, considered his father's methods to be old-fashioned and limiting. Vittorio's first vintage in 1928 comprised two vats with a total capacity of 1800 gallons, and by 1936, capacity was twenty vats holding 25 000 gallons. By 1959, however, Deen had increased capacity to 110 vats holding 795 000 gallons.

In 1958 Deen married Emeri Cunial, whose parents had also emigrated from Northern Italy. The 1960s saw the birth of Deen and Emeri's four children: Darren, Leanne, Kevin and Victor. With four young children growing up, surrounded by vineyards and the winery, Deen could see the promise of another dynasty that could expand the family business even further.

Whenever Vittorio and Giuseppina were away, Deen would talk to the bankers to arrange finance and get contractors in to install new equipment and expand the winery. When his parents returned there was always a furious war of words between father and son. This happened many times, but not once did Vittorio demand a reversal of the changes or warn Deen not to modify the winery while he was away.

Emeri recalls some fiery arguments between Deen and Vittorio. 'Life was always an argument between Deen and his father. They didn't listen to each other. They were both basically saying the same thing, but they were too busy arguing to realise that they agreed. Darren and Deen were the same, and Darren is now seeing the same with his son, Ben.'

Deen and Emeri De Bortoli on their wedding day in 1958.

A range that sparkles

De Bortoli's sparkling wines were relaunched in the late 1990s as the Emeri sparkling range, a collection of fresh, vibrant and fruity wines made in the tradition of Deen's Vittorio Spumante. Named after Emeri, matriarch of the De Bortoli family, this range is made with fruit sourced from the company's vineyards and external growers throughout Australia. The Emeri sparkling range includes Chardonnay Pinot Noir, Moscato, Pink Moscato, Pinot Grigio, Sauvignon Blanc and Shiraz.

Deen energetically expanded the family business, relentlessly implementing many innovations, introducing new wine styles and pioneering new winemaking and viticultural practices. The expansion accelerated when Vittorio purchased a licence that enabled the company to once again package and sell wine in New South Wales and Queensland. Florrie and her husband, Silvio, became managers of the wine distribution company set up in Sydney. Eola and her husband, Ian, later took over the business in Sydney after Florrie and Silvio moved on.

De Bortoli Wines was well placed to lead the way in the production of dry table wines when they became popular during the 1960s and 1970s, at the expense of the previously dominant fortified wines. Deen released a fruity Italian wine called Vittorio Spumante, which introduced a whole new generation to the delights of wine.

When Vittorio passed away in 1979, Deen inherited the winery and Florrie and Eola inherited the Sydney assets. Today, Florrie and Eola are no longer involved in the family business, but continue to live in Sydney.

In 1982 Deen and Emeri's eldest son, Darren, newly graduated from South Australia's Roseworthy Agricultural College with a Bachelor of Applied Science in Oenology, sat down with his father

Opposite: The vineyards at Bilbul today.

to discuss taking advantage of a surplus of grapes that year and making a botrytised wine. Deen had always harboured ambitions to make use of the botrytis mould, otherwise known as 'noble rot'. The weather conditions that year turned out to be perfect for the growth of botrytis, and an Australian legend, De Bortoli Noble One was conceived.

> ‘ If it hadn't been for my father, there would have been nothing for me to carry on. ’
>
> Deen De Bortoli

In 1987 De Bortoli Wines purchased a winery and vineyard in Victoria's Yarra Valley. The intention was to establish a premium wine brand for the company in a cool-climate region. Two years later, Darren's sister Leanne and her winemaker husband, Steve Webber, moved from Bilbul to the Yarra Valley to manage the development of the estate.

The Yarra Valley venture has proved to be both exciting and successful. The original thirty-two acres of vineyards has grown to more than 500 acres, planted with an impressive range of varieties that includes Chardonnay, Riesling, Sauvignon Blanc, Gewurztraminer, Semillon, Pinot Grigio, Pinot Noir, Cabernet Sauvignon and Shiraz, as well as lesser known varieties such as Viognier, Nebbiolo and Sangiovese.

During the 1990s, Deen De Bortoli established a 450-acre vineyard in the King Valley wine region of north-eastern Victoria. Located on the banks of the King river, this large vineyard is exposed to warm days and cool nights during the growing season, providing ideal conditions for growing premium fruit. As well as established varieties such as Chardonnay, Riesling, Sauvignon Blanc, Shiraz, Merlot and Cabernet Sauvignon, the King Valley vines include some Italian and Spanish varieties such as Sangiovese, Pinot Grigio and Tempranillo.

Ever expanding, in 2002 the family purchased a winery and vineyards in the Hunter Valley, with the aim of crafting the distinctive Shiraz and Semillon styles for which the region is famous. The vineyards occupy ninety acres and include a mature vineyard with Semillon vines more than forty years old.

Deen De Bortoli expanding the winery in his parents' absence and without their knowledge.

The De Bortoli winery at Bilbul in 1966.

A truly noble one

Noble One, the white wine made from botrytised Semillon, has become De Bortoli's flagship wine and Australia's benchmark sweet white wine.

Noble One was De Bortoli's first international success story. Its first vintage, crafted by Darren and his father Deen in 1982, has won more trophies and medals internationally than any other Australian wine. By 2007, the year of its twenty-fifth vintage, Noble One Botrytis Semillon had won more than 100 trophies and 352 gold medals both nationally and internationally.

The success of Noble One is even more remarkable given that conventional wisdom at the time was that a wine of this style and quality could not be made in Australia. Noble One has been produced in every year since the first vintage in 1982, except for the 1989 vintage when heavy rains resulted in the growth of numerous other moulds on the Semillon fruit.

Deen De Bortoli passed away suddenly at the age of sixty-seven in October 2003, leaving behind his wife Emeri, their four children and ten grandchildren. Earlier that year he had proudly celebrated the seventy-fifth anniversary of De Bortoli Wines. Deen had carried on the legacy of his hard-working parents by growing the family business into an internationally recognised and respected producer of premium wines.

Largely self-taught, Deen was a visionary whose involvement in the Australian wine industry spanned fifty years. As well as being active in the company's vineyards, he was a member of the Vine Improvement Society and the Murrumbidgee Irrigation Area Sustainable Development Committee, which is concerned with land management issues, including salinity control, drainage, recycling and the streamlining of irrigation systems.

Deen received many awards and other accolades for his contributions to the wine industry, including the Graham Gregory Award for Services to the New South Wales wine industry in 1995

Deen De Bortoli
(1936–2003).

and the inaugural Golden Plate Award in recognition of his
contribution to the wine industry in the Riverina wine region. While
they were not something Deen had set out to achieve — he simply
wanted to make good, affordable wine — he was immensely proud
of the awards and recognition he and the family business received.

✿   ✿   ✿

The third generation, Deen and Emeri De Bortoli's four children,
are the current custodians of De Bortoli Wines. With Emeri as
chairperson, they form the family board of directors. Darren is
managing director, Leanne manages the Yarra Valley arm of the
business, Kevin looks after the company vineyards in the Riverina
and Victor is export director.

Darren was only thirty-three years old when he was appointed
managing director of the business in the mid 1990s. He is still
involved with winemaking and works closely with his team of
winemakers. Darren is a member of numerous wine industry
organisations, including the New South Wales Winemakers'
Association, the Riverina Winemakers' Association and the
Winemakers' Federation of Australia and serves on the Wine
Industry Research & Development Consultative Committee to
the New South Wales minister for primary industry.

De Bortoli's Yarra Valley vineyards.

Like her brothers, Leanne started working in the winery as a teenager during school holidays. She studied wine marketing at Roseworthy Agricultural College and graduated with an associate diploma with honours. Leanne then spent time travelling, and worked for the family business in Griffith and with De Bortoli's agents in the United States. After marrying Steve Webber in 1989, the couple moved to Coonawarra, where Steve was working for Lindemans at their Rouge Homme winery.

Third-generation managing director Darren De Bortoli.

When Darren asked Leanne and Steve to manage the Yarra Valley project in 1989, they didn't hesitate. 'We were so excited to be asked', Leanne says. 'The plan was to make a range of premium wines and develop the vineyard.' In the same year, building commenced on a new cellar door and restaurant complex, which was officially opened in early 1990.

Bring something to the table

Deen De Bortoli created his original Vat series with the idea of developing a range of wines to be enjoyed over a meal with family and friends. The wines were named after the identifying chalked numbers on the vats.

The Deen Vat series comprises traditional varietal wines, as well as wines made from interesting varieties that are newer to Australia. This multi-award-winning range was inspired by Deen's original Vat series and includes eight single varieties, including the highly awarded Vat 1 Durif, Vat 5 Botrytis Semillon and Vat 8 Shiraz. Five additional wines in this range are produced exclusively for export markets.

Today the De Bortoli Winery and Restaurant is recognised as one of the premier wine and food attractions in the Yarra Valley and has received numerous accolades, including being named Best Tourism Winery in 2007, 2008 and 2009 at the Victorian Tourism Awards, being inducted into the Victorian Tourism Awards Hall of Fame in 2009 and receiving the Tourism Wineries award at the 2008 and 2009 Qantas Australian Tourism Awards.

Leanne's roles include overseeing and directing the restaurant and cellar door businesses, public relations for De Bortoli and the Yarra Valley region, marketing and product development. She is involved with Victorian tourism networks, is an active member of the Yarra Valley Wine Growers Association and a director of the Yarra Ranges Regional Marketing Group.

Chief winemaker Steve Webber oversees all wine production at De Bortoli's Yarra Valley Estate, Hunter Valley and the King Valley. Assisting Steve at the Yarra Valley winery is Sarah Fagan, who was awarded the 2009 *Gourmet Traveller WINE* magazine Young Winemaker of the Year and was named rising star in Matt Skinner's 2011 *Wine Guide*. One of Sarah's mentors was David Slingsby-Smith, who was appointed one of the senior winemakers at the Yarra Valley winery in 1992. David was a valuable part of

Leanne De Bortoli and Steve Webber with some loyal followers in the Yarra Valley vineyards.

The fruits of maturity

The fruit used to craft the De Bortoli Yarra Valley Estate wines are exclusively sourced from the family-owned vineyards in the cool-climate of the Yarra Valley. The mature and low-yielding vines in these vineyards deliver fruit of exceptional quality fruit to the winery, which is preserved with gentle, low-intervention winemaking techniques. Each wine in this highly rated range—which includes Chardonnay, Sauvignon Blanc, Viognier, Cabernet Sauvignon, Pinot Noir and Shiraz—is designed to be an expression of vineyard detail and purity.

the team and instrumental in mentoring young winemakers until he passed away following a short illness in August 2010.

Steve had developed an interest in horticulture, viticulture and winemaking at an early age, influenced by his late father, Ron. After completing school in South Australia, Steve worked in the cellar at Leo Buring under the tutelage of John Vickery before starting a degree in Oenology at Roseworthy in 1980. Following his graduation in 1982, Steve worked for Lindemans Wines at their Karadoc and Coonawarra wineries before moving to the Yarra Valley with Leanne.

He aims for finesse and detail in his wines. 'We have addressed most aspects of our site, the way we tend our vineyards, ensuring perfect fruit is received into the winery; all in the quest to preserve detail in our wine', he says. He admits to being obsessed with wines made from Pinot Noir. 'Pinot, while time consuming and expensive to grow, when handled gently and not overly macerated is a wine that articulates the characters of the site so well'. Between 2003 and 2005, Steve travelled to Burgundy in France several times to make some small batches of Pinot Noir. His experiences in Burgundy taught him about the importance of the vineyard and wines having a 'sense of place'.

Opposite: De Bortoli's multi-award-winning cellar door at Dixons Creek in the Yarra Valley.

Steve is highly regarded in the Australian wine industry, and his wines and winemaking skills have been recognised with numerous awards, including the *Gourmet Traveller WINE* magazine's 2007 Winemaker of the Year. In 2008, Steve was appointed chairman of judges at The Royal Melbourne Wine Show and has been instrumental in fostering change within the show system to make it more relevant to the Australian wine industry today.

> ❛ Deen was forever on the lookout for new opportunities and wanting to make sure the business was set up well to make the most of those opportunities. ❜
>
> Leanne De Bortoli

Kevin De Bortoli is responsible for the family vineyards that surround the original De Bortoli winery and head office in Bilbul. As a youngster he loved life on the farm and there was never any doubt that he would work in the business. He started work in the family winery immediately after completing high school and undertook part-time studies at Charles Sturt University, graduating with a diploma in viticulture.

Deen De Bortoli with the 1997 Jimmy Watson trophy.

Kevin is always looking for ways to improve quality and productivity in the vineyard using environmentally sustainable practices. Kevin has been instrumental in diversifying the De Bortoli portfolio through the introduction of new varieties appropriate to the region such as Verdelho, Petit Verdot and Durif. He has overseen huge improvements in the quality of mainstream varieties such as Chardonnay, Sauvignon Blanc, Cabernet Sauvignon and Shiraz in recent years, and demonstrated that production can be effectively scaled back to produce lower yielding, higher quality crops.

Kevin De Bortoli
in the vineyards
at Bilbul.

The De Bortoli winemaking philosophy is that great wine begins in the vineyard. The focus is on careful site selection, vine maturity and hands-on viticulture with a move towards biological farming principles. It recognises the value of sustainable practices that deliver vast improvements in fruit quality, as well as real environmental benefits. In the winery there is minimal interference, allowing the wine to 'make itself'. In short, the policy is hands-on in the vineyard and hands-off in the winery.

Implementing environmentally sustainable practices is an essential element of De Bortoli Wines' operations. Leanne De Bortoli explains: 'As a family company we believe this is important to respect the environment. Such an approach, I believe, will lead not only to the full expression of terroir, or sense of place, in our wines, but also to the consciousness that we are, after all, only custodians of the land'.

De Bortoli Wines has developed a world's best practice biological treatment system for wastewater at the Bilbul site, allowing it to be used for irrigation. Similar systems have been implemented in the family's Yarra Valley, King Valley and Hunter Valley sites. The use of chemicals in all of the vineyards is minimised and, in some of the vineyards, not used at all. Composting and mulching is being used more and more to reduce water usage, suppress disease and improve soil nutrition

Like many other Australian wineries, De Bortoli Wines is a signatory of the National Packaging Covenant. It has made a commitment to minimise the impact on the environment from the disposal of used packaging, to conserve resources through improved design and production processes, and to facilitate the re-use and recycling of used packaging materials.

Composting in the Yarra Valley.

Unlike his older siblings, Victor De Bortoli was uncertain about joining the family wine company. While he helped out

from an early age, his future appeared to lie elsewhere. 'I have some great memories, but life as a youngster in a family winery can be hard work. When I was twelve and Darren was having his first crack at Noble One, the old man grabbed us all to spend a day in the vineyard hand-picking those rotten grapes, while my mates were out having fun', Victor recalls. After completing high school, he enrolled at the Australian National University in Canberra, where he studied commerce and gained his degree in 1993.

After graduating, Victor spent some time in a non-wine-related family venture, and then moved to Canberra to work for De Bortoli Wines as area sales manager. Following this grounding in sales, Victor relocated to London in 1996 to establish the family's first offshore office, De Bortoli Wines (United Kingdom) Ltd. Offices in Belgium and the United States soon followed. 'This was an exciting time for me,' he says, 'but I must admit there were many distractions. I think the old man finally had a gutful so he brought me back home in late 1997. It was probably at this time when I was back in the winery that my understanding of the industry grew at an exponential rate to the point where I was able to take over the total export operations in 2001'.

> ❛As a family wine company we take a long-term view; we are determined to pass on a sustainable business for the next generation.❜
>
> Darren De Bortoli

As export director, with the task of developing and expanding De Bortoli's international business, Victor is based in Bilbul but travels extensively to the United Kingdom, Europe, North America and other international markets. 'I can visit as many as fifteen countries in a year, but the best part is not necessarily the exciting or exotic locations but the characters you meet', he says. Today, De Bortoli exports to more than seventy countries, including major markets for Australian wine such as the United Kingdom, the United States, New Zealand, Europe, Canada and Japan, as well as emerging markets such as India, Vietnam and Korea.

De Bortoli Wines has successfully overcome numerous setbacks since it was first established in 1928. In the early years, the gritty determination of Vittorio took the family business successfully through the Great Depression, and the family endured hostility towards Italian migrants and government restrictions during World War II, and the imprisonment of Vittorio. In recent years the family has again demonstrated its strength and resilience following the sudden passing of Deen, who was so influential in the growth of the company and the preservation of its heritage.

The third generation — Darren, Leanne, Kevin and Victor — under the watchful eye of their mother Emeri, is carrying on the legacy left by Deen and has already met more than its fair share of challenges, including droughts, frosts, hailstorms, bushfires,

Export Director
Victor
De Bortoli.

The De Bortoli family in the winery gardens at Bilbul. From left: Darren, Kevin, Emeri, Leanne and Victor.

climate change and the global financial crisis. Darren feels the company is well placed to withstand most of the extreme variations in the weather because its vineyards are in four very different regions. Steve Webber is philosophical about the weather, commenting, 'There are setbacks — long summers, cold winters, extreme variations — that challenge you, but that's also what makes wines different. The seasonal stuff gives wine great character'. Leanne adds, 'With each year, we learn more from the seasons and from the decisions we make (good and bad), as has been done for centuries in Europe'.

> 'Wine should be about a place. It should taste of the site and the seasons.'
>
> Steve Webber

Emeri De Bortoli and her family now look to the future, consolidating and expanding on their considerable achievements and fulfilling Deen's vision. While Emeri prefers a behind-the-scenes role, she was a sounding board for Deen when he was alive and remains very influential in contributing to the success of the family company as chairperson.

The future of De Bortoli Wines seems secure with Emeri and Deen's ten grandchildren waiting in the wings. 'Some will want to come into the family business and some won't', comments Leanne. 'We are just trying to set up a great family business that can be passed on to the next generation. How they go forward with it is up to them.'

Matching wine and cheese

What better way to relax on a chilly winter's night than with a bottle of wine and a platter of perfectly matured cheeses? At our custom-built Cheese Maturation Room, our cheese selection changes from day to day, depending on which are in peak condition. Under the guidance of renowned cheesemaker Richard Thomas we match these against our wines. Here are just a few of Richard's recommendations.

Enjoy Pinot Noir with morbier, washed rind or brie. The formidable Epoisses washed rind of Burgundy provides serious contrast to the complexity of a well-made Pinot. Sadly, most Australian brie styles are too clean and lack the forceful flavour of the French style.

Enjoy sparkling wine with fresh, salty goats' cheese. Salt complements and lifts the flavours of sparkling wine and most cold, acidic white wines. Unripened salty, acidic goats' cheese, or dishes containing it, is there to make your fizz look good.

Enjoy big red wines with Grana or Parmigiano. This is a historic match. If you don't enjoy this your palate requires readjustment. The salt–sweet, rock-hard character of the Grana family of cheeses can withstand the onslaught of a Shiraz.

Enjoy dessert wines with cheese and honey. This is another fantastic experience based on a simple Italian mountain lunch of Gorgonzola, truffled honey and sweet wine.

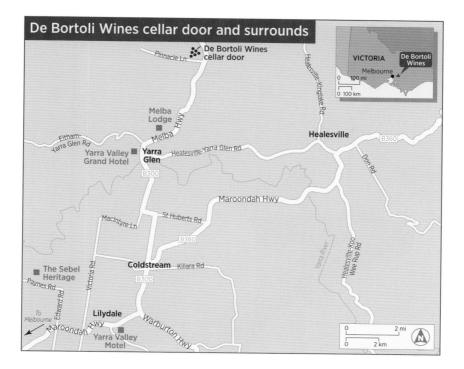

De Bortoli Wines cellar door and surrounds

Cellar door

Pinnacle Ln
Dixons Creek Vic. 3775
t: 03 5965 2271
w: www.debortoliyarra.com.au

Opening hours
Monday to Sunday: 10 am to 5 pm

Accommodation options

Melba Lodge
939 Melba Hwy
Yarra Glen Vic. 3775
t: 03 9730 1511
w: www.melbalodge.com.au
e: enquiries@melbalodge.com.au

The Sebel Heritage
Heritage Ave
Chirnside Park Vic. 3116
t: 03 9760 3333
w: www.mirvachotels.com/
      sebel-heritage-yarra-valley

Yarra Valley Grand Hotel
19 Bell St
Yarra Glen Vic. 3775
03 9730 1230
w: www.yarravalleygrand.com.au
e: hotel@yarravalleygrand.com.au

Yarra Valley Motel
418–420 Maroondah Hwy
Lilydale Vic. 3140
t: 03 9735 3000
w: www.yarravalleymotel.com.au
e: stay@yarravalleymotel.com.au

Jim Barry
Wines
More than a lifetime

‘Sometimes it takes longer than a lifetime to do a lifetime's work ... it's now up to my children.’

Jim Barry, founder of Jim Barry Wines, 1925–2004

When Peter Barry, second-generation winemaker at Jim Barry Wines, says that he is absolutely devoted to and passionate about Riesling, it comes as no surprise. After all, nine of the eleven vineyards belonging to this small family-owned company are in South Australia's beautiful Clare Valley, known as the capital of Australian Riesling.

The Clare Valley is about two hours' drive north-west of its much larger cousin, the Barossa Valley, and, despite the dominance of Riesling, variation in soil and climate within this region make it particularly suited to growing some red varieties. Indeed, Jim Barry Wines uses Clare fruit to produce some of the best red wines in the land, notably the Armagh Shiraz, the McRae

Peter Barry in the winery.

Nancy and Jim Barry signing a barrel in the Armagh vineyard during the Armagh Weekend in July 2000.

Wood Shiraz and the Benbournie Cabernet Sauvignon. Since it was established more than fifty years ago, the company has built up a rich portfolio of regionally distinctive wines.

Jim Barry Wines was founded in 1959 when Jim and Nancy Barry purchased an eighty-acre property on the northern outskirts of the Clare Valley. (The couple had met some years earlier, when Jim was living in Clare and working at the Clarevale Cooperative Winery as a winemaker and chemist.) Their intention at this stage was simply to plant vineyards.

When Jim started at the cooperative in 1946, he was the first fully qualified winemaker in the Clare Valley. He graduated from Roseworthy Agricultural College at the end of that year, with only the seventeenth oenology diploma in Australia. Jim was one of six students in his oenology class — at that time, Roseworthy could accept only six students for the oenology course due to limitations in equipment and glassware. In some instances, students even had to make their own glassware.

A family affair

The first release of the Armagh Shiraz was produced from the 1985 vintage. The Armagh has achieved extraordinary success and is regarded as one of Australia's highest quality wines. The fruit for this flagship wine is sourced exclusively from the Armagh vineyard.

The development of this wine was a true family affair—a collaboration between Jim Barry and his three sons, Mark, Peter and John. The Armagh is a vineyard that the family has a particular attachment to. Peter recalls, 'There was a terrible drought when we planted it and we were all carting forty-four-gallon drums of water from the house three miles away and hand-watering the vines to get them through those tough early days'.

This vineyard now requires little intervention. It is low-yielding, but produces rich and concentrated fruit. It lies on a north-west facing slope, which acts as a natural suntrap, ensuring that the fruit is always fully ripened when picked. 'We've only had a couple of lesser years—we won't release a wine if the fruit's not good enough', says Peter.

The Armagh Shiraz is hand-crafted to be enjoyed on release, but it is also well suited to long-term cellaring. Since it was first released twenty-five years ago, the Armagh has won dozens of awards and received many accolades worldwide.

Following the successful planting of their eighty acres, in 1964 Jim and Nancy purchased seventy acres of prime land in the Armagh area of the Clare Valley. The area was first settled by Irish migrants in 1849 and named after the lush rolling hills of their homeland. Further to his plan to make premium red wine, in 1968 Jim planted eight acres of Shiraz and named it the Armagh vineyard. This vineyard would go on to be the foundation for Jim Barry's red wine production.

Widely respected as a red and white winemaker, in 1969 Jim was approached by the Taylor family to help them establish their 440 acres of vines and new winery at Auburn, further to the south

Peter Barry
hand-pruning
in the Armagh
vineyard.

of the Clare Valley. At the same time, he and Nancy continued to develop their own vineyards and expand the range of wines under their Jim Barry label. Their wines were being produced at the nearby Wendouree Cellars with facilities borrowed from Jim's mate and Clare Valley identity Roly Birks. However, it became clear that to continue to grow they would need to build their own winery. Five years later, in 1974, the first wines were produced at their new winery, built on a hillside with spectacular views over the northern Clare Valley.

Jim quickly gained a reputation as a far-sighted and innovative winemaker who embraced cutting-edge technology. This included using cold fermentation for red wine and cool fermentation for white wine. He was also one of the first to recognise how significantly the Australian wine market was changing in the post-war environment and what steps were necessary to accommodate those changes. As a result, he attracted the attention of many other winemakers from around Australia, who were keen to see the winery and how Jim operated.

Aware that the Clare Valley's soil and climate lent itself particularly well to Riesling, Jim always kept an eye out for promising areas of land. In 1977 he bought another farm, known as Lodge Hill, high in the eastern ranges of the Clare Valley, with the intention of planting it entirely with Riesling. At an altitude of 480 metres, Jim was sure that it would produce some of the best Riesling in Clare. However, while pottering around on the property, digging here and there with his shovel to get a better feel for the soil he would be working with, he discovered a different soil profile on a north-facing slope. Because it was warmer than

Truly inspired

The McRae Wood Shiraz was developed in 1992 with fruit sourced from a selection of locations in the Clare Valley, including the Armagh vineyard. Since the purchase of the Lodge Hill vineyard and further expansion, the fruit is sourced from a wider selection of locations in the Clare Valley, including the Armagh.

This premium full-bodied Shiraz honours Jim Barry's vision of making the highest quality premium table wines. Jim purchased the land that became the Armagh vineyard from Duncan McRae Wood, after whom the vineyard is named. The choice of location for planting Shiraz was truly inspired. John Barry considers one of his major achievements to be helping his brother Peter create the McRae Wood Shiraz.

the rest of the property, Jim decided that it was the perfect place to plant Shiraz. Consequently, the Lodge Hill vineyard was planted with both Riesling and Shiraz.

Like the children of many other winemakers and viti-culturists, Jim and Nancy's three sons — Mark, Peter and John — all grew up immersed in the business. They went on to study at Roseworthy Agricultural College before officially joining the winery. Mark helped his father plant vineyards on the family property while he was still at school. After completing high school in 1974, he worked as a vineyard and cellar hand for three years before embarking on a winemaking course at Roseworthy. In 1980, after having spent several years as vineyard manager and serving his winemaking apprenticeship with his father, he became chief winemaker. Mark retired from winemaking after the 2002 vintage, but during his time in the role won many gold medals and trophies for his Riesling (including the Watervale Riesling), Sauvignon Blanc, Cabernet Sauvignon and Shiraz (including the Armagh Shiraz). He took great pride in being recognised on the Australian wine show circuit for his winemaking skills.

Both of the Lodge Hill varieties are consistent gold medal winners at wine competitions in Australia and abroad.

The rolling greenery of Jim Barry's Lodge Hill vineyard.

Jim Barry checking barrel samples in the cellar.

Peter and Mark Barry.

Peter completed his first vintages as a cellar hand at the winery in 1977 and 1978 after finishing high school. His interest in winemaking led him to undertake a degree in oenology at Roseworthy. While studying he completed vintages at Rothbury Estate in the Hunter Valley with David Lowe, and Bilyara in the Barossa Valley with Wolf Blass and John Glaetzer. Peter returned to Jim Barry Wines in 1982 after graduating and took on a marketing and viticultural role. 'When I first decided to join the business, Dad took me to the Adelaide Wine Show and introduced me to his winemaking friends', Peter recalls. 'When he introduced me to Max Schubert he told Max that I was going to be a winemaker. I didn't realise how proud he must have been at that moment until my own sons decided to join the family business.'

> ❛My father always said, "The secret to making good wine is shoe leather—walk the vineyard, check the barrels, it's all hands on".❜
>
> Peter Barry

The youngest of the Barry brothers, John, also joined the business after finishing high school, in 1982. His interest lay in viticulture, and he worked in the vineyard for six years before studying at Roseworthy. He graduated in 1990 with a diploma in farm management, viticulture and horticulture, and worked alongside Mark as assistant winemaker for three years before undertaking vintages in France and in Oregon in the United States.

John's desire to learn as much as possible about the different aspects of the wine industry led him to spend time selling Jim Barry wines in the Adelaide market before returning to Clare and taking on a marketing role. In 1994 John was appointed company viticulturist, which involves overseeing the family vineyards in the Clare Valley. He also ensures that all vineyard personnel are kept up to date with the latest vineyard practices, including pest and disease management.

In 2001 John and his wife, Gayle, purchased a small property at the northern end of the valley, just a few kilometres from the winery. They planted thirty acres of Shiraz and this fruit is now used in some of the Jim Barry Wines portfolio. John and Gayle also run a bed and breakfast on their property.

Jim and Nancy Barry also had three daughters — Susan, Julie and Dianne — who have all worked in the family business in sales and marketing.

In 1985, at the age of sixty, Jim decided to take a back seat and Peter took his place as managing director. His love of the business undiminished, Jim continued to take an active role in the winery until he passed away at the age of seventy-nine in 2004.

In 1986 Peter, Mark and John purchased the Florita vineyard at Watervale, in the southern end of the Clare Valley. The Florita vineyard was renowned for its superb Riesling grapes, but the purchase was made at a time when there was an oversupply of grapes and the South Australian government had initiated a vine pull scheme. To make matters worse, Riesling was being overshadowed by a surge in the popularity of Chardonnay. The three brothers were prepared to swim against the tide because they knew the Florita vineyard had been the source for the great Leo Buring Rieslings of the 1960s and 1970s.

The little flower

The Barrys' Florita vineyard was established in the 1960s and had been owned previously by the renowned Leo Buring. Leo had registered the trademark 'The Florita' in 1946, however, which meant Mark, Peter and John were forced to wait until 2004 when they were able to procure the trademark and use the name of the vineyard on the labels.

The Florita Riesling is made in small batches from the best parcels of fruit selected from individual rows of the vineyard. An underlying floral characteristic is always evident in this Riesling, making the name 'Florita' (which means 'little flower' in Spanish) all the more appropriate. Peter Barry describes it as 'delicate as perfumed rosewater'.

John and Peter,
circa 1985.

Peter and John
in the Armagh
vineyard.

Jim Barry Wines commenced a steady program of expansion that by 1977 grew the company's holdings in the Clare Valley to 600 acres, comprising ten different vineyards spread over four distinctive climatic and geographical sites. The following year an opportunity arose to purchase a property in the Coonawarra region of South Australia, famous for its terra rossa, or red soils. Jim Barry had always had an affection for Coonawarra and its ability to produce excellent Cabernet Sauvignon fruit, so the thirty-three-acre property was purchased and planted with Cabernet Sauvignon. Not your typical farmland, the Coonawarra property was once the Penola cricket ground. The pitch was still intact, so to preserve a piece of cricketing history the vineyard was planted around the cricket pitch and the original pavilion left standing.

Howzat!

THE COVER DRIVE ✽ JIM BARRY

The first wine sourced from the Old Cricket Ground vineyard was the 2001 The Cover Drive Cabernet Sauvignon, which was blended with selected fruit from the company's Clare Valley vineyards and launched in 2003. 'The Cover Drive' honours one of the most beautiful batting strokes in cricket—the flashing cover drive played in defiance of a fierce fast bowler. This rich and approachable red is currently Jim Barry's biggest selling wine.

In keeping with the theme, The First Eleven Cabernet Sauvignon, released four years later and sourced only from the Old Cricket Ground vineyard, honours the legends of Australian cricket—those elite sportsmen who have represented their country at the highest level.

FIRST
750ML XI 2000
ELEVEN

The First Eleven Cabernet Sauvignon
honours the legends of Australian cricket.

John, Peter, Jim and Mark Barry in the winery, circa 1985.

The acquisition of vineyards is based on the Barrys' philosophy of winemaking: own the vineyards to develop the best fruit flavours possible and retain these flavours during winemaking. 'Sourcing fruit from our family-owned vineyards, ensures we have complete and utter control over every stage of production from vine to wine', notes Peter.

> ❛We get the flavours from different soils. We blend all these parcels of fruit together to make a more complex wine.❜
>
> Peter Barry

Indeed, quality, not quantity, is all-important at this winery. Peter notes that their aim is to 'stick to what we do well and keep working to improve it'. 'If something doesn't work in the vineyard we study it, make a few changes and re-evaluate the following year', he says.

The drive to do 'what we do well' does not preclude experimenting with new varieties. In 2008, the company became the first wine producer in Australia to import the popular Greek wine variety, Assyrtiko. Peter is growing Assyrtiko on a small scale and experimenting with the fruit in his own micro-batch winery with a view to eventually planting it in a small vineyard. 'We don't try something new like this very often because it's an expensive risk', explains Peter. However, a visit to the Greek island of Santorini in 2008 and a taste of the wine convinced him it was a worthwhile venture. 'Assyrtiko is to Santorini what Riesling is to Clare', he continues. 'I liked the fresh, crisp, acidic qualities of the wine, as well as its low pH and steely backbone. I particularly liked the unwooded style.'

'My family has been making wine for a long time', Peter says. 'My late father was a pioneer winemaker in Clare and was a passionate believer of keeping with the times and making interesting wine. Like my father, I have an interest in growing grapes that have a future in our region.'

Hand in hand with the Barry family's desire to be innovative is their commitment to ensuring responsible environmental practices. Jim pioneered the use of drip irrigation in Australian vineyards in 1969 after reading about it being used in Israel to grow crops in the desert by placing small amounts of water next

Peter and Tom checking the fermentations and assessing experiments in the micro-batch facility, March 2010.

Mature and refined

The Benbournie Cabernet Sauvignon is a top-end drop and one of Jim Barry's flagship wines. First crafted in 2002, is named after the Benbournie district of the Clare Valley. The district was settled in 1853 by a group of German migrants and originally comprised about fifteen mud huts surrounding a chapel. The settlers were dependent on the local copper mining industry, but after its rapid decline at the end of the nineteenth century the original settlement was abandoned. Nothing is left of it now except for a few ancient vines, and fig and almond trees. The hand-picked fruit for this mature and refined Cabernet Sauvignon is wholly sourced from Jim Barry Wines' Clare Valley vineyards.

to the root zone of a plant. The water comes from dams on the properties and aquifers. Today, the winery recycles water and waste, and uses organic fertilisers. 'It's pretty much traditional viticulture', explains Peter, adding 'I own the vineyard — of course I'll look after it!' Such practices are also a necessity to preserve their vineyards for future generations.

Since Jim passed away, Nancy has continued to play an important and much-valued role in the everyday running of the business. Five of their six children still live in the Clare Valley and all are actively involved in the family business. Peter and John work together as winemaker and viticulturalist, respectively, and, although retired, Mark still calls in to the winery several times a week.

Peter and Jim had worked very closely together. For the last fifteen years of Jim's life, he and Peter shared an office. Peter fondly recalls, 'We used to end each day talking and laughing over a glass of wine. On weekends we'd catch up for a beer or a glass of wine and talk about projects. It was a great relationship'.

Opposite:
A friendly
neighbour in
the Jim Barry
vineyards.

Jim Barry Wines exports to more than twenty-five countries, and about 50 per cent of the winery's total production is exported. Although Peter Barry spends as much time as he can in Clare, the company's international focus requires him to travel extensively, attending wine shows, conducting tastings and master classes, and doing media interviews. He also tours markets in Australia on a regular basis.

Peter is also actively involved in the local wine industry. He has been the longest ever serving chairman of Clare Valley Winemakers Incorporated, and has served as chairman of the South Australian Wine Industry Association Export Committee. He was one of the founding members of the Australian Society of Viticulture and Oenology, and was also instrumental in establishing the annual Clare Valley Gourmet Weekend, which celebrated its twenty-fifth anniversary in 2009.

Jim Barry Wines as a company, and Peter Barry personally, are keen supporters of the community and local businesses. Peter comments, 'You can't help it. All family companies do this. Your kids go to school in the area, play football and other sports. So do

Beats waiting for the kettle to boil!

The Nancy Sparkling Pinot Noir is named in honour of Nancy Barry. 'Growing up, our home was the hub of family entertainment', explains Peter. 'No television, just dinner parties and the obligatory game of cards enjoyed by my mother and her friends every week. There was always an open bottle of sparkling wine at such gatherings. "Beats waiting for the kettle to boil!" my mother would say. To honour Mum I have produced a gentle, sparkling wine.'

The fruit is sourced from the Clare Valley vineyards and only one vintage has been produced. It is made in a delicate, easy drinking style.

The Barry family. From left: Olivia, Sam, Peter, Tom and Sue.

the kids of our employees.' It's near impossible to go anywhere in the town of Clare without seeing prominent signs bearing the name Jim Barry Wines. 'We are proud of the Clare Community and feel privileged to live in and be a part of it', says Peter.

Peter and Sue Barry's three children — Tom, Sam and Olivia — were all captivated by the family business from a young age. The diversity is what appeals the most. Notes Peter, 'The wine business can include viticulture, winemaking, marketing, sales, journalism, engineering, photography and logistics. On some days you're involved in all of these aspects, which makes it exciting … and challenging'.

Tom joined the company as a winemaker in 2009 after graduating from the University of Adelaide (of which Roseworthy College is now part) with a Bachelor of Oenology, making him the third generation of the family to graduate from Roseworthy. Sam is studying commerce at the University of Adelaide, but works at the winery

> ❛It's an honour to work in the same winery as my grandfather did and alongside my father today. ❜
>
> Tom Barry

during vintage. Tom and Sam are also winemakers and proprietors of clos Clare, a boutique winery in Watervale, which they run with the help of their sister Olivia, who is completing a Bachelor of Arts at the University of South Australia. 'Running a boutique winery gives them valuable experience before returning to the family business', notes Peter. Sue Barry is also part of the business, providing support in promotions and travelling and sharing the load, and runs her own conveyancing business in the Clare Valley.

> ❛ It's a wonderful industry to be part of ... I'm obviously very proud that Tom has joined the winemaking team. ❜
>
> Peter Barry

Jim Barry Wines celebrated its fiftieth anniversary, with its third generation all entrenched in the business and determined to build on the strong foundations established by their grandfather. With an innovative approach to viticulture and strong commitment to technological excellence in winemaking, the company is well positioned to thrive for many years to come. Peter Barry looks forward to seeing his children continue the tradition of achieving international recognition by making wines of the highest quality.

Jim Barry, at home in his vineyards.

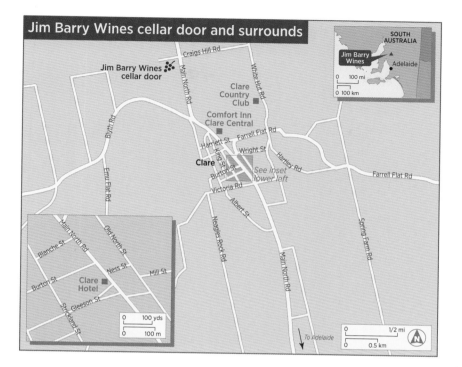

Cellar door

Craigs Hill Rd
Clare SA 5453
t: 08 8842 2261
w: www.jimbarry.com
e: jbwines@jimbarry.com

Opening hours
Monday to Friday: 9 am to 5 pm
Saturday, Sunday and public holidays:
9 am to 4 pm
Closed: Good Friday and Christmas Day

Accommodation options

Clare Country Club
White Hut Rd
Clare SA 5453
t: 08 8842 1060
w: www.countryclubs.com.au/clare
e: clare@countryclubs.com.au

Clare Hotel
244 Main North Rd
Clare SA 5453
t: 08 8842 2816
w: www.clarehotel.com.au
e: scaggs@clarehotel.com.au

Comfort Inn Clare Central
325 Main North Rd
Clare SA 5453
t: 08 8842 2277
w: www.clarecentral.com.au
e: centralmotel@chariot.net.au

Taylors
On the banks of the Wakefield

> ❛At Taylors we really believe "the wine is everything". It is this simple mantra that provides the cornerstone to our winemaking philosophy and is behind every decision taken within the business.❜
>
> Mitchell Taylor, third-generation managing director

Located on the banks of the Wakefield River in the beautiful Clare Valley, Taylors Wines (known as Wakefield Wines in most of the Northern Hemisphere) has established itself in just over four decades as one of Australia's most successful family-owned wine companies. It is the largest family-owned winery in the Clare Valley.

Taylors has built a reputation for wines of delicacy and finesse with outstanding consistency, quality and value. Its success is reflected in the numerous awards it has received at national and international wine competitions. Taylors is recognised within the wine industry as innovative and a leader in environmentally responsible practices.

Before founding Taylors in the Clare Valley, Bill Taylor Senior, together with sons John and Bill, operated hotel and wine-distribution businesses in Sydney. Bill Senior had grown up in the town of Bega, about 400 kilometres south of Sydney. His grandfather, Henry Taylor, had been transported on the last convict ship to sail from England to Australia in 1849. On arrival at Sydney Cove, Henry was given the choice between gaining his freedom on the condition that he move to the new settlement of Bega (this was common practice to assist with the opening up of new settlements) or remaining a convict in Sydney. Naturally, he chose the former.

An intelligent and athletic young man, Bill Senior won a scholarship to attend St Josephs College in Hunters Hill, Sydney. He later won an academic and sporting scholarship to study law at Sydney University. After graduating, he worked as a judge's associate where he met Mary Isabella Whelan, whose family owned and operated numerous hotels. He and Mary later married, and together they operated one of the many Whelan and Taylor pubs before starting their own wine-distribution business.

As wine merchants and publicans, the Taylor family had long held a fascination for wine and winemaking. Bill Senior, John and Bill set up a new business called South Australian Wine Distributors. Through an arrangement with the Clare Valley

Second-generation proprietor of Taylors, Bill Taylor.

Cooperative during the 1960s, they bottled and distributed Clare Valley table wines under the Chateau Clare label.

However, the inspiration for Taylors came from France in 1969 — from a 1966 Chateau Mouton Rothschild from Bordeaux, to be precise. Bill Senior was convinced that it was possible to produce a premium Cabernet Sauvignon in Australia to rival the best from Bordeaux, and made it his personal mission to prove it. It was an ambition that was shared by John and Bill Junior.

The Taylor brothers set about finding an exceptional site in the Clare Valley to realise their dream, with the assistance of Jim Barry and a local real estate agent. In 1969 they purchased a holding of 440 acres, formerly a dairy farm, by the Wakefield River near the town of Auburn. With an altitude of 350 metres, rich terra rossa (red soils), and warm to hot summer days and cool summer nights, it was ideal for growing the 'noble' Cabernet Sauvignon and Shiraz varieties. The Taylors planted 400 acres with Cabernet Sauvignon and forty acres with Shiraz. Mitchell Taylor describes the planting of red table wine varieties by his father (Bill), grandfather and uncle as 'A gutsy move, given that at the time almost everyone else was producing the fortified wines that Australian consumers were familiar with'.

The Taylors winery has a distinctively Spanish influence. The whole winemaking process all the way through to the bottling line takes place in this building.

Taylors' undulating Clare Valley vineyards.

From humble beginnings

The first range of wines launched under the Taylors label in 1973 was an estate-grown and bottled range, which consisted only of a Cabernet Sauvignon and a Shiraz. The awards won by the first vintage of Taylors Cabernet Sauvignon established a reputation for Taylors Estate wines that continues today, with every vintage winning medals at national and international shows.

Taylors Estate Cabernet Sauvignon, still made from the original vineyard, is consistently among Australia's best-selling premium red wines. The range, designed to deliver superb quality and wide appeal, now includes Shiraz, Chardonnay, Pinot Noir, Riesling and, most recently, a Pinot Gris.

Construction of the Taylors winery was completed and equipped with state-of-the-art technology just in time for the first vintage in 1973. The 1973 Taylors Cabernet Sauvignon went on to win gold medals at every national wine show in Australia. A 1973 Hermitage (Shiraz) was also released. Two years later, having worked several vintages and seen his company find its feet and achieve success, Bill Senior passed away at the age of sixty-five.

However, planting the entire property with red varieties most suited to table wines proved to be a problem. Even in the 1970s, Australian consumers still had a preference for fortified and sweet white wines. Then, in 1978, the medical establishment announced that the histamines in

> 'I'd never seen a chainsaw go through a vineyard before. I still remember the tears in my father's eyes as he watched his precious Cabernet vines being chopped.'
>
> Mitchell Taylor

red wine were 'damaging'. The family business was in danger of collapsing after only nine years. Changes had to be made and Bill Taylor wept as large sections of his beloved vineyard planted with Cabernet Sauvignon were grafted over to Riesling.

More of the Cabernet Sauvignon vines were grafted with white varieties, including Crouchen, Gewurztraminer and Chardonnay. 'Just as we were completing the regrafting program the doctors did a 180-degree turn,' recalls Mitchell Taylor, 'claiming that the antioxidants in red wine were good for you. Fortunately, we had only removed about half of our Cabernet vines.'

The first Taylors Estate Riesling was released in 1980. In that same year, Taylors Estate Cabernet Sauvignon won its first international award — a gold medal at the 1980 Bristol Wine Show in London. As a result of the increasing demand for Taylors wines, an adjacent property of 280 acres was purchased in 1981 and quickly planted with Cabernet Sauvignon and Chardonnay. It was named the Promised Land vineyard.

The promised land

The Promised Land vineyard and range of wines are so named because of the promise of what the extra 280 acres could do for the business. The family adopted three seahorses as the company logo after the fossilised remains of three tiny seahorses were found during the excavation of the vineyard dam on the Clare Valley estate. Today, they are found on Taylors and Wakefield labels all over the world.

The first Promised Land release was the 1996 Unwooded Chardonnay, launched in 1998. That was followed by the release of the 1999 Promised Land Shiraz Cabernet in 2000. The contemporary range consists of ten different wines, all crafted from quality fruit sourced from the family's Clare Valley estate and other South Australian regions, including Coonawarra, Padthaway and the Barossa.

Planting Chardonnay in the Broadway vineyard, circa 1989.

In 1989 another adjoining property was purchased, allowing the planting of a further eighty acres of the increasingly popular Chardonnay. This marked the beginning of a period of rapid expansion of the Taylors estate vineyard. During the 1990s the Taylors estate became the largest continuous estate vineyard in the Southern Hemisphere with strategic acquisitions of neighbouring properties, including the historic St Andrews vineyards.

The increased acreage allowed Taylors to extend its range of varieties, with plantings of Merlot and Semillon. By 1995, consumer demand for red wine had surged and Bill Taylor's vision for Cabernet Sauvignon was once again achievable. Vines of Cabernet Sauvignon, Merlot, Shiraz and Riesling were planted in the vineyards.

❛Our heart and soul will always be in the Clare Valley and with Cabernet, the noble grape.❜

Mitchell Taylor

In 1998, the first vintages sourced from the new acquisitions and plantings of the previous decade began to roll out, beginning with the launch of the Promised Land Unwooded Chardonnay and the first Taylors Estate Merlot. The first release of Taylors Semillon and the launch of the premium St Andrews Range took place the following year. In 2000, Bill Taylor stepped down as managing director to take on the new role of chairman.

Through his earlier hotel and wine-distribution businesses, Bill had brought to Taylors an intimate knowledge and appreciation of what wine consumers wanted. Although he is now less involved in the day-to-day operations of the family business, Bill remains a driving force behind the company. His brother John moved on from the business in 1992.

Mitchell Taylor joined the family business in 1988 after completing a Bachelor of Commerce at the University of New South Wales and working as a stockbroker for a number of years. His initial role at Taylors was in financial and export management, but he became increasingly fascinated with winemaking and wanted to be part of that side of the business. Mitchell had always enjoyed working in the cellar and the vineyard during school holidays, and had built up a good basic knowledge of the winemaking process. Keen to learn more, he enrolled in a winemaking course at Charles Sturt University, and while studying part-time completed vintages as winemaker in the Clare Valley.

What's in a name?

Taylors began to spread its wings in 1985 by exporting to the United Kingdom. However, it was forced to export under a different label due to international trademarks held by another Taylor family from Portugal. The name chosen for the new label was Wakefield, after the river that flowed through their estate in the Clare Valley.

The river was named after Eric Gibbon Wakefield, one of the founders of South Australia. 'We liked him because he was a bit of a rogue', explains Mitchell Taylor. 'He'd sell land titles to settlers from the United Kingdom before they set sail for Australia. When they arrived they'd find that the titles were worthless. Wakefield was thrown into prison. Despite this, one of Adelaide's main streets is named after him. Although he was a rogue, I think that in Australia we see him as an entrepreneur and that's what his name on our label represents.'

A labour of love

St Andrews is Taylors' flagship range of premium wines, crafted from carefully selected parcels of fruit that encapsulate the regional uniqueness of the Clare Valley and represent the best of the fruit from the Taylors Estate vineyard. The vines on the St Andrews property are watered from a natural spring and set against the backdrop of a disused winery that was founded in 1896. The old winery is currently used for functions, special tastings and the storage of vineyard equipment. Mitchell describes the St Andrews range as 'a true labour of love'.

The first release of the range in 1999 included a 1996 Cabernet Sauvignon, a 1996 Shiraz, a 1997 Chardonnay and a 1994 Riesling. Since its launch, the range has accumulated an impressive number of awards and is recognised in Australia and internationally for its consistently outstanding quality. Indeed, the Taylor family was disappointed when the 1994 St Andrews Riesling was Runner-up Wine of the Year at *Winestate* magazine's Wine Awards—until they discovered it was second only to the iconic Penfolds Grange.

The first decade of the new millennium consolidated Taylors' reputation for innovation and quality, with more new releases and a rapidly growing collection of trophies and medals. In 2000, frustrated with the amount of premium wine being ruined by cork taint, Taylors and a group of eleven other Clare Valley winemakers announced that they would all be releasing their 2000 Clare Valley Rieslings under the Stelvin screw cap closure. Four years later, Taylors became the first major Australian wine company to bottle all of their wines under the screw cap. Also in 2000 Taylors added to the Promised Land range with the 1999 Shiraz Cabernet.

In 2003, the Taylor family was thrilled when leading Australian wine writer James Halliday recognised Taylors as an example for others to follow. Halliday's assessment noted,

Opposite:
Mitchell Taylor
in the winery's
barrel room.

The old
St Andrews
winery.

'Taylors, the long-established family owned and run winery in South Australia's Clare Valley has consistently over-delivered against expectations during the past few years. In broad terms, this is what the industry has to achieve during the rest of this decade if it is going to maintain its growth and narrow the gap between it and the two giants, France and Italy'.

Today, the winery is managed by Mitchell, who holds the dual roles of managing director and winemaker. He oversees a management team that includes his brothers Justin as director and United States business development manager, and Clinton as director and sales and production project manager.

With a background in commerce, a degree in oenology and a passion for the wine industry, Mitchell is exceptionally well qualified to oversee all aspects of the business. He supervises the whole winemaking process and maintains a hands-on role at the winery. Mitchell is a board member of the Winemakers' Federation of Australia and chairman of the National Alcohol Beverage Industry Council. Through his involvement in these organisations, and Australia's First Families of Wine, Mitchell hopes to influence positive change for Australian wineries and wine consumers.

Justin joined the family business in 1995 after working for three years in sales and service at stockbroker JBWere and six years as an advertising sales representative for Channel Nine. After four years in sales at Taylors, he was appointed national sales manager in 2000.

The United States and Canada are key markets for Taylors' future growth under the Wakefield name, and Justin and his family moved to Atlanta in 2008, where he established the Wakefield United States office and continues to manage the company's export growth in North America. Although currently working in business development, Justin has maintained a keen interest in winemaking following his years of working in the family winery. He has continued his formal wine education, including completion of the Wine Executive program at Monash University, as well as various advanced wine appreciation courses.

> ❝My brothers and I still marvel at the vision shared by our grandfather, father and Uncle John in establishing our winery in the Clare Valley in 1969.❞
>
> Mitchell Taylor

Mitchell Taylor considers awards to be both humbling and worthy of celebration.

Down to earth

The newest range from Taylors Clare Valley estate is the Eighty Acres range, launched in 2007 and named after the traditional eighty-acre blocks in which Bill senior first got his hands dirty in 1969. This range, which currently consists of two reds and two whites, was created to celebrate that heritage. The label features the terra rossa that is the foundation of all of the Taylors Estate vineyards. Mitchell Taylor describes the Eighty Acre range as being 'refreshingly down to earth, as is the heritage that it celebrates'.

The Eighty Acre range is completely carbon-neutral. All carbon emissions associated with the production, sale, consumption and disposal of each product in the range are neutralised by purchasing government approved Verified Emission Reduction units (VERs) and tree planting. 'This is just the beginning', says Mitchell. 'We are custodians of the environment for our children and have a responsibility to leave it in a better condition than we found it.'

Clinton joined the business with Justin in 1995 and was appointed national account director, managing the company's relationships with Australia's wine retailers. In 2007 he was appointed sales and production project manager, making him responsible for a number of aspects of sales and marketing, as well as risk management, winery development, environmental committee and off-premise new business development. Like his elder brothers, Clinton has an inherent interest in winemaking and often pitches in with general winemaking duties at the winery during vintage. 'Growing up we lived in Sydney, and Dad would travel back and forth as the winery was being set up', he recalls. 'When he came home Justin and I would hop into bed and he would tell us stories about foxes on the property and how they would hunt swans on the dam. It conjured up some amazing images of the place in our minds.'

The Taylor brothers have three sisters, Victoria, Angela and Edwina. Their eldest sister, Victoria, worked in the family business in administration after completing an arts degree. Angela had a career in the media and worked for several years at Channel Nine. Edwina also worked in the television industry until she passed away at the age of thirty-eight after a battle with cancer. Taylors has named three vineyards on the St Andrews block after Victoria, Angela and Edwina.

The Taylor boys in the winery. From left: Clinton, Bill, Justin and Mitchell.

From left: Clinton and wife Justine, Bill, Adrienne and husband Mitchell.

Two of a kind

In 2003 the new Jaraman range of wines was released, adding a new dimension to the Taylors portfolio. 'Jaraman' is a local aboriginal word for 'seahorse', the logo adopted by the Taylor family. The wines in the Jaraman range is created from the fusion of exceptional parcels of fruit from two iconic wine regions of Australia.

Each of the single-variety wines in the range is an expression of the vineyards from two different and distinct regions. According to Mitchell Taylor, the aim is to achieve a blend of perfect symmetry and balance that highlights the nuances of two terroirs. The regions from which the fruit is sourced include the Clare Valley, Adelaide Hills, McLaren Vale, Coonawarra, Eden Valley, Margaret River and the Yarra Valley. The varieties currently in the Jaraman range are Cabernet Sauvignon, Shiraz, Pinot Noir, Riesling, Chardonnay and Sauvignon Blanc.

The vineyard team is led by vineyard manager Ken Noak and viticulturalist Colin Hinze. Ken has worked in the Taylors Clare Valley vineyards since he left school at the age of fifteen in 1978. Ken's parents and sisters had all worked in the business. Bill Taylor recalls, 'Ken's father worked with us. His sisters were on the bottling line, our first bottling line when we started. I remember Ken's mother kneeling down in the dirt when we were grafting, showing the others how to do it. That's the spirit, the whole spirit of the business'.

By 1989 Ken had worked his way up to assistant vineyard manager. He was appointed vineyard manager in 1997, and over the years he has seen the property grow from the original 440 acres to almost 1800 acres. He has also seen the vineyards recover from droughts, devastating frosts, and a memorable and destructive hailstorm. Ken is philosophical about the setbacks. 'You know, this is agriculture; you've just got to push on', he says.

Vineyard manager Ken Noak.

Hand-picking in the vineyard.

After more than thirty years, Ken remains passionate about the vineyards. 'I've had that many different roles — that's why I'm still enjoying it', he explains. 'I still think I've got a bit to offer.'

> 'Think of nothing else but the source when crafting a wine, for it is in the vineyard that great wines are made.'
>
> Bill Taylor Senior

The winemaking team at Taylors is led by chief winemaker Adam Eggins, who joined the company in 1999 after graduating from Roseworthy Agricultural College in 1991 and crafting vintage sparkling for Roederer Estate in California. He had also worked at Yellowglen in Ballarat, Mildara Blass in the Barossa Valley and Rothbury Estate in the Hunter Valley. After a tough first vintage due to drought, many of the wines made by Adam have won international trophies and medals. In 2006 he was named *Winestate* magazine's winemaker of the year.

Senior winemaker Helen McCarthy, who joined Taylors in 2002, has also enjoyed considerable recognition for her skills.

Chief winemaker Adam Eggins.

Senior winemaker
Helen McCarthy.

In 2006, the respected United Kingdom author and writer,
Matthew Jukes, recognised her in his Future of the Wine
Industry speech as one of the top young Australian winemakers
to watch out for. In 2007 and 2008 she was named a finalist for
the Wine Society Young Winemaker of the Year award, and in
2008 was awarded the Kemeny's Medal by *Gourmet Traveller
WINE magazine* for Australia's most outstanding up-and-coming
winemaker. The Kemeny's Medal is one of only three major
prizes that make up the annual *Gourmet Traveller WINE* awards
and has been won by many of Australia's finest established and
emerging winemakers.

In recent years, Taylors has adopted an environmental action
plan, which includes a number of key initiatives to ensure that
it functions in a considered and responsible manner in each
environment in which it operates, including its head office in
Sydney. One of those initiatives is the development of the 100 per
cent carbon-neutral Eighty Acres range. Others include a water
recycling plant, which recycles all waste water from the winery
and bottling plant; composting all organic waste produced in the
winemaking process; vineyard mulching with compost from the
property, local farmers and other third parties; revegetation of the

Carbon-rich compost is spread in the vineyard to condition and improve the soil.

Wakefield River; the reintroduction of sheep into the vineyards to control winter grasses and weeds; and using eco-mapping, a system that helps to design and prioritise environmental problems and issues for action.

To ensure the future success of its family business, the Taylor family has developed a constitution that reflects its values and sets out the processes and conditions of succession from one generation to the next. Mitchell steadfastly believes that working for the family business is a privilege that must be earned and not a right. He remembers from his early days with the company overhearing one of the older employees saying, 'Remember, he's a Taylor and you have to treat him differently. There's one rule for the Taylors and another for the rest of us'. Mitchell was shocked by what he had heard, and states that today, 'Non-family employees know that we have mechanisms in place to ensure that there is no nepotism'.

> ❛Our family has a passion to run the business the right way, to do something we love and do the best we can. We instil this approach in our staff and they really get a buzz out of working in a family business. ❜
>
> Mitchell Taylor

Opposite:
A gnarled vine.

There is an elected family council that assures best practice for a family business and also deals with any family conflicts that might affect the performance of the business.

Mitchell is acutely aware of his family's heritage. A blend of old-world estate philosophy and new-world winemaking innovation, combined with an almost fanatical attention to detail and obsession with quality in all aspects of the business, has kept his grandfather's dream alive. According to Mitchell, the future of Taylors lies in exploring and expanding on new and existing opportunities in the international market, and 'taking our family-owned business to the world'.

Glassware and wine

Choosing the right glassware can really add to the enjoyment, as well as the flavour, of wine. Generally, glassware is differentiated by wine style or grape, with some manufacturers having a specific glass for every varietal.

The glassware for red wine allows a generous amount to be poured, while still leaving plenty of air in the glass. This heightens the sensation of the wine's aromas, an important factor when tasting wine. White wine glassware is generally smaller and narrower. It directs the wine to the centre of the tongue, diminishing the acidic flavours that are tasted at the sides of the tongue. So you'll enjoy a crisp Riesling or Sauvignon Blanc in a narrower glass. The same is true of sparkling wine.

Wide-rimmed, shallower glassware favours Chardonnay or Pinot Noir, which typically have lower tannins and lower acid levels. Shiraz is best served in larger capacity glassware with a narrower rim to minimise the tannins. Cabernet Sauvignon, often the most tannic of reds, also benefits from a larger capacity glass, though with a narrower rim than Shiraz glassware. Don't hold the glass by the bowl—place your fingers around the stem or base so that your body temperature won't affect the serving temperature of the wine.

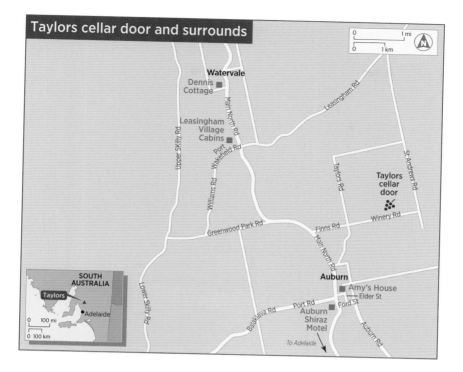

Cellar door

Taylors Rd
Auburn SA 5451
t: 08 8849 1111
w: www.taylorswines.com.au
e: cdsales@taylorswines.com.au

Opening hours
Monday to Friday: 9 am to 5 pm
Saturday and public holidays: 10 am to 5 pm
Sunday: 10 am to 4 pm
Closed: Christmas Day and Good Friday

Accommodation options

Amy's House
Corner Church and Elder Sts
Auburn SA 5451
t: 0408 492 281
w: www.amyshouse.com.au
e: quiet@amyshouse.com.au

Auburn Shiraz Motel
Main North Rd
Auburn SA 5451
t: 08 8849 2125
w: www.auburnshirazmotel.com.au
e: admin@auburnshirazmotel.com.au

Dennis Cottage
St Vincent St
Auburn SA 5451
t: 08 8843 0048
w: www.denniscottage.com.au
e: neil@denniscottage.com.au

Leasingham Village Cabins
94 Main North Rd
Leasingham SA 5452
t: 08 8843 0136
w: www.leasinghamvillagecabins.com.au
e: foxlee@rbe.net.au

Howard
Park
New blood

I'm proud of what we've achieved in such a short time and proud that our children are taking on the mantle.

Amy Burch, marketing director, Howard Park

*H*oward Park is the youngest of Australia's First Families of Wine and the only representative of the Western Australian wine regions. This is not surprising, however, as the establishment of vineyards for the production of premium wines only began in the Margaret River and Great Southern regions in the 1970s.

Established by John Wade in 1986, Howard Park began humbly, with no winery and no vineyards of its own. When Amy and Jeff Burch joined John as partners in 1993, the company was buying grapes to make wine in a shed in the town of Denmark (about three and a half hours' drive from Margaret River), producing a modest three tonnes of Riesling and Cabernet

Labels from Howard Park's first vintage in 1986.

Sauvignon. Since then, Jeff and Amy Burch have built Howard Park into Western Australia's largest family-owned wine company, with a reputation for producing premium wines of distinct regional character.

Howard Park now boasts two architecturally distinctive wineries, several vineyards and a loyal band of growers — almost all of them in the wine regions of Margaret River and Great Southern. As well as the Howard Park label, the business produces the MadFish range of wines and, in a joint venture with Pascal Marchand of Burgundy, the Marchand and Burch range.

Beginning with its first vintage in 1986, the fruit used to produce Howard Park Riesling has been sourced from premier vineyards in Great Southern, which are ideally suited to Riesling. The fruit used to produce Howard Park Cabernet Sauvignon is sourced from a handful of the oldest vineyards in Margaret River and the Mount Barker subregion of the Great Southern. Both the Cabernet Sauvignon and Riesling have been recognised as some of the best in the world, winning numerous medals and trophies within Australia and internationally. Howard Park Cabernet Sauvignon is a record-breaker, attracting record bids at wine auctions.

The Cabernet Sauvignon remains the flagship of Howard Park.

Having already won multiple awards at the Concours Mondial de Bruxelles (including gold medals and the Best Red Wine trophy), it was relabelled Howard Park Abercrombie Cabernet Sauvignon in 2005.

Jeff Burch's interest in winemaking can be traced back to his passion for surfing. As a youngster growing up in the Adelaide Hills, within easy reach of some of South Australia's surf beaches, Jeff learned to surf and it quickly became his favourite pastime. He was never a beer drinker, instead developing an appreciation for fine wine, of which there was plenty in South Australia. That combination of surfing and his love of wine would eventually lead him and his family to Margaret River.

Jeff moved to Western Australia with his parents in the late 1960s and met Amy at university in Perth in the 1970s. The couple spent many weekends on the south-west coast, visiting different beaches, including Three Bears, The Farm, Injidup and Yallingup. In later years they would often set off early in

The jewel in the crown

Abercrombie is the jewel in the crown for Howard Park. Named after Jeff Burch's great-grandfather, Walter Abercrombie, this highly praised wine continues to win Australian and international awards. Jeff proudly points out that Abercrombie is 'produced from the top 2 per cent of available Cabernet Sauvignon, and then only in the years when grapes of extraordinarily high quality are available'.

The Abercrombie Cabernet Sauvignon is one of Australia's most collected wines. Langton's Classification of Australian Wine rates the Abercrombie as 'excellent', which denotes 'high-performing wines of exquisite quality'. The wine has also received many top ratings from leading wine writers, including James Halliday and Robert Parker.

Jeff Burch surfing at Margaret River.

John Wade and Jeff Burch in 1996.

the morning with their young family to drive down to Margaret River where Jeff would surf while Amy and the children enjoyed time on the beach.

In the 1980s they built a home in Yallingup, north of Margaret River, so the family could spend more time away from the city and Jeff could spend more time surfing. At the same time Margaret River was beginning to establish itself as a wine region, so when the surf wasn't up, Jeff and Amy pursued their shared passion for regional wines. They joined tasting groups and began to collect premium wines. At tastings in the newly established vineyards they met and became friends with some of Western Australia's other wine pioneers, including Kevin and Di Cullen, Vanya Cullen and John Brocksopp of Leeuwin Estate. The Burches would often invite them to Yallingup to drink — and talk about — wine and enjoy Amy's cooking.

Jeff and Amy bought a pastoral property in Margaret River in 1988 (destined to become Howard Park Leston) with the vision of creating vineyards and a winery to produce their own wines. This move was inspired by experts, such as the internationally acclaimed Dr John Gladstone, who identified similarities between Margaret River and the Bordeaux region of France, and was influential in promoting grape-growing in Western Australia. Featuring the Willyabrup Creek, a run-down Group Settlement cottage and some woolsheds, the Leston property needed plenty of tender loving care. One of the first things the Burches did was plant a line of trees to form a spectacular driveway.

A chance meeting with John Wade led Amy and Jeff to cement their growing commitment to wine production by becoming partners in Howard Park in 1993. They purchased French oak barrels, a modern press and tanks, and established a winery in a rented shed at Denmark Agricultural College in the Great Southern wine region, where the 1994 vintage was completed.

A new label is born

Howard Park's MadFish label is distinctively Western Australian. The artwork was originally designed by the late Maxine Fumagelli, an Indigenous artist of the Noongar people of Western Australia's south-west. The design reflects the Indigenous Australian understanding of the unity between land, sea, stars, animals and people. All of these elements are portrayed on the label.

The MadFish name comes from Madfish Bay, an inlet fifteen kilometres from the town of Denmark. The traditional Noongar people believe that the bay's tranquillity is broken when two tides meet. The fish, confused by the changing currents, can be observed leaping into the air as if in a state of madness. The traditional Indigenous water turtle design on the label is a symbol of perseverance and tolerance—some of the characteristics displayed by the fish in Madfish Bay.

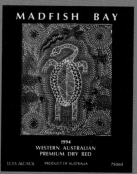

The popular MadFish range is made from cool-climate varieties, and the wines are well known for their pure, fresh and clean characteristics. The first MadFish release was in 1992 with the MadFish Premium White, followed by the MadFish Premium Red in 1993. Today, the MadFish portfolio includes Riesling, Sauvignon Blanc, Semillon, Shiraz and Pinot Noir.

Leading Australian wine writer James Halliday awarded a rare 19.5 points out of 20 for the 1994 Howard Park Cabernet Merlot in his annual *Wine Companion*, which was a huge turning point for the company. By this time a new range of Howard Park wines with an emphasis on enjoyment, fruit flavour and drinkability had been released under the MadFish label.

Jeff views MadFish as a different style for a different market and hopes it will bring the Howard Park label to the attention of a new group of consumers. He explains, 'The Howard Park wines are of super-high quality and exceptionally well balanced; the best that I can make of each variety with no expense spared. The MadFish style is approachable and offers very high quality for the price point. The labels complement each other and allow us to reach a diverse market'.

In 1996 Amy and Jeff purchased Parkhead, a rural property not far from Madfish Bay and just two kilometres from Denmark. From modest beginnings in borrowed and rented sheds, the Burches began to realise their vision, planning a brand new winery and cellar door for Howard Park. The winery, elevated and surrounded by the iconic, towering Western Australian Marri and Jarrah trees, was completed the following year.

The Leston vineyard at Margaret River at sunrise.

Inside the cellar door at the Denmark winery.

Also in 1996 the first vines were planted at the Margaret River property purchased by Amy and Jeff in 1988. They named it the Leston vineyard after Jeff's father and mentor. The vines were planted by Jeff's brother, David, a former principal dancer with the Australian Ballet.

Until 1999 all wines under the Howard Park and MadFish labels were made from externally sourced fruit. The first reasonable crop from the Leston vineyard was harvested in 1999. The whole family took part in this small harvest as Leston, who was ill, wanted to share the moment of harvesting the first fruit from the vineyard bearing his name with his children and grandchildren.

The last few years of the twentieth century saw two landmarks in Howard Park's history. Senior winemaker and business partner John Wade left Howard Park in 1998 and was replaced by Michael Kerrigan as senior winemaker. In 1999 the Single Vineyard series was launched with the first release of the Leston Cabernet Sauvignon from Margaret River and the Scotsdale Shiraz from the Great Southern. This range was extended in 2000 to a Shiraz and Cabernet from both regions.

Leston Burch after a day in the vineyard.

Howard Park opened its second winery and cellar door, built on the highest point of the Leston vineyard, in 2000. The Leston winery and cellar door in Margaret River has spectacular panoramic views over the vineyards and adjacent valley.

An extraordinary pair

Howard Park Leston Cabernet Sauvignon and Leston Shiraz are named in honour of Jeff's father and are sourced exclusively from the Leston vineyard. The vines in this vineyard are given extraordinary attention. Canopy management is designed to maximise exposure of the fruit to sunlight and yields are kept low to achieve concentration in the grapes. Grapes are harvested according to flavour with little regard for analytical data. After fermentation the wines are matured in French oak barriques for about eighteen months. Both Leston wines have been acclaimed by critics in Australia and internationally. In 2007, the 2004 Leston Shiraz was awarded a gold medal at the prestigious Concours Mondial de Bruxelles wine competition.

HOWARD PARK
LESTON
MARGARET RIVER
WESTERN AUSTRALIA
2004
SHIRAZ

14.5% VOL.
WINE OF AUSTRALIA FROM WESTERN AUSTRALIA   750ml

It is a tourist attraction in its own right having received acclaim for its unique architecture, winning the commercial category award from the Royal Australian Institute of Architects in 2000.

Reflecting Amy's Asian heritage and passion for design, the design and orientation of the Leston winery and cellar door combines contemporary Australian ingenuity with traditional Feng Shui principles. The building was constructed under the direct supervision of Professor Cheng Jian-Jun of the Department of Architecture at the South China University of Technology.

'I knew I would never have the opportunity to build something special like this again', says Amy. 'I wanted it to harmonise with the landscape as anyone with Chinese origin wishes to do, and working with architects and Feng Shui experts was very interesting as we worked towards our goal of synergy with the environment combined with the best of modern Australian architecture.' The new winery and cellar door opened on 6 February 2000, an auspicious date for such an event according to the Chinese calendar.

The Howard Park winery and cellar door at Margaret River. The design combines traditional Feng Shui principles with contemporary Australian ingenuity.

Amy Burch pouring at Howard Park's Margaret River cellar door.

A golden range from the West

The success of the MadFish portfolio inspired the development of the new range of premium wines under the MadFish Gold Turtle label. The first vintage of this series was the 2004 Gold Turtle Shiraz, made exclusively from fruit grown in the Frankland River subregion of Great Southern.

The Gold Turtle range has since expanded to include Pinot Noir from Mount Barker, Tempranillo from Geographe, and Cabernet Sauvignon and Chardonnay from Margaret River. Each of the wines in the Gold Turtle range is a true varietal expression sourced from specific sites in the Great Southern or Margaret River regions.

Amy and Jeff saw potential in the Great Southern region for the supply of quality fruit for their premium Cabernet Sauvignon and Riesling. They began to search for a suitable property and, after talking to local farmers, viticulturists and other vineyard owners, found a sheep station that fitted the bill near the foothills of the Porongurup Range, near Mount Barker.

They purchased the property in 2004 with the intention of establishing a super-premium cool-climate vineyard with plantings of Chardonnay, Riesling, Sauvignon Blanc and Pinot Noir in the ancient ironstone soils. Reaching 380 metres above sea level and receiving less extreme summer temperatures than the rest of the region, this is one of the highest vineyard sites in Western Australia. The vineyard, which was named the Mount Barrow vineyard, first produced grapes in 2008 and has already become the core source of fruit for the Howard Park Riesling and the Sauvignon Blanc. Experimental plots have also added complexity to fruit sourcing, not least with the elusive Pinot Noir.

Always keen to sharpen his viticultural knowledge and skills, Jeff Burch has been a frequent visitor to France. On one of those visits in 1991 he met winemaker and biodynamic ambassador Pascal Marchand. They instantly connected through a mutual passion for Pinot Noir. Born in Montreal, Pascal is renowned in wine circles for his success in managing the vineyards of Burgundy's Premier Cru 'Clos-des-Epeneaux' in the village of Pommard. He transformed the little-known vineyards into the most sought after in Burgundy and eventually took over from his employer Comte Armand as winemaker.

> ❛We have a simple philosophy: premium wine can only come from excellent fruit. Simply put, we go to wherever the fruit grows best.❜
>
> Jeff Burch

Jeff and Pascal have since established a close working relationship, and in 2007 a new Howard Park label — Marchand and Burch — was launched with the release of a Chardonnay, Pinot Noir and Shiraz, produced in Western Australia, and a Meursault, Gevrey-Chambertin and Grand Cru Chambertin-Clos de Bèze, produced in Burgundy. 'I've really enjoyed the joint venture', notes Jeff. 'He comes out here to make wine with me and I go to France to make wine with him.'

The cool-climate Mount Barrow vineyard.

Jeff Burch and Pascal Marchand.

At first Jeff wondered why a renowned winemaker such as Pascal, having made Pinot from the Grand Cru vineyards in Burgundy, would be interested in coming to Western Australia and regions not known for Pinot. Pascal's explanation reveals an adventurous streak. 'In Burgundy we have 500 years of history', he says. 'Everything has been done. Here I am, a Frenchman, having the opportunity to work with [Jeff] in a brand-new area in a brand-new vineyard setting, putting in our own clones and laying it all out ourselves. I'm a pioneer and an explorer. I find that fantastic, exciting and invigorating — and I hope that we are successful at it.'

'Biodynamics brings you closer to the forces of nature and helps you observe nature better, work with nature and not try to control it or work against it.'

Pascal Marchand

Pascal Marchand has been instrumental in introducing sustainable organic and biodynamic practices to Howard Park's vineyards in both Great Southern and Margaret River. Some of the initiatives taken

A new direction

In 2009 Howard Park launched the MadFish Sideways range of wines. The Sideways range showcases wines from specially chosen vineyards in Margaret River. The name 'Sideways' was inspired by vineyards planted with north–south orientation, perpendicular to the original MadFish vineyard plantings, which were planted in an east–west orientation. The Sideways range includes Cabernet Sauvignon Merlot, Sauvignon Blanc Semillon and Shiraz, and is produced using sustainable and organic viticultural practices. Cartons are made from 100 per cent recycled material and lightweight bottles, which provides significant savings in energy and water, as well as reduced emissions during transportation.

by Howard Park to improve sustainability in the vineyards and winery include reducing water consumption, installing a waste-water recycling plant, composting all grape waste, reducing dependence on synthetic fertilisers and pesticides, adopting biodynamic practices and organic methods throughout the vineyard operations, introducing sheep to control weeds in the vineyards, and reducing the use of heavy machinery through the vines to avoid compacting the soil.

In addition, Howard Park, like many other Australian wineries, is a signatory of the National Packaging Covenant. It has made a commitment to minimise the impact on the environment from the disposal of used packaging, to conserve resources through improved design and production processes, and to facilitate the re-use and recycling of used packaging materials.

MARCHAND&BURCH

CLOS DE BÊZE
2007

The Burch family are the first Australians to gain ownership in the production of a French Burgundian Grand Cru.

⚜ ⚜ ⚜

Amid the success, Howard Park has had some serious setbacks, one of the most memorable for Jeff and Amy being the 2006 vintage. It was a very cool summer, as Jeff recalls. '[We] waited and waited and waited. The leaves started falling off, and of our top five reds, we only produced one. It was financially disastrous. We thought it was all over for Howard Park.' Jeff contends that to release inferior wine in 2006 would have done a lot of damage to the brand's credibility and the loyalty of customers who expect an excellent product. 'We chose to endure the financial pain of 2006 and have been rewarded with great vintages in subsequent years.'

> ‘We have to keep improving—everyone else is doing better things too. You can't stand still or they will pass you by.’
>
> Jeff Burch

In 2007 Tony Davis joined Howard Park as chief winemaker when Michael Kerrigan left to launch his own business career as a partner in a new venture at Hay Shed Hill, not far from the Leston vineyard. Tony had previously completed vintages at other Australian wineries including Yalumba, Plantagenet, Brown Brothers and Millbrook, as well as in France and the United States. Genevieve Mann, a viticulture and oenology graduate of Curtin University in Western Australia, also joined Howard Park in 2007. She was appointed Margaret River winemaker, having had winemaking experience in France, her native South Africa, California and McLaren Vale in South Australia.

According to Jeff Burch, the challenge facing Howard Park now is to keep improving. 'We benchmark ourselves by tasting the best wines from around the world and avoid resting on our laurels. You can't make internationally acclaimed wines unless you know what's happening in the international market.'

Today one-third of Howard Park's grapes come from its own vineyards. The remainder are sourced from a loyal band of growers, almost all from the Margaret River and Great Southern regions.

A huge effort goes into finding the right fruit for the wine. Amy explains, 'The advantage of sourcing grapes from contract

Chief winemaker Tony Davis with Natalie Burch
at the Margaret River winery.

Genevieve Mann,
winemaker at
Margaret River.

growers is that we can always source the very best fruit. We chase it and we learn about it. We don't have to try to change our own fruit into something that it's not'.

Andrew Milbourne, winemaker at the Denmark winery.

The Howard Park vineyards are managed by Jeff's younger brother, David P Burch. He is assisted by David Botting, chief viticulturalist, known to some as the Grape Doctor. David came to Howard Park with more than thirty years' experience consulting to vineyards all over Australia. At first quite skeptical about biodynamic practices, his visits to Burgundy to study Pascal Marchand's approach to natural, holistic viticultural management have convinced him of their benefits. Jeff's sister, Lesley Scogna, also has a role in the company as brand ambassador, developing and maintaining relationships with retail customers and restaurants, a role that suits her bubbly personality.

Jeff is chief executive officer, overseeing all aspects of production with his teams. Amy is marketing director and oversees the cellar door. The Burches are both proud that their two older children are now directly involved in the business with them.

Their daughter, Natalie, formally joined Howard Park in 2005 after many years of helping out. She has the challenging task of managing operations at the Margaret River site, including the office, cellar door, stock control and exports.

> ❛ In an increasingly globalised wine market people are looking for the stories, the sense of individuality and place, the family history and a taste that's different. That's where the future lies. ❜
>
> Jeff Burch

Their son, David, known as David W to distinguish him from Jeff's brother, has worked in multiple areas of the business since the age of fourteen — from the cellar door and the vineyard

David P Burch,
vineyard
manager,
and David
Botting, chief
viticulturalist,
in the Leston
vineyard at
Margaret River.

to winemaking and running dispatch. He formally joined the business in 2006 as part of the sales and marketing team.

The youngest Burch, Richard, has recently finished studying marketing at university. He plans to gain experience working elsewhere first, and the rest of the family is confident that he will have the skills to make a significant contribution if he decides later to join Howard Park.

Natalie remembers doing all sorts of jobs at the winery when she and her brothers were growing up. 'We were dragged in to do anything — odd jobs in the cellar door, tastings at random shows, handing out leaflets, taking phone calls in the office, chasing cows out of the vineyards and helping to put out the occasional fire.' David enjoyed the trips to Europe. 'Growing up, we travelled to Europe where we were exposed to the cultures, food and wines of Italy and France. On a houseboat trip through Burgundy we stopped off in villages — Dad would check out the wine shops and we all went to little cafes where we sampled the cuisine and tried to speak French.'

'As a family', says Amy, 'we are always talking about wine, drinking it, enjoying it with food and discussing strategies for the wineries and vineyards. Our children were never forced into

David W (front right) with the Denmark winemaking crew working the 2009 Howard Park vintage at the vibrating grape-sorting table.

the business, but were surrounded by the conversation. They used to complain on longer trips, though.' She remembers the many winery visits with all three children in the back of the car complaining, 'Do we have to go to another winery?' and 'Not another winery!'.

Amy, Natalie and David W all agree that Jeff is the driver of Howard Park. They describe him as tenacious, single-minded, demanding and blustering — as Amy says with affection 'rather like a bulldozer'. Amy is the creative member of the family, 'Great with people, communication and relationships and has the energy to make things happen. She's like a whirlwind'. Natalie is the 'Jack of all trades' who resolves daily issues with 'a wicked sense of humour'.

On reflection, Amy proudly describes the range of wines under the Howard Park, MadFish and Marchand and Burch labels as unparalleled in south-western Australia. The range includes seven Rieslings, three Sauvignon Blancs, five Chardonnays, six Pinot Noirs, five Shirazes and six Cabernets. Jeff is quick to add, 'They are all good. There are no dogs in our kennel'.

> ❛We have worked towards establishing Howard Park as a premium family wine company. Our success will be measured by the work we do now for future generations.❜
>
> Jeff Burch

The staff at Howard Park are an integral part of its success story. As Natalie says, 'They all feel like they have input. We regularly ask for their thoughts on issues. It's a team effort and everyone should be part of the decision-making process. This is crucial to the success of such a complex activity.' Jeff adds, 'The staff are on this journey with us. As a family, you have to have a huge passion and long-term commitment to making really good wine and working with your staff. You fall in love with this industry, you fall in love with your people. This is the heart and soul — not the dollars'.

Giving back to the region is a top priority and Howard Park has become well known for its sponsorship of events such as the Logie Awards, Tropfest (with screenings of winning films at both of the Howard Park vineyards), the Sydney Writer's Festival and the Pascall Prize for Critical Writing. Readings are regularly held in the vineyards with leading authors such as Alexander McCall Smith and Li Cunxin. Concerts also feature in the busy Howard Park events calendar.

The Burch family. From left: Jeff, Richard, Natalie, David and Amy.

The Burch family represents the 'new blood' of Australia's First Families of Wine. They are the newest pioneers in a relatively young region. Jeff explains, 'We have the long-term vision, the passion and the determination to leave a sustainable legacy for the next generation, and the next. We are doing what some winemaking families were doing more than 100 years ago'. As Amy notes, 'We are creating history now'.

The growth and development of Howard Park is exciting to see. The challenges are different from those faced by Australia's early winemaking pioneers. In the early years of the twenty-first century there are new challenges. The industry is established, competition abounds and there are just too many grapes. To survive under these conditions is a huge challenge, in fact it is almost impossible. Yet, Howard Park is defying the odds — not only surviving but truly flourishing.

Enjoying vintage wine

There is much pleasure to be had from drinking correctly aged wine. Before you go out and make the all-important purchase for long-term cellaring, it's important to work out what it is you're looking for.

Think about which varieties you like to drink and how long you want to age the wine before drinking. It's not a lot of fun aging wine if you choose a style that doesn't age well or that you don't enjoy drinking. To give you some idea, generally, Rieslings will age longer than Chardonnay, while Cabernet Sauvignon and Shiraz will age longer than Pinot Noir.

To assist in your decision-making, build a relationship with knowledgeable retailers and use the internet to research your preferred varieties. Pick a focus for your cellar, such as Margaret River Cabernet Sauvignon, and talk to the wineries—they can advise you on how long their wines will age.

Visit the region you decide to focus on and get involved with some of the wineries. You will find there's nothing quite like sitting down to enjoy a bottle of wine you bought on a visit to a winery ten years earlier.

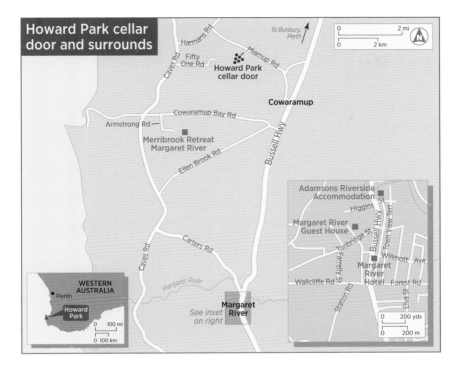

Cellar door

Miamup Rd
Cowaramup WA 6284
t: 08 9756 5200
w: www.howardparkwines.com.au
e: margaretriver@hpw.com.au

Opening hours
Monday to Sunday: 10 am to 5 pm
Closed: Good Friday and Christmas Day

Accommodation options

Adamsons Riverside Accommodation
71 Bussell Hwy
Margaret River WA 6285
t: 08 9757 2013
w: www.adamsonsriverside.net.au

Margaret River Guest House
22 Valley Rd
Margaret River WA 6285
t: 08 9757 2349
w: www.margaretriverguesthouse.com.au
e: info@margaretriverguesthouse.com.au

Margaret River Hotel
125 Bussell Hwy
Margaret River WA 6285
t: 08 9757 2655
w: www.margaretriverhotel.com.au
e: bookings@margaretriverhotel.com.au

Merribrook Retreat Margaret River
Armstrong Rd (off Cowaramup Bay Rd)
Margaret River WA 6284
t: 08 9755 5599
w: www.merribrook.com.au
e: info@merribrook.com.au

Epilogue

The twelve inaugural wineries of Australia's First Families of Wine are all family owned. They all produce iconic wines that have stood the test of time, are custodians of some of Australia's oldest vineyards and are committed to environmental best practice. In addition, they are, or have been, active in wine industry bodies and are committed to export markets. But their similarities run much deeper than that.

The founders of these wineries were ambitious, resourceful and determined, and possessed unshakable self-belief and an astounding work ethic. Some could also be described as gung-ho adventurers and larrikins. They were all risk-takers in one way or another. Some of them travelled across the world to a country vastly different from their homeland. Others were ridiculed for planting vineyards in locations thought to be totally unsuitable for viticulture, while still others started with nothing but their clothes and a few coins.

Subsequent generations also have much in common. Almost all have grown up in and around the vineyards and wineries. As toddlers they played in the cellars and as teenagers they earned pocket money by working in the family business. Some of them rebelled, swearing that they would never again work with their parents or in the wine industry. Yet, more than a few of the rebels returned and absorbed themselves completely into the business. They have seen the ups and downs, and the blood, sweat and tears of their parents and grandparents. There is no substitute for this kind of education.

Over the generations, the members of Australia's First Families of Wine have served up some colourful characters. There's the cheerful, debonair, game-hunting adventurer Walter Smith of Yalumba and his grandson, Robert Hill Smith, who has inherited his family's passion for thoroughbred racing; the gruff and 'larger than life' Murray Tyrrell and his reputedly pugnacious son Bruce; the shrewd man with the booming voice, JJ McWilliam, and his good-humoured grandson, Don, who worked his way up from bottle hand to chairman; the elegant, energetic and ambitious John Francis Brown and his only son, John Charles, who steered the company through depression, war and drought with gritty determination; and, more recently, the much-loved and respected d'Arry Osborn of d'Arenberg and his colourful, creative and daring son Chester. These are just a few of many.

These wine companies have also had some quiet achievers, such as stockbroker turned winemaker Mitchell Taylor, and Peter Barry, who just wants to let his wine 'do the talking'. And there have been, and still are, some great partnerships — extraordinary winemakers Eric Purbrick and his grandson Alister of Tahbilk; father-and-son team Vittorio and Deen De Bortoli who took their wine company to the top despite arguing every step of the way; creative husband-and-wife team Stephen and Prue Henschke as winemaker and viticulturist, respectively; brothers Malcolm and Colin Campbell, also a viticulturist and winemaker partnership; and husband-and-wife team Jeff and Amy Burch, both perfectionists in their respective fields of winemaking and marketing and design.

The longevity of all family-owned wine companies depends on characters such as these, generation after generation. They endure the setbacks that all who live off the land are faced with, staring them down defiantly. They have experienced vintages doomed by the whims of nature — the frosts, hail, drought, floods and bushfires, and infestations of insects such as phylloxera — and they have all bounced back. Now they are challenged with problems including climate change, grape surpluses and a global economic crisis. John Graham Brown, third-generation winemaker at Brown Brothers, takes a view typical of the twelve families when he notes, 'We've had our fair share of setbacks, but each setback has resulted in a giant step forward'.

Knowledge and skills are passed on from one generation to the next — usually beginning from a very young age — along with some insight into the business's long-term vision and how to deal with the challenges. There is also an immense pride in each generation when they see their sons and daughters officially become part of the family business. Equally, the new generation is proud of what previous generations have achieved.

There is much more to a family-owned winery than the vineyards, the buildings, the equipment and the wine. Stephen Henschke explains it well. 'The true value of a multi-generation family business is much more than its financial value. There is the toil, the perseverance and the belief in what previous generations did. You know you wouldn't be here if it wasn't for the blood, sweat and tears that they went through to make it all happen.' About his own family business he comments, 'What we've got is something with unimaginable value, a truly beautiful historic property full of family tradition and heritage'.

There is a common belief among the wine companies in this book that the land should be carefully nurtured and left for the next generation in a condition as good as, or better than, it was found. They all consider themselves custodians of the land and are determined to leave their legacy for the next generation.

All of the members of Australia's First Families of Wine are determined that their businesses will remain in family hands. Some of the families have planned for the future by putting succession policies in place, defining conditions under which new generations can enter the family business. Brown Brothers, for example, requires that new generations work for at least four years outside the family business before joining the company full-time. Succession plans are designed to protect the long-term interests of the business.

One of the unanticipated benefits of the collective of twelve families has been the interaction between the new generations at Australia's First Families of Wine functions. Although some of the families have known each other for many years, the exposure of the younger generations to each other has been limited. As Jeff Burch of Howard Park explains, 'AFFW is a brilliant networking platform for the younger generations. They will help and inspire each other. It encourages those not yet directly involved with their family businesses to step up as members of their family'.

The families that make up Australia's First Families of Wine are sending a clear message to the world that Australian wine can be interesting, compelling and full of personality, not unlike the people who make them. What is more, they are also demonstrating that the Australian wine industry has a fascinating history, a family heritage and an innovative and adventurous streak. Indeed, families are the heart and soul of Australia's wine industry.

Glossary

acidity a quality of wine that gives it a sharp, crisp taste due to the presence of natural fruit acids. Acidity also contributes to the successful maturing of wine. Too much acid makes a wine too sharp, while too little can make it dull and flat.

apera the Australian name for the fortified wine formerly known as sherry. *See* sherry.

appellation the legally protected name given to a wine region. Regulations and terminology vary from country to country. In Australia regions are defined by Australian geographic indications (GIs) as part of the Register of Protected Names.

barriques wooden barrels of a style that originated in Bordeaux, France. Barriques have a capacity of 225 litres.

basket press a wooden basket-shaped receptacle used to separate juice from skins by squeezing. It is believed to be the first mechanical device used for this purpose. A plate is lowered onto the grapes in the press and the juice flows out through openings in the basket. For red wines, basket pressing occurs near the end of fermentation, once the desirable tannin extraction is complete.

biodynamic a method of horticulture that is ecologically sound and sustainable and excludes the use of artificial fertilisers and chemicals in favour of natural substances such as manure and compost.

botrytis a fungus that, if conditions are suitable, grows and feeds on grapes, leaving them dehydrated, shrivelled and with increased sugar concentration. The affliction is called noble rot. Unripened grapes are ruined by botrytis, but some ripe botrytis-infected grapes can be used to make sweet dessert wines.

bush vines free-standing vines grown without a trellis or wires.

canopy the uppermost part of grape vines, dominated by leaves.

canopy management the management of the canopy, including selective leaf removal, trimming and pruning. Good canopy management controls the amount of direct sunlight falling on the foliage and fruit, improves air circulation and controls diseases.

Chablis a style of white wine named for the Chablis appellation in the region of Burgundy, France and made from Chardonnay grapes. It was also known in Australia as White Burgundy. The name 'Chablis', like those of 'Burgundy', 'Champagne' and other European appellations, are no longer used in Australia.

character a tasting term used to describe distinctive wines that possess interesting elements that reflect the grape varieties, vineyards, regions and winemaking processes.

claret a medium-bodied red wine style that originated in the Bordeaux region in France, where Cabernet Sauvignon and Merlot are the dominant red varieties.

clone the offspring of vines of a particular variety that have changed by either naturally adapting to the environment or through controlled breeding to change characteristics such as ripening period, flavour, the need for water or resistance to disease.

complexity a tasting term that describes a wine that has many layers of interest in taste and aroma, all nicely balanced.

cooper a person who makes or repairs barrels and casks.

depth a description of the intensity of flavour or colour of a wine.

distillery a plant in which the alcohol content of a wine is increased by distillation, which separates the water from the alcohol and other substances that provide flavour. The remaining liquid is called 'spirit', and is used to produce brandy and fortified wines such as apera (formerly sherry), port and topaque (formerly tokay).

drip irrigation a form of irrigation in which vines are watered drop by drop at the soil surface or directly to the roots through a system of underground pipes.

dry a wine with little or no sweetness.

dry grown vines watered only by rainfall without the support of irrigation.

fermentation a biochemical reaction in which sugar is converted into alcohol and carbon dioxide by yeast. Fermentation is the reason for the difference between grape juice and wine and is a process that is controlled by the winemaker to achieve the desired wine style.

filtration in winemaking, filtration is used after fermentation to remove solid impurities such as sediment and dead yeast.

fining the use of clarifying agents such as egg whites, gelatin (an animal protein) and casein (a protein found in milk), which remove solids suspended in the wine that cause cloudiness. The agents cause the suspended solids to sink to the bottom of the tank or barrel, making the wine clear.

fortified wine wine produced by adding spirit to increase the alcohol content. The spirit can be added before or after fermentation. If the spirit is added before fermentation is complete, the fortified wine has a distinctive sweetness because it contains unfermented sugar.

full-bodied a tasting term that describes a wine that fills the mouth with flavour. Tannins and high alcohol content contribute significantly to the body of a wine.

gravity feeding a process that uses gravity to advantage reducing handling and labour. For example, crushed grapes can be fed into presses on one level and the juice allowed to run into casks on the next level down. Building a winery into the side of a hill can facilitate gravity feeding.

Hermitage a wine made from the Shiraz (known as 'Syrah' in France) grape. It is not a variety, but named for the Hermitage appellation of the Rhone Valley in France, which is famous for the Shiraz variety.

hock a term formally used to describe a wine made in the tradition of the Rhine Valley white wines of Germany.

hogshead a wooden barrel that, in Australia, holds 300 litres of wine. Throughout the rest of the world hogsheads have a capacity of about 240 litres.

intensity a tasting term describing the power or concentration of the flavour of a wine.

late-picked refers to grapes that are picked later than usual. Late-picked grapes are riper, have higher sugar levels and are well-suited to making dessert wines.

length a tasting term that loosely describes how long the taste of a wine lingers in the mouth after being swallowed. Generally speaking, length is a desirable quality.

meso-climate the climate of a small area, typically that of a vineyard or collection of continuous vineyards.

micro-climate the climate of a tiny area within the vineyard, small enough to be influenced by the vine canopy.

noble rot a fungal infection caused by the parasitic *Botrytis cinerea* fungus, which feeds on grapes, leaving them dehydrated, shrivelled and with increased sugar concentration. Although many grape varieties are devastated by noble rot, some infected varieties can be used to make dessert wines, usually bearing the word 'noble' or 'botrytis' on their label.

oak the flavour and aroma of a wine that results from being fermented or matured in barrels or casks made from oak. Although oak can provide flavour and complexity to a wine, it can also be overwhelming. Older oak imparts less oak flavour to wines than newer oak.

oenology the science of winemaking.

open fermentation the traditional method of fermentation of red wine, in an uncovered vat or tank.

palate a tasting term describing the taste sensations experienced when you sip wine. People who are said to have a good palate are able to detect many different taste sensations.

palate weight a tasting term describing the degree of body in a wine. A wine having a full palate weight can also be described as full-bodied.

personality a highly subjective tasting term that describes a high level of interest and character in a wine.

pH a measure of acidity. Distilled water, with no acidity, has a pH of 7. As acidity increases pH decreases. For example, the pH of orange juice is about 3, while the pH of lemon juice is about 2.

phylloxera a tiny insect that feeds on the roots of grape vines, depriving the vines of nutrients and water and ultimately destroying them.

port a sweet fortified red wine that originated in Portugal. The name 'port' will be phased out in Australia and replaced with 'tawny', 'ruby' or 'vintage'.

regionality a characteristic of wine that reflects the climate, topography and soils of vineyards in a particular region.

regional style a style reflecting the characteristics of the wine made from grapes that are well suited to the region.

reserve a term used to describe a wine that is of higher quality than other comparable wines. The term has no legal status and its proper use depends on the integrity of the wine producer.

rich a tasting term used to describe a fullness of flavour. In a dry wine, richness is delivered by alcohol content, glycerine and oak.

rootstock vine roots and lower stem onto which cuttings from other vines can be grafted.

sherry a fortified wine originating in Spain. It is made from the juices of the white grapes Palomino, Pedro Ximenez and Moscatel. Palomino is the primary grape in dry sherry, while Pedro Ximenez is the primary grape in sweet sherry. In Australia sherry is now officially known as apera.

soft a tasting term that describes a gentleness in taste, which could be the result of low acidity, low alcohol content or low levels of tannins.

solera a series of barrels used for ageing fortified wines at different levels of maturation. The wine progressively makes its way from one barrel to the next over a period of years.

Stelvin screw cap a brand of screw cap commonly used instead of cork to eliminate the threat of wine spoiling due to cork taint, which imparts unpleasant characteristics to the wine.

structure a tasting term that describes the way in which the different characteristics of the wine work together. The characteristics, which include acidity, tannins, alcohol content, flavour and body, should be in balance and work together to provide a positive drinking experience.

table wine wine that is not sparkling or fortified.

tannins substances found in grape skin, stems and seeds. They give red wines colour, astringency and provide a puckering sensation in the mouth. They also act as a preservative. Tannins can also find their way into wine from oak barrels, especially new ones. Tannins in wine dissipate with age, which is why wines high in tannins are meant to be cellared for at least a few years.

tawny a sweet fortified red wine that has been aged in wooden barrels, giving it the brownish colour from which it gets its name. Tawny was previously known as tawny port.

terra rossa a fertile soil that is produced by the weathering of limestone and is high in iron oxide, which gives it a reddish brown colour. Terra rossa soil is considered ideal for the growth of Cabernet Sauvignon vines.

terroir the climatic and geographical characteristics of a vineyard site including temperature, rainfall, exposure to sunlight and wind, topography, soil and drainage.

tokay a sweet, fortified dessert wine made from the Muscadelle grape, which until 1976 was mistakenly thought to be the same variety used to make the famous Tokaji dessert wine made in Hungary, hence given the name 'tokay'. It is now known as topaque.

topaque *see* tokay.

top-grafting the grafting of a new vine onto the top of the stem of an existing vine.

varietal a wine made from a single variety of grape. Varietal character describes the flavours, aroma and other qualities of a particular variety.

vigneron a French term for a vine grower, which is also widely used by English speakers for winemaker.

vinification the process of transforming grape juice into wine.

vintage the harvesting of grapes or the year in which grapes were harvested to produce a particular wine.

viticulture the science of grape growing, a branch of the broader science of horticulture.

Acknowledgements

This book would not have been possible without the constant encouragement, support and patience of my wife, Dianne Lofts.

I would like to thank all twelve members of Australia's First Families of Wine, who provided the opportunity to write this book and access to their publications and archives. I am also grateful to all of the family members who gave so freely of their time to tell their stories. The families — the Browns, Campbells, Osborns, De Bortolis, Henschkes, Burches, Barrys, McWilliams, Purbricks, Taylors, Tyrrells and Hill Smiths — are truly inspirational and, in my mind, living legends. I would especially like to thank the inaugural chairman of Australia's First Families of Wine, Alister Purbrick, for his ongoing support and encouragement.

I am also indebted to many at John Wiley & Sons; in particular, Katherine Drew, who shared my enthusiasm for this book and provided invaluable support, editor Kate Romaniotis, who made numerous suggestions for improvements, and Elizabeth Whiley, who sourced the wonderful images that help bring the pages to life.

Credits

Front cover image: courtesy of Tyrrell's photographic archives. Back cover image: © iStockphoto.com/Benjamin Goode.

Yalumba Feature box on p. 32: courtesy of Yalumba. Image on p. 8: created by John Henry Chinner (1865–1933), published in 1927. All other images: courtesy of Yalumba photographic archives.

Tyrrell's Wines All images: courtesy of Tyrrell's photographic archives.

Tahbilk Image on p. 64: Lois Marsh. Images on pp. 66–67 and p. 89: Angela Trapani. Image on p. 86: The Herald and Weekly Times Photographic Collection. Image on p. 74: Helen Campbell. All other images: courtesy of Tahbilk photographic archives.

Henschke Feature box on p. 114: courtesy of Henschke. Images on pp. 94, 96, 100, 107, 108 and 110–111: Dragan Radocaj Photography. Image on p. 113, top: Adam Bruzzone. Image on p. 113, bottom: Stephen Henschke. All other images: courtesy of Henschke photographic archives.

Campbells Feature box on p. 142: courtesy of Campbells Wines. All images: courtesy of Campbells photographic archives.

McWilliam's Feature box on p. 170: courtesy of McWilliam's Wines Academy. All images: courtesy of McWilliam's photographic archives.

Brown Brothers Feature box on p. 200: courtesy of Brown Brothers. Image on p. 199: published with permission from ACP Magazines, photographer: Amanda McLauchlan, published in *Gourmet Traveller Wine*, Oct/Nov 2009, p. 74. All other images: courtesy of Brown Brothers photographic archives.

d'Arenberg All images: courtesy of d'Arenberg photographic archives.

De Bortoli Wines Feature box on p. 252: courtesy of De Bortoli Wines. All images: courtesy of De Bortoli photographic archives, including photography by Andrew Chapman and Adrian Lander.

Jim Barry Wines Images on pp. 254, 260–261 and 271: Don Brice Photographer. Image on p. 274: © Newspix/Lindsay Moller. All other images: courtesy of Jim Barry photographic archives.

Taylors Feature box on p. 298: courtesy of Taylors Wines. All images: courtesy of Taylors photographic archives.

Howard Park Feature box on p. 320 courtesy of Howard Park. All images: courtesy of Howard Park photographic archives.

Index